PORTFOLIO DEVELOPMENT AND
THE ASSESSMENT OF PRIOR LEARNING

PORTFOLIO DEVELOPMENT AND THE ASSESSMENT OF PRIOR LEARNING

Perspectives, Models, and Practices

Elana Michelson, Alan Mandell, and Contributors

STERLING, VIRGINIA

Published in 2004 by

Stylus Publishing, LLC
22883 Quicksilver Drive
Sterling, Virginia 20166-2102

**Library of Congress
Cataloging-in-Publication-Data**

Portfolio development and the assessment of
    prior learning : perspectives, models, and
    practices / edited by Elana Michelson and
    Alan Mandell.— 1st ed.
        p. cm.
    Includes bibliographical references.
    ISBN 1-57922-089-4 (alk. paper)
    ISBN 1-57922-090-8 (pbk. : alk. paper)
    1. Portfolios in education—Case studies.
    2. Adult education—Case studies.
    3. Educational tests and measurements—
    Case studies. I. Michelson, Elana, 1949–
    II. Mandell, Alan, 1950–
    LB1029.P67 P665 2004
    374'.126—dc22   2003021087

First edition, 2004
10 9 8 7 6 5 4 3 2 1

ISBN: 1-57922-089-4 (cloth)
ISBN: 1-57922-090-8 (paper)

Printed in the United States of America
All first editions printed on acid free paper
that meets the American National Standards
Institute Z39-48 Standard.

CONTENTS

ACKNOWLEDGMENTS

This book has been a long-term project, and many people have had a role in bringing it to completion. In 1990, the Council on Adult and Experiential Learning (CAEL) published our *Portfolio Development and Adult Learning: Purposes and Strategies*. That work drew on the expertise of many colleagues in the CAEL network and included chapters by Bernardin Deutsch, Mary Kay Kramp, James Roth, Brenda Krieger, Muriel Dance, Betta LoSardo, Dee Steffans, Gail Hall, Robert McKenzie, Betsy Steltenpohl, Suzanne Boyd, Leah Harvey, Clark Taylor, and the late Jane Shipton and Richard Roughton. Our coauthors in that volume helped us begin to conceptualize a taxonomy of approaches to portfolio development and at the same time demonstrated, through their creative and varied practices, that the richness of portfolio development belies any categorization.

At the 1999 CAEL conference in Seattle, a group of colleagues from across the United States met with us to discuss their portfolio practices and the resources they had developed. From those conversations, we were able to make connections with others who were creating their own portfolio forms. Thanks are due to Tai Arnold, Sharyn Boornazian, Debbi Dagavraian, Austin Doherty, Cecelia McDaniel, Tessa McDonald, Victor Montana, Susan Oaks, Chris Rounds, Susan Simosko, Gary Smith, Nan Travers, Joy Van Kleef, Urban Whitaker, and, as ever, Morris Keeton. In later stages, Robert Frisby helped us greatly with his competent and patient technical support, and Jonah Mandell lent timely aid to the preparation of the Index. Through all the stages of preparing this book, Tom Flint of CAEL has been a supportive and loyal friend.

Three of the contributors to this book, Lee Herman, Diane Hill, and Ruksana Osman, have especially informed and broadened our understanding of adult learning in ways that go far beyond their chapters here. In thinking about this book, we have been fed by the commitment, comradery, and insights of Banakonda Kennedy-Kish Bell, Nena Benton, Richard Benton, Michelle Buchler, Linda Cooper, Xenia Coulter, Larry Daloz, Judy Harris, Mechthild Hart, Lorenzo Humenshul, Clive Millar, Roger Mills, Fathima

Osman, Rachel Prinsloo, Alan Ralphs, Lyn Slonimsky, Alan Tait, Shirley Walters, and Paul Zakos. Esme Moses and Dave O'Reilly, whose untimely deaths have impoverished the world of adult learning, influenced these pages in diffuse and important ways.

Finally, we thank our colleagues at Empire State College for their ideas and for the years of thoughtful and imaginative engagement. Our deepest thanks go to our students, who always challenge us to question what we think we know and how we understand the purposes of education.

I

INTRODUCTION
PORTFOLIO DEVELOPMENT
IN HISTORIC CONTEXT

Portfolios and Adult Learning

It is no longer unusual to read about "portfolios" in many areas of education. Elementary school students are helped to create portfolios of work they have done in a project. Secondary school students are asked to use portfolios as systematic compilations of written work. In both lab- and research-based university courses, students are required to demonstrate their progress by choosing materials to be included in a final end-of-term portfolio. In effect, the portfolio has become a distinctive model of performance assessment, serving as a meaningful alternative to conventional papers and standardized testing (Kohn, 2000).

The role of portfolios in adult learning, however, has an additional dimension. It is not only a way of recording what is learned in the classroom; it also serves as a means of articulating and evidencing the prior, often experiential learning of a skilled and knowledgeable adult. The portfolio offers the adult learner an opportunity to identify knowledge and skills gained over years of work experience, community involvement, or individual study. In this way, through the creation of a portfolio, the adult learner can be credited with legitimate learning that has occurred outside the contours of the university while also gaining information about and insight into the qualities of learning and communication that are expected of college-level study. Thus, the portfolio becomes a record of a life of learning, providing a student with a perspective on both prior and future learning and, indeed, on him or herself.

To be sure, the assessment of an adult's prior learning does not require a portfolio. Educational institutions and organizations have developed a variety of instruments to measure prior learning: national standardized exams, campus-based "challenge" exams, generic evaluations of apprenticeships and on-the-job training, interviews, demonstrations, and simulated activities. All of these instruments allow for the assessment and recognition of learning in some form, and all of them allow for the recognition that creditable learning can be gained outside the walls of the academy. The value of the portfolio, however, lies in the ability to bring the student into active engagement with academic and nonacademic cultures of knowledge by providing a "reflective bridge connecting the learner, higher education, and the workplace" (Brown, 2001).

Portfolio development provides that "reflective bridge" by encouraging self-exploration, dialogue, and critique. The creation of a portfolio requires that students assess their own prior learning in the process of presenting evidence to others. It offers them a significant context in which to experience themselves as knowledgeable and skilled. At the same time, by understanding the relationship between what they already know and what they need to learn, students are also learning to take greater control of their own educational needs. As the contributors to this book attest, this is rarely an easy or uncontentious process. But the challenges, possibilities, tensions, and successes of the portfolio-development process enriches both the adult learner and the institution in ways that less learner-centered forms of assessments cannot do.

Prior Learning Assessment in Historical Perspective

The assessment of students' prior experiential learning has always been a product of its time and place. In its origins, it is deeply rooted in both the American university system and in the broader social and economic context within which that system evolved. Sporadically after World Wars I and II, and more systematically beginning in the late 1960s, adults were entering academic institutions with what was clearly academically equivalent knowledge that had been acquired through life experience, noncollegiate training, and work. A number of social forces put the potential accreditation of this knowledge on the agenda of colleges and universities. Among them was the wish to respond to the demands of veterans after each world war, the greater emphasis on formal credentials beginning at midcentury, and the calls for both relevance and access that characterized higher education reform in the late 1960s and 1970s.

The first edition of this book, titled *Portfolio Development and Adult Learning* (Mandell & Michelson, 1990) and published through the Council on Adult and Experiential Learning (CAEL), is a reflection of that moment in the history of American higher education. Founded for the most part in the early 1970s, all but one of the institutions represented in that edition were the brainchildren of either large state university systems or progressive liberal arts colleges affiliated with the Catholic Church. The spirit that had characterized the development of prior learning assessment (PLA) at that historical moment was perhaps best captured by Gail Hall, in the first paragraph of her description of portfolio development at the University of Massachusetts–Amherst:

> In 1972 the Commonwealth of Massachusetts gave the vote for president to George McGovern and its university gave the green light to a number of campus-based liberal experiments. One of these, the University Without Walls, was charged to open the doors of the university to those who were eager to learn but who had been excluded because of discrimination, logistics, or other reasons. A staff of four, mostly working part-time, set up an office in an old farmhouse on the edge of campus. We sought students who were intelligent and skilled and whose accomplishments we respected, but who were outsiders, students for whom college was both attractive and mysterious. At the same time we sought to stretch the boundaries of the campus to include new places to learn: work, home, the artist's studio, the streets. Armed with grant money from the Ford Foundation and the United States Office of Education, the enthusiasm of the university's best faculty, and the strength of our students, we set out to make a university education available to all. As part of our mandate, we started designing a process for crediting what our "outsider" students had learned from the world of work. (Hall, 1990, pp. 88–89)

Hall's words here can serve as a kind of benchmark against which to chart the new academic and social context within which PLA is now practiced. The past years have been a period of economic and political transformations, of demographic and economic dislocations, and of new cultural and intellectual landscapes. The world of adult and experiential learning has changed. On the one hand, higher education for adults is a far less marginalized practice; the PLA office is less likely these days to be located, as it was at UMass–Amherst, in "an old farmhouse on the edge of campus." On the other hand, the forces of marketization, the shrinking of resources, and the competition for adult students have taken PLA out of the hands of a small group of dedicated, energetic believers for whom access, educational quality, social equity, and student-centeredness were all of a piece. The more than 1,000 U.S. colleges and universities that responded to CAEL's recent study of PLA practices (Zucker, Johnson, & Flint, 1999) represent a far broader range of institutions than we once could have imagined: private and public, urban and rural, community colleges and research universities.

In the same way, the new alphabet soup of acronyms for PLA— PLAR and RDA in Canada; APL and APEL in Britain and Ireland; RPL in

South Africa, New Zealand, and Australia; and EVC in the Netherlands, among others[1]—bears witness to the truly international domain within which the assessment of prior learning now functions. Whereas the first edition of this book grew out of CAEL's advocacy efforts in the American Midwest, as part of the College and University Options Program of the United Auto Workers and Ford Motor Company, the second edition finds U.S.-based PLA practitioners working collaboratively with colleagues in Canada, Britain, Australia, and South Africa.

In the face of these changes, Hall's words invite us to explore the implications of a changing landscape, not only for PLA and portfolio development but also for adult learning generally. In so doing, we can discern both continuities and discontinuities and identify the challenges, threats, and possibilities represented by portfolio development today. This volume is an attempt, among other things, to recognize and honor the variety of emerging traditions in the still-innovative field of PLA. But it is also an attempt to grapple with the challenges raised by new practices and to use the experience and insights of our colleagues in the United States and around the English-speaking world to expand and deepen how we understand what we do.

Stretching the Boundaries: PLA in a Changing World

Many of the contributors to this book began their careers at a time at which the assessment of experiential learning for academic credit was still an innovative practice. They would have shared the energy and conviction with which Hall and her colleagues "set out" to provide access to higher education, and her sense of being "armed" with the enthusiasm of the faculty typifies a spirit that many veteran PLA practitioners shared. By seeing PLA, in whatever form it took, as promoting both access to education and the humanistic values within it, many of us viewed our assessment practices as unproblematically promoting the still-revolutionary claim that *what* one knew was more important than *where* one had happened to learn it. Learning, including academically creditable learning, was understood to be the by-product of ordinary, vital human activity.

In a sense, the second edition of this book is evidence both of the triumph of that idea and of new challenges to it. Like other educational and social

---

[1]PLAR-Prior Learning Assessment and Recognition; RDA-Reconnaissance des Acquis; APL-Accreditation of Prior Learning; APEL-Accreditation of Prior Experiential Learning; RPL-Recognition of Prior Learning; and EVC-Erkennen van elders of informeel Verworven Competenties.

experiments that become institutionalized, PLA has run the risk of losing some of its imaginative and creative vitality in the face of systematization, complacency, and an altered socioeconomic environment. At the same time, new sources of energy and innovation continue to emerge. Attempting to capture PLA practice today is like trying to hit the proverbial moving target. New institutions are formulating fresh forms of practice, while venerable programs are struggling to sustain long-held commitments to the complex nature of adult learning. The evolving community of PLA practitioners can no longer take a shared vision or shared practices for granted. This, in turn, raises both possibilities and troublesome questions for our growing professional community.

PLA is itself evidence of the fact that changes in education never occur in isolation. New PLA practices are the product of a changed historical moment in which both the economic picture and the intellectual climate have altered markedly. In what follows, we would like to explore the effect of some of these changes on PLA practice in North America and abroad. First, we are interested in identifying the ways in which economic changes have both created a new imperative for PLA and threatened some of its most time-honored principles. Second, we need to understand the contributions being made by PLA practitioners internationally, especially in view of the relationship between educational reform and social equity. Third, we would like to trace the influence of new understandings of knowledge, curriculum, and the human knower that are intimately linked to the way we understand experiential learning. In the process, we want to ask ourselves and our colleagues how we have matured as a community of practitioners, what worries us, what we are proud of, and who we are.

PLA Practices and Economic Change

In the past decades, new economic realities have deeply affected the lives of adult learners. While some have prospered, others have lost ground as globalization, technological change, and corporate decision making have led to a decline in numerous economic sectors and, for many people, less job security. Deindustrialization and the decline in the manual trades have increased the percentage of workers designated as managers, administrators, and what Reich refers to as "symbolic analysts" (1992). Economic shifts and political instability have similarly led to geographic dislocation, including the movement of populations across national boundaries.

One result of these changes is a new focus on "employability" that runs through the discourse on adult learning and adult education policy. The very titles of recent works in adult education tell the story. Barry Sheckley, Lois Lamdin, and Morris Keeton's *Employability in a High Performance Economy* (1993) is a case in point, as are collections of essays edited by two international colleagues: Shirley Walters's *Globalization, Adult Education and Training* (1997) and Norman Evans's *Experiential Learning around the World: Employability and the Global Economy* (2000). CAEL's president, Pamela Tate, captures this new spirit in her foreword to Sheckley et al.:

> What we want to do, what we must do, is ensure that every person currently in the workforce or approaching working age has access to the resources to achieve employability on his or her own terms. That is, all must have not only the skills and competencies to fulfill the needs of their present jobs but the ability, flexibility, and means to learn new skills and competencies as required. (1993, p. xvi)

The new economic realities reflected here have had many implications for educational institutions serving adults. On the one hand, they have often led to increased student numbers as, for better or worse, adults return to education to help them retain old jobs, access new ones, and create maximum stability in their lives. This, in turn, has been both cause and effect of what many see as positive developments in adult education, such as greater cooperation among business, labor, and academic institutions to provide education and training to adults. A significant number of these adults use these educational opportunities to create exciting and satisfying new lives, finding new and enhanced possibilities in the face of change. As described by Nicky Solomon and Julie Gustavs in Model 10 of Part 3,[2] the Work-Based Learning initiative offered at the University of Technology, Sydney, exemplifies a partnership in which work is seen as the "site of learning" and in which the curriculum is developed through a three-way negotiation between the learner, the workplace, and the university.

At the same time, adult educators have also been in a position to witness the devastation created by economic dislocation in the lives of students and their families. In Model 2, Carolyn Mann of Sinclair Community College in Dayton, Ohio, for example, discusses the importance of PLA in a shrinking employment landscape in which a degree has become what one Sinclair student refers to as an "insurance policy." In Model 6, Helen Peters, Helen Pokorny, and Linda Johnson report from Great Britain on a portfolio-development program geared toward refugees and immigrants at the London Metropolitan University (LMU). For these students, the exploration of their

---

[2]All models are collected in Part 3.

prior learning has been necessitated by profound disruptions in their lives and expectations, often tempering their sense of possibility with anxiety, bitterness, and disillusionment.

A focus on work and career has long been a staple of portfolio-development courses. Indeed, the curricula of many portfolio-development courses join a practical attention to the economic realities to an investigation of values and goals inspired by humanistic psychology. To be sure, there has always been a tension between the instrumentalist and humanistic imperatives of portfolio development. But that tension has often been a fruitful one, encouraging students to explore their own values, priorities, and possibilities and to gain a clearer understanding of both themselves and the broader world.

In times of significant economic change and economic insecurity, however, both students' own legitimate worries and the rhetoric of "the market" threaten this delicate balance. One potential result is the narrowing of the definition of learning. Competence quickly becomes equated with the skills needed by employers, and curriculum planning becomes preoccupied with economic instrumentalism rather than with Dewey's dream of personal development for workers as foundational to an informed and active citizenry. In some cases, changing PLA practices reflect such a narrowing of focus. In many institutions, for example, portfolios themselves have come under attack. Institutions that had once prized them as opportunities for reflection have grown suspicious of their claims, weary of their inefficiencies, and troubled by the lack of easily measurable outcomes that they provide. Here again, the ascendancy of a more instrumentalist strain obsessed with costs, tests, and measurements has threatened both the humanistic promise of PLA and its ability to accredit knowledge that does not fit neatly into academic disciplines, courses, or departments (Mandell, 2000).

That threat is heightened by the current decline in public support for higher education as programs for adults, in the United States and elsewhere, become ever more dependent on tuition fees and corporate support. As learners are, in effect, redefined as consumers, and as PLA becomes central to the marketing strategy of an institution, the demand for new student constituencies and the tuition they bring with them becomes an ever-greater factor in policy and curriculum development.

There is no doubt that the goals and practices of PLA are vulnerable to being altered by these developments. For the student, PLA becomes a way of equating skills and knowledge with predefined course expectations, of "selling" oneself to a potential employer, or of molding oneself to the requirements of an externally imposed curriculum. In so doing, PLA loses its power as a way to significantly engage with the full range of life experiences and the broad meaning of one's personal history. As the rhetoric of the market becomes the *lingua franca* of academe, PLA also becomes a way for institutions to "sell" themselves to potential customers rather than, as Hall (1990) puts it, a way of "open(ing) the doors . . . to those who were eager to learn."

Portfolio-mediated PLA is especially vulnerable to current economic and political realities. Portfolio development is a time- and labor-consuming activity. Staff requirements alone—course instructors, assessors, advisors, and writing tutors—put strains on institutions struggling with shrinking budgets and growing demands. It is worth noting that Hall and her colleagues were "armed" not only with enthusiasm and a belief in their students, but also with substantial monies from the Ford Foundation and the federal government. As the efficient use of limited resources becomes the order of the day, and as standardization of "outcomes" and assessment instruments becomes more widespread, the very labor-intensiveness and open-endedness of portfolio development threaten its continuity. In such an environment, PLA programs come under increasing pressure to return to less costly, instrumentalist methods of assessment: standardized tests and generic evaluations, to name but two. The effort to maintain portfolio development as a central assessment option is part of a larger struggle being waged at many institutions to sustain student-centered, individualized, and academically rich educational services for adults. That struggle will not be an easy one.

Model 7 by Susan Rydell of Metropolitan State University is both a reflection on and evidence of these changes. Metropolitan State was founded as a nontraditional, adult-oriented institution characterized by student-centeredness, individualized assessment, and a broad understanding of competency. As Rydell's model makes clear, Metropolitan State continues to make important efforts to respond to the needs of an ever more diverse population of adult learners, but the highly individualized, adult-oriented program she describes is no longer at the center of Metropolitan State's academic life. It now exists at the periphery, one option for a small number of students within a largely mainstreamed, newly conventional university.

These changes can also manifest themselves in Model 9 by Theresa Hoffmann on the EXCEL Through Experiential Learning program of University of Maryland University College (UMUC). The Web-based version of EXCEL uses new technologies to respond to new economic imperatives and to deliver PLA to students from business and the U.S. armed forces around the world. Hoffmann's discussion of UMUC's highly successful format raises fascinating questions for the hands-on traditions of student service in PLA. What does "student support" mean in a massified, computer-based system? How does one create a venue for the intimacies of self-reflection and self-disclosure, so cherished in the early years of PLA, on the Web? How does one replicate the camradery among students or the nurturing relationship between student and faculty that PLA courses are often designed to create and so often provide?

While UMUC has been in the forefront of Web-based PLA, a number of the institutions represented in this book are also initiating Web-based and other distance-learning versions of portfolio development, among them SUNY–Empire State College, Sinclair Community College, and the Vermont State Colleges. One can expect that, as with UMUC, these institutions will seek to draw on rich traditions of student-centered learning to create nuanced and supportive Web-based practices. But what of other institutions that do not bring such traditions to computer-mediated delivery models or that do not have the resources, expertise, history, or philosophical commitment to develop effective systems of student support? UMUC's experience suggests that economic and technological change is altering the PLA landscape in ways that are filled with both possibility and danger. There is the danger, eloquently raised by Judy Fitch in Model 12 regarding the Vermont State Colleges, that open-handed practices will narrow, that group camaraderie will be compromised, and that technicist solutions will be imposed on what are in fact very human problems. But there is also the hope that new solutions will be found to fulfill PLA's traditional promise: to keep the student, the student's experience, and student access at the heart of educational inquiry.

PLA and Social Equity

Like employment and the world of work, the relationship of PLA to equity, social justice, and diversity was a focus of many of the PLA practices that arose in the 1970s. The greater openness to adult learners, for many institutions, was part of the effort to reach out to constituencies that had traditionally been underserved by higher education. This social vision was matched, in many cases, by a curriculum that explicitly recognized that there is no such thing as "the" adult learner and that experience is shaped by categories of social privilege and marginalization including those of "race," gender, class, national origin, age, and sexual orientation. Reading assignments in portfolio-development courses often focused on culture and ethnicity—autobiographies such as Maxine Hong Kingston's The Woman Warrior (1999) were prominent, for example, and class discussions explored the learning that grew out of the experience of life as a woman or "minority."

Given the internationalization of PLA, however, one of the striking aspects of this approach to social equity is how very *American* it is. Higher education in the United States has long been characterized by comparatively greater attention to access, greater fluidity and portability among different forms of postsecondary education, and a greater commitment to serving non-elite communities, be they Midwestern farmers, Southern sharecroppers, East and West Coast immigrants, or, as Gail Hall (1990) described her New England students, "outsiders for whom college is both attractive and mysterious." Related to all of these characteristics—and, in a sense, both their cause and effect—has been a widely held recognition of the role of higher education in "Americanization" and upward mobility. These traditions, both practical and ideological, are rooted in the nineteenth century, in the founding of the first land-grant colleges, historically Black institutions, community colleges, and public urban universities. But they took on new and heightened meanings in the last third of the twentieth century as many groups within American society contested the meaning and purpose of knowledge and the role and status of the university. The emergence of PLA, in this sense, was part of a strongly critical and socially progressive tradition in the history of American education.

Equally striking is how grounded these PLA practices are in American theories of education, most notably, how much they have been influenced by John Dewey. The impulse, as Hall put it, to "open the doors" and "stretch the boundaries of the campus to include new places to learn" speaks to the belief in the educative value of experience, in the perceived relationship between learning and life, and in the vision of education as fundamentally egalitarian. Virtually any PLA program finds its legitimacy through the relationships upon which Dewey insisted—between experience and learning, between vocational and liberal studies, between the activities through which men and women organize and manage their social existence and the kinds of educational practices that help them do so. PLA is non-elitist in a particularly American way, reflecting the belief that there are many ways of creating knowledge and countless sites at which academically credible knowledge is created. In a practical and also deeply symbolic way, PLA announces the possibility of access, second chances, improvisation, and know-how as part of the educational meld.

As was the case with economic change, the relationship of PLA to social equity, multiculturalism, and educational opportunity has become more complex, and this is due to a number of reasons. One factor has been the increasing role of PLA in countries other than the United States, in which the role of PLA in the struggle for social justice has played out within disparate social histories. In Britain, for example, PLA was introduced at a time in which an elitist, class-bound tradition of higher education was giving way to greater access and in which the movement of peoples within what was once the British Empire was rapidly remaking Britain into a multicultural society. In

Canada and New Zealand, the assessment practices of historically white institutions quickly entered into dialogue with the traditions of learning in Aborigi-
nal/Native communities; it is no coincidence that the Canadian contribution of
Model 5 comes from the First Nations Technical Institute, an Aboriginally
owned community college located on the Tyendinaga Mohawk Territory. In
South Africa, PLA has explicitly been promoted by the Black trade union
movement and the African National Congress as a vehicle for overcoming the
legacy of apartheid by providing access to education and by formally recognizing the skills and knowledge of Black South Africans. In many of these countries, the use of PLA to promote social change is complicated by the absence of
a tradition of mass higher education and the continued power of rigid, non-
adult-friendly institutional policies and curricula. But new PLA practices have
also been enabled by the work and spirit of educators, represented in Model 11
by Ruksana Osman of the University of the Witwatersrand in South Africa
whose commitment to PLA grew directly out of an effort to contribute to a systematic process of social change that would "bring about educational and
vocational redress and contribute to social justice."

This text is being produced at a conservative moment in American higher
education. As Lee Herman reports in Model 3, even nontraditional institutions such as SUNY–Empire State College are faced with the imposition of
restrictive curricular policies that limit the range of student options and
threaten the historical relationship between educational access and social
equity. At such a time, the experiences of our international colleagues can
inspire U.S.-based practitioners by reminding us of PLA's unique and important role as a vehicle for academic critique and social change.

The experiences of our international colleagues can also challenge U.S.-
based practitioners to be self-critical concerning our own assumptions,
encouraging us to ask fundamental questions about which adult learners our
PLA programs are serving and which they are serving well. Do our unexamined expectations, for example, inadvertently privilege the knowledge of some
people over that of others, so that we value the knowledge of personnel managers over that of shop stewards, or classical oboists over jazz clarinetists, or
paid lobbyists over grassroots community organizers? Similarly, do our conventional assumptions about accreditable knowledge—assumptions that stress
the "public" realm over the "private," for example—discourage the full
recognition of women's knowledge? Our international colleagues continue to
remind us that we need to be institutionally and personally self-critical concerning differential success rates among students and that we need to ask how
those rates are the result not of students' deficits but of our practices and of
the assumptions that inform and sustain them.

PLA *and the Isolated Self*

While no formal studies have been published to our knowledge, there is much anecdotal evidence to suggest that portfolios are more difficult for some students than for others. This difficulty is typically understood to stem from two predicaments. One often-cited problem is lack of time. The labor-intensiveness of portfolios disadvantages those students—single parents, for example—whose multiple roles and lack of an adequate support network make sustained portfolio development particularly difficult. Moreover, as the pressures on adult lives continue to grow and as adults return to education for reasons of economic survival, the self-exploratory imperative of portfolios can seem a luxury at best. Originally intended to accelerate degree completion for busy adults, for some, the portfolio is experienced as an impediment.

The other common explanation for differential completion rates is lack of academic skills. It is understood that the denial of educational opportunity earlier in life has brought adults to higher education who have little experience with the written conventions and conceptual norms of academe. Indeed, it is for this latter reason that many institutions use portfolio development itself as an orientation to academic ways of thinking and writing. For many practitioners, represented in this volume by Kate Crowe of the Evergreen State College (Model 4), portfolio-development courses that focus directly on such academic preparation or on the strengthening of academic skills are part of a commitment to social equity, a second chance for those previously denied an education because they were poor, or people of color, or "just a girl."

A number of schools of contemporary scholarship, however, give us reason to believe that lack of time and lack of academic preparation are not the only barriers to the completion of portfolios. The portfolio narrative itself may inadvertently be part of the problem as well. Specifically, the conceptual and narrative frame of much portfolio development is based on assumptions about experience and selfhood that are, arguably, culturally and socially narrow, so that practices we assume to be student-centered may actually undercut the very students we claim to want to support.

As an assessment method, the portfolio has its origins in a particular vision of adult education as "a cooperative venture in non-authoritarian, informal learning, the chief purpose of which is to discover the meaning of experience" (Eduard Lindeman, quoted in Brookfield, 1987, p. 196). It is rooted in liberal humanist ideals of autonomy and "the wholeness . . . and uniqueness of Self" (Rogers, quoted in Knowles, 1990, p. 8). These roots, in turn, tie portfolio development to another paradigmatically American belief, namely, the value of the individual. It is no coincidence that David Kolb begins his influential *Experiential Learning* (1984) by evoking Dewey on the liberatory value of the inner life of the individual:

> The modern discovery of inner experience, of a realm of purely personal events . . . is also a great and liberating discovery. It implies a new worth and sense of dignity in human individuality, a sense that an individual is not merely a property of nature, but that he (sic) adds something, that he makes a contribution. (quoted on p. 1)

More than any other assessment methodology, portfolios stress the importance of what Dewey here calls the uniqueness of "inner experience." The unit of knowledge—that is, the knowing self who is both the author and the subject of the portfolio narrative—is understood to be the autonomous, self-aware individual.

Understood in this way, portfolio essays are not neutral records of learning that a student has gained. As autobiographical documents, they can't help but require students to narrate a specific form of selfhood, one that both assumes and reflects specific ways of understanding the relationship of self to others, of experience to learning, and of personal accomplishment to history. The conventional logic of portfolio narratives assumes, first, that students can identify specific learning experiences that contribute to a cohesive and highly individualized sense of self. Second, they require that students be able to separate what they have done and learned from collective actions and insights. This logic takes for granted that the individual can create a record of personal attainment and accomplishment.

Recent studies of autobiography suggest, however, that this narrative of a coherent individual selfhood characterizes a relatively narrow range of autobiographies. Autobiographies written by women and by members of non-European cultures, for example, tend not to distinguish the writer's own accomplishments from shared challenges and triumphs. Women's autobiographical writings tend to use circuitous narrative patterns that reflect the multiple roles women play simultaneously rather than extract specific insights from unitary experiences (Michelson, 1996). Moreover, accounts of lives spent in intense collective action rest on far different assumptions concerning the relationship of action, knowledge, and the historical circumstances within which knowledge is given value (Michelson, 1999). Thus, portfolio essays are difficult for many students not because learning and self-awareness are lacking but because students are being asked to represent that learning and self-awareness in narrative forms that actually belie their experience of self.

In some cases, this difficulty is intensified by two familiar requirements: that portfolios be exclusively written documents, and that they be organized around the movement from "what I've done" to "what I've learned." A broader range of students might be better served by portfolios with narrative structures designed to capture the relationship between knowledge, action, and decision making in other, more nuanced ways. Rather than requiring students to separate their learning from the context in which it was gained, for example, portfolio-development activities might encourage them to place their action-as-knowledge within the context of shared experiences and goals. Thus, portfolios might utilize forms—such as case studies—that tie learning more closely to strategic action based on the ability to evaluate the social environment with accuracy. Similarly, we might envision portfolio designs that mime the dialogic and performative qualities of knowledge. In this way, students could be encouraged to present their learning as the product of active, shared engagement rather than of the singular inner life.

This is not, of course, to gainsay the portfolio as an important venue for helping students connect their learning to academic writing styles and conceptual frames. Nor is it to devalue the importance of providing what Helen Peters et al. in Model 6 call a "structured time" for synthesis and integration. It does suggest, however, that such synthesis can come in many guises. Put in another way, we need to distinguish between legitimate attention to quality and the requirement that students demonstrate their learning in ways that are incongruent with their own experience of self. One alternative is evident by the ways in which Marixsa Alicea, Deborah Holton, and Derise Tolliver of DePaul University take inspiration in Model 8 not only from "an individualistic model of lifelong learning but also from a philosophy of life that stresses interdependence and collective responsibility." In this effort, the authors are aided by DePaul's recognition of competencies "that focus on collaborative learning, social justice, cross-cultural issues, globalization, and service learning." Their approach is supported by a different kind of context, one in which the collectivity is as central as the individual.

PLA *and Evolving Theories of Knowledge*

As records of learning, portfolios rest not only on particular tacit assumptions about selfhood but also on assumptions about the nature of legitimate knowledge. Moreover, they depend on institutional relationships in which evaluators have both the right and the responsibility to "translate" experiential learning into acceptably academic terms. The past twelve years have seen challenges to academic definitions of knowledge that are both unsettling and fruitful. An awareness of the politics of knowledge—that is, how knowledge is created, used, and valued—is reflected in many of the chapters in this book.

For all their innovative social spirit, however, the PLA practices that arose in the 1970s actually kept quite close to conventional definitions of academic learning. The students were often outsiders in that they came from communities historically ill-served by higher education. Yet PLA practitioners largely assumed that what students knew could be assessed because it closely resembled the "insider" knowledge familiar to the academy. Thus, while learning was understood to happen everywhere, and while academics worked hard with students to help make their knowledge "fit" into academic norms, an examination of the assumptions concerning what knowledge "counts" was rare. Academic equivalence required that knowledge be generic, transferable, and abstract and that it conform to academic traditions that valued theory over practice, concepts over feelings, and learning over "mere" experience. Portfolios were valued, in part, because they encouraged students to internalize—or at least learn to mimic—the value judgments and communicative practices of the academy. In many significant ways, the nature of academic knowledge itself remained unexamined, as did the social relationships within which that knowledge was assessed and accredited.

To be sure, such assumptions about knowledge and about the efficacy of portfolios are still central to these pages, but they are balanced—and, we would argue, enriched—by new understandings of knowledge that challenge the distinctions between theory and practice, between "universal" and local knowledge, and between the intellectual and emotional realms. As Alicea, Holton, and Tolliver put it in Model 8, even in today's world of scholarship, knowledge has come to be understood as "subjective, constructed, and contextual" rather than abstract and transcendent.

These new approaches to knowledge have their origins both in social and professional practice and in developments in a variety of academic fields. Cognitive psychologists, for example, have come to challenge the valuing of theory over practice, arguing that experts in fields from medicine to teaching do not rely on their ability to apply context-independent theory to a range of situations, but rather draw on a rich, context-specific pool of experiences, practical examples, and past activities (Chi, Glaser, & Farr, 1988; Lave & Wenger, 1991). Feminist scholars and scholars from a range of ethnic and antiracist studies have simultaneously challenged the ideal of abstract and universal knowledge, arguing that much knowledge depends on where one is standing and on the social and historical perspectives available from one's grounded human life (Collins, 1991; Harding, 1991; Mudimbe, 1988). Thus, "outsider" students produce "outsider" knowledge that is valuable not because it mimics the concepts and language of academics but precisely because it is distinctive.

This suggests a vital role for PLA in an academy that seeks to broaden the dimensions of what can be known. It suggests that PLA can offer a fuller exploration of how knowledge from the margins can amend and deepen human understanding. Perhaps it matters where one has learned something after all.

This volume represents a number of ways in which portfolio-mediated PLA is being enriched by such new understandings. The first of these is the relationship between PLA, outsider knowledge, and the curriculum. At First Nations Technical Institute (FNTI), for example, firsthand knowledge of the social and psychic scars of Native peoples is part of the genuine expertise students bring to their work as social service professionals. At SUNY–Empire State College, an understanding of the needs of their communities is foundational to the development of many students' individualized curriculum. Both of these programs build on the knowledge students have both as members of and as professionals within the society they serve. In effect, the experience of students becomes the very stuff of the curriculum. This occurs not only because experiential learning forms an important bridge between experiential and academic learning, which, indeed, it does; it also occurs because students are informed participants in curriculum development based on both their deeply felt personal and collective memories and their distinctive professional expertise.

Secondly, these developments help us to broaden our understanding of a concept that has been central to U.S. forms of portfolio development, namely, "self-reflection." In liberal humanist approaches to portfolio development, self-reflection is understood as the largely personal, highly rational exploration of memory and experience. As such, self-reflection is supposed to help students achieve distance from their own experience and transform it into knowledge and to empower students to become agents of their own lives and learning. Such uses of self-reflection have their origins in the influence of humanistic psychology and are echoed in notions that are familiar to PLA practitioners, such as Kolb's learning cycle (1984) and Schon's reflexive practitioner (1983).

Recent scholarship, however, encourages us to go beyond the personal and purely cognitive in the ways we approach portfolio development. Rather than seeing "reflection" as the moment of detached, individual cognition, more recent theories understand it as one node in a rich "relational interdependency of agent and world, activity, meaning, cognition, learning, and knowing" in which "learning, thinking, and knowing are relations among people in activity in, with and arising from the socially and culturally structured world" (Lave & Wenger, 1991, pp. 50–51). In arguing for "the inherently socially negotiated character of meaning and the interested, concerned character of the thought and action of persons-in-activity" (pp. 50–51), contemporary cultural and cognitive theory redefines self-reflection as an active, dialogic understanding of oneself in relationship both to others and to one's own sensate, emotional, and corporeal humanity.

A number of the programs represented in this second edition draw on these expanded notions of reflection through which students are asked to locate their own learning not only as a moment in a personal development but as part of a shared cultural history. The questions asked of students as they draft their portfolios not only focus on the process through which experience is transformed into knowledge through individual acts of cognition, but also ask how our knowledge of the world is shaped through concrete, shared forms of identity and experience. The potential richness of this approach is clear from the chapter by Helen Peters et al. (Model 6) on the PLA program at the London Metropolitan University. Peters et al. use the example of two physically disabled students to explore the relationship between the personal and the social, in this case, between "experiencing their disability" and at the same time "experiencing being a disabled person in society." Students in the program "are encouraged to make links between a life history and relevant social, historical, or cultural frameworks and perspectives." Peters et al. offer other examples as well: a survivor of childhood abuse who now works for the protection of battered women, and a refugee who works as an advocate for those seeking political asylum in Great Britain. In this way, self-reflection becomes an invitation to explore not only what makes us unique but also what we share with others. The portfolio-development course thus functions as something of a meeting ground between the cognitive and the affective and between personal and social history.

Other programs represented in this volume challenge our notions of self-reflection by revisiting the conventional distinction between what we have done and what we have learned. In Model 1, as presented by James Roth, Georgine Loacker, Bernardin Deutsch, Suzann Gardner, and Barbara Nevers, for example, the PLA philosophy and portfolio-development practices of Alverno College posit a close relationship between mind and body and between knowing and doing. Grounded in the notion that all knowledge is performative, Alverno's practices emphasize "active performance" rather than distanced contemplation in the demonstration of learning. Its curriculum seeks to help students "to develop abilities that facilitate the 'doing' of what they know." Important as new cultural and cognitive theory is in this regard, however, equally important is the growing visibility of non-European concepts of being. Drawing on Native North American teachings about knowledge, Diane Hill, in Model 5, describes FNTI's whole-person approach to the portfolio-mediated demonstration of competency as necessarily including body, emotions, and spirit, as well as mind.

PLA Practice and the PLA Practitioner

As academics, our two individual careers have been spent in a nontraditional institution for adults and as consultants, writers, and trainers in the field of PLA. Our working lives have been both constrained and enriched by the changes discussed above. As we complete this volume, perhaps the most striking change over the years is in the voices of the PLA practitioners themselves. The contributors to our first edition were proud of their programs, confident of their ability to meet all challenges, and secure in the sense that the future was on their side. Today, the energy and pride remain, but they exist side by side with new solicitude. Perhaps that is simply evidence of our maturing as a professional community. We are now secure enough in our understanding to be honest about our concerns and about the challenges to past habits that are sure to transform future practice, no doubt for both good and ill.

The PLA advocates with whom we first worked saw themselves as facing two directions simultaneously. On the one hand, they identified themselves as advocates for adult learners and for the academic legitimacy of experiential learning. On the other hand, they saw themselves as upholders of the benefits of academic ways of knowing, even as those gates were being opened wider. Indeed, they typically valued PLA because it was seen as mediating between experiential and academic learning by giving students the opportunity, as the late Richard Roughton put it, "to integrate worklife skills and knowledge with a strong academic base and to experience the connections between the traditional subject matter of academe and their social and personal experience of the world" (1990, p. 81).

That dual loyalty, to experiential *and* to academic forms of knowing, is still visible in this volume. As Peters et al. put it (Model 6) the future of PLA "lies in breaking down the boundaries between learning from experience and learning through academic study" and in enabling students "to undertake a process of synthesis between their previous experience and their integration into the sphere of academic study." PLA advocates continue to see themselves as mediators of this process and see PLA as uniquely positioned to form a bridge between those two worlds.

At the same time, there is disquietude in this volume that was not perceptible in the past. The role of mediator has been destabilized. The authors of these new chapters are more aware of the contradictions in their roles and in their own social and institutional locations. In this way, too, our community has come of age. These chapters reflect a growing understanding that the recognition of knowledge is always negotiated among disparate social interests and that many groups now demand a voice in answering questions once considered the sole purview of academics: What is the relationship of theory to practice? What should colleges and universities teach? Whose knowledge is academically legitimate? No longer seeing themselves as neutral filters through which students and institutions meet, a number of these authors understand that they, like their students, are socially and historically specific human beings whose learning has been shaped by experience, whose identities are the products of personal and social history, and whose knowledge is necessarily incomplete. Thus, Alicea, Holton, and Tolliver (Model 8) insist that they must tell us about themselves in order to help us understand their approaches to portfolio development. They speak not only as academics but also as artists and as women of color with "memories of and commitments to personal development, community identity, and connectedness to others." Nor is this new self-awareness simply the result of new sensitivities to race, class, and gender. Herman (Model 3) makes a similar point invoking that most Western and male of thinkers, Plato: In asking students to "know themselves," we require them to think about what they love, believe in, and most value. We, as educators, must do the same.

References

Brookfield, S. (1987). *Developing Critical Thinkers*. San Francisco: Jossey-Bass.

Brown, J. O. (2001). "The Portfolio: A Reflective Bridge Connecting the Learner, Higher Education, and the Workplace." *The Journal of Continuing Higher Education* 49 (2), pp. 2–13.

Chi, M., Glaser, R. I., and Farr, M. (eds.) (1988). *The Nature of Expertise*. Hillsdale, NJ: Lawrence Erlbaum.

Collins, P. H. (1991). *Black Feminist Thought*. New York: Routledge, Chapman, and Hall.

Evans, N. (ed.) (2000). *Experiential Learning around the World: Employability and the Global Economy*. London: Jessica Kingsley.

Hall, G. (1990). "The University of Massachusetts–Amherst." In A. Mandell and E. Michelson, *Portfolio Development and Adult Learning: Contexts and Strategies,* pp. 88–98. Chicago: CAEL.

Harding, S. (1991). *Whose Science? Whose Knowledge? Thinking from Women's Lives*. Ithaca, NY: Cornell University Press.

Hong Kingston, M. (1999). *The Woman Warrior: Memoirs of a Girlhood among Ghosts*. New York: Vintage.

Knowles, M. (1990). *The Adult Learner: A Neglected Species*. Houston, TX: Gulf.

Kohn, A. (2000). *The Case against Standardized Testing: Raising Scores, Ruining the Schools*. Portsmouth, NH: Heinemann.

Kolb, D. (1984). *Experiential Learning: Experience as the Source of Learning and Development*. Englewood Cliffs, NJ: Prentice Hall.

Lave, J., and Wenger, E. (1991). *Situated Learning: Legitimate Peripheral Participation*. New York: Cambridge University Press.

Mandell, A. (2000). "Saving What Is Messy: PLA in a World of Testing." *Journal of Continuing Higher Education* 48 (2), 48–50.

Mandell, A. and Michelson, E. (1990). *Portfolio Development and Adult Learning: Purposes and Strategies*. Chicago: CAEL.

Michelson, E. (1996). " 'Auctoritee' and 'Experience': Feminist Epistemology and the Assessment of Experiential Learning." *Feminist Studies* 22 (3), pp. 17–18; 33–35.

Michelson, E. (1999). "Expanding the Logic of Portfolio-Assisted Assessment: Lessons from South Africa." *CAEL Forum and News* 23 (1), pp. 17–18, 33–35.

Mudimbe, V. Y. (1988). *The Invention of Africa: Gnossis, Philosophy, and the Order of Knowledge*. Bloomington: Indiana University Press.

Reich, R. (1992). *The Work of Nations*. New York: Vintage Books.

Roughton, R. (1990). "The American University." In A. Mandell and E. Michelson, *Portfolio Development and Adult Learning: Contexts and Strategies*, pp. 77–81. Chicago: CAEL.

Schon, D. A. (1983). *The Reflective Practitioner: How Professionals Think in Action*. New York: Basic Books.

Sheckley, B. G., Lamdin, L., Keeton, M. T. (1993). *Employability in a High Performance Economy*. Chicago: CAEL.

Walters, S. (ed.) (1997). *Globalization, Adult Education and Training: Impacts and Issues*. London: Zed.

Zucker, B. J., Johnson, C. C., and Flint, T. A. (1999). *Prior Learning Assessment: A Guidebook to American Institutional Practices*. Dubuque, IA: Kendall/Hunt.

APPROACHES TO PORTFOLIO DEVELOPMENT

Introduction

Framing the Portfolio-Development Course

Much of the work of a portfolio-development course is inherently difficult. Students must be initiated into the "how-to" of assessment, helped to understand the policies and procedures of a given institution, and guided through the long process of documenting what they know. In most institutions, moreover, portfolios must be structured in such a way as to go beyond a narrative of experiences. Students are expected to think about the differences between what they "learned" and what they "have done." They are called upon to find connections between the practices and the formal and informal conceptual frameworks that guide their fields.

In many respects, the real power of a portfolio-development course is grounded in the intimate connection to a student's life and learning and in the practice of thoughtful self-awareness that its activities seek to encourage. Indeed, it often represents a student's single most significant opportunity to explore the role of learning in his or her life, whatever the origin and shape of that learning might be. Perhaps more explicitly and directly than in other learning contexts, therefore, the portfolio course requires that we focus on our students. We may draw on our own experiences, know our purposes, and hold onto our own fantasies of best practices, but we can never easily slip away from the goal of grappling with how to listen to what our students have to tell us. That is, we can never forget our basic goal of helping them to articulate, organize, and document what they know.

Yet, as the division of this section into six different "approaches" implies, there is more than one way to do this. Students think, feel, and speak about their lives through complexly textured lenses formed by memories, points of pride and sorrow, and individual and group aspirations. Those lenses are contoured according to the particularities of gender, class, nationality, "race," and generation, and by students' share of the fears and hopes of families and communities. Thus, the focus on prior learning invites an exploration of the multiple relationships between a student's personal history on the one hand and, on the other hand, social institutions, stages of human development, bodies of knowledge, and understandings—however tacit they may be—of the world. The "approaches" attend to these relationships in different ways, from different angles, and with different emphases. In the process, they offer students the opportunity to construct a particular narrative of self.

Put in yet another way, the value of the portfolio course can be seen, in large part, as a function of a kind of "in-between-ness." It situates students between knowing and unknowing, between past and future, between cherished attitudes and new insights, between practical imperatives and broader understandings, and between their unique selfhood and the ongoing life of the world. Thus, the real challenge of the course is to attend to and seriously work with these inherent tensions. When one side is accented at the expense of the other (for example, the personal and not the social, the contemporary and not the historical, the job and not the socioeconomic context within which it exists), students and faculty lose the critical opportunity that the portfolio-development course offers to introduce and work with myriad questions about knowledge, self, and society that are at the heart of serious academic learning.

The sections that follow describe six approaches to portfolio-development courses, or rather six ways of framing the integration of prior learning assessment (PLA) into more broadly based understandings of education, work, and society. These approaches do not represent separate curricular outlines, nor are they intended to serve as "stand-alone" and fully articulated syllabi. Rather, they are emphases within a single intellectual exploration—clusters of interrelated concerns around which a range of appropriate and relevant subject matter and activities can be organized. There are many points of overlap, topics form continuities from theme to theme, and individual activities and assignments will work with many approaches. The ideas and examples are offered as ways to begin and samples of work that might stimulate new efforts and relevant course designs.

In effect, this section is a kind of primer. Drawing on the contributions of our colleagues in our own and many other institutions, we have tried to present an extensive array of assignments, readings, and classroom exercises. Such materials are designed to help students work with questions, not only about what they know, but also about how what they know has been learned, about the meaning of that learning, and about its place in their personal, professional, and academic lives. They are included here as occasions to both affirm what has long been important for our students and to encourage them to imagine their lives in new ways.

Selecting an Approach

How we think—and encourage our students to think—about the worlds of work and learning, the fostering of personal growth and meaningful work, the role of academic knowledge, and the experience of social inclusivity and marginalization serves as a foundation on which the portfolio-development course rests. The way we examine these most central issues frames the kind of exploration of personal experience that the course seeks to encourage. Particularly because it is in the very nature of this course to raise these issues for ourselves and with our students, we cannot put them aside. They are always with us, whatever explicit topic we are addressing.

Like many practitioners of adult education, the faculty and staff who teach portfolio-development workshops tend to be guided by deeply held convictions concerning the rightness of what we do and the role of adult education in giving second—and sometimes first—chances to the learners whom we serve. We are always drawing on and influenced by our own intellectual and social backgrounds, the myriad global traditions of adult education, the ways and rules of the institutions within which we work, and our particular life commitments to the communities we serve.

Thus, the specific curricular focus and structure of the course is far from a neutral matrix. All of us necessarily approach its broad design and its specific activities with a set of implicit or explicit assumptions. Our judgments about the nature of student learning, the academic skills that students need, the requirements for a college degree, and perhaps even the role of the university in society play a part in the portfolio course we construct and offer. Our course designs are predicated on an understanding (once again, however implicit or explicit) of the relationship between experience and knowledge and between an individual and the broader social contexts of education and work. Even when we are not consciously drawing upon a specific theory of adult development or curriculum formation, decisions about how any portfolio course will be shaped are informed by our value judgments. That is, such decisions reflect the stated or unstated ideological frameworks that mold our understanding of the social, cultural, economic, and historical contexts within which we and our students live.

Yet there is something else that exists alongside these deeply felt influences on our work as adult educators. Even when we try to attend to these influences, even when we are consciously and self-critically aware of what we are attempting, there is always a gap between the most well-thought-out theories we can call upon and the nature of our everyday activities. We can lure ourselves into believing that our strongest attitudes, most deeply held beliefs, and best intentions directly manifest themselves in our practice as guides to portfolio development. But the realities of our institutional mandates, of our own learning (both what we know and how we know it), and of the students we work with strongly affect our plans and choices. As hard as we might try to put into practice what we believe is right and true, we are faced with complexities and challenges we probably had not imagined beforehand. We are forced to improvise, rethink our plans, wonder what went wrong, and come up with alternative strategies that could be more responsive to those we wish to serve. And just when we think we have it, we may just have to change again.

Thus, the approaches and examples that follow are places to start, clues to working with learners in the portfolio-development course. They must be tailored to the needs of particular learner populations, faculty interests, academic and professional areas, social realities, and institutional parameters. They are meant to be picked apart and recombined, amended, and supplemented by new materials and new activities. We expect these approaches will be improved upon continually as our experiential base in prior learning assessment deepens, as it surely has since the first edition of this book was published more than a decade ago.

Whatever approach we take, whatever imaginative materials we use or develop, however we are formed by the ideological underpinnings of our societies, there is a set of shared values that should inform our work in *any* portfolio course we create and facilitate. First, in what is a complex and usually demanding process, learners need our support and our energy. Isolation and a one-sided obsession with institutional policies and procedures only exacerbate the fears that learners may bring to the process. Learners also need our clarity and honesty, even as we listen for and empathize with the demands, joys, and pains of their lives. Thirdly, whoever guides the portfolio course needs to respond with a critical eye and, to use Schon's (1983) helpful phrase, to gain new experience as "reflective practitioners." Because this study often serves as an entry point for the learner, the course and the work of the faculty related to it become, for better or worse, models of the entire academy. As Theodore and Nancy Sizer (1999) put it in a different context, "The students are watching."

And finally, whatever design we may choose, we must remember that the portfolio course and the entire portfolio process are about *access*. The course should be about finding comforting, effective, and academically rich ways to welcome new learners and new experiences into the academy. The portfolio course is always about taking seriously what learners have done and rethinking our own assumptions and values based on new populations, new needs, and new circumstances. At its core, the portfolio course is thus about the democratization of education, about finding ways to encourage our learners to find a voice and to become active participants in their learning and in their schooling. With this critical end in mind, the portfolio course offers all of us a vital and significant opportunity.

Focusing on the Learners

Because of the deeply student-centered nature of portfolio development, no approach can appropriately be formulated without reference to the learners it is designed to serve. For that reason, we have identified three adult learners, three quite specific individuals who at the same time are representative of the needs, life commitments, interests, and circumstances of many adults in higher education. In the sections that follow, we explore the ways in which various approaches might meet the different needs of these three individuals. Equally importantly, we try to suggest the ways in which the approaches themselves seem to change shape, emphasis, and meaning when filtered through the life circumstances of disparate individuals.

The three learners are:

CHERYL

Cheryl is a 42-year-old single African American woman who lives in a Southern city. She worked in the garment industry for a company that has closed because it is moving its main plant abroad. Cheryl is a first-generation urbanite; the older members of her family remain in the country. She is an extremely skilled seamstress who has a small business in her neighborhood making wedding dresses.

JOHN

John is a 34-year-old New York City police officer who has been working as a police department substance abuse counselor for the past three years. He came to that work through his own recovery. John is a second-generation Polish American. He's divorced with two children. He is the child of an alcoholic father who died when John was in his teens. He has ten more years in the department before he can retire at half-pay and is interested in a new career, not necessarily in substance abuse. John volunteers as a "big brother" for fatherless boys.

MARIA

Maria is a 51-year-old teacher's aide who lives in California and has recently been involved in a successful organizing drive for unionization. She is now chief shop steward at her school and serves on the negotiation committee. She is from Latin America and came to the United States as a teenager. She is married and has three grown children. Maria has come back to school via new education benefits that offer higher salaries for gaining an associate's degree and a career path from teacher's aide to teacher upon gaining a bachelor's degree. Maria is afraid she will be too old by the time she graduates, but she always wanted to be a teacher and is determined to do it, if she can.

A Note on Resources

In the approaches that follow, we have tried to address issues in adult learning and portfolio development that have resonance in multiple, national, and cultural contexts. The sample texts referred to in the activities, however, are intended largely for adult learners in a North American context. Parallel texts are, of course, available in other national contexts, but we have made no consistent effort to identify them.

Academic Orientation

Our students come to us with an array of strengths and limitations. Some adults can already write with ease and clarity, but have never used a scholarly database. Others have had years of computer training, but have never read an entire book. Still others regularly produce complex company reports, but have never been asked to develop and defend their own ideas. In these and many other ways, adult students find themselves with uneven levels of comfort in an academic environment. A new look, more practice, and the development of additional skills in academic literacy can all make a signifi-cant difference for the adult learner. Indeed, many institutions have housed the portfolio course in the English Department, recognizing that helping stu-dents gain experience and confidence as college-level writers is one significant goal of the portfolio-development course.

The portfolio-development course offers multiple opportunities for stu-dents to identify and work on a broad range of academic skills. The portfo-lio essays may be the first sustained writing students have done, or at least the first they have done for many years. In such cases, the portfolio can pro-vide the opportunity for remediation, introductory work in writing, and practice in building arguments and finding evidence. Students with more "advanced" writing skills can gain more familiarity with the language of academia and with academic conventions for reasoning that may differ from the analytical systems they may employ competently and appropri-ately in other contexts. Whatever their level of formal academic literacy, the drafting of essays can provide the occasion for students to explore and articulate a range of knowledge, not only the narrowly vocational skills that may be initially the most obvious but also their broader conceptual understanding of the structures and communities within which they live and work.

Creating a portfolio using this approach, moreover, helps students to think about their skills in fuller terms. It can help them both to identify the academically transferable skills they already possess and to become aware of other competencies they need to develop as they continue their studies. In this way, the Academic Orientation approach can provide a constructive bridge between present skills and understandings and future choices of study. It can also provide the occasion for some serious dialogue about the place—and the limits—of academic knowledge in a world that requires many forms of expertise and about the hard-earned ambivalence that many adults have about academic forms of knowledge.

Sample Activities

1. Review the various organizational forms for written communications: narration, description, explanation, comparison/contrast, argumentation, and definition. Assign students pieces of their portfolio essays using each form. Possible assignments could include:

   - Narrate the steps of a procedure you have created or worked with and explain the importance of each step;

   - describe the structure and function of your company, community, or an organization with which you are familiar;

   - compare and contrast your job before and after a major structural or technological change;

   - define a concept or an idea important to your work; and

   - argue for or against a proposed change in your community, organization, or workplace.

2. Assign a free-writing exercise in class or for homework, such as:

   - I like my job because . . .

   - I feel good about myself at work when I . . .

   - If I were the boss at work, I'd change the way . . .

   - The tasks I perform in a week include . . .

   - I believe in this organization because . . .

   - The value that most motivates my work in the community is . . .

   Ask volunteers to share their free-writing. Help the class to tease out ideas for further development and new writing. (Peter Elbow's *Writing with Power: Techniques for Mastering the Writing Process* (1998) and *Everyone Can Write: Toward a Hopeful Theory of Writing and Teaching Writing* (2000) are helpful resources for both teachers and students.)

3. Give assignments that help students to focus on the roles they play rather than on themselves. (Note: This is especially useful given that some students find writing easier when the attention is not directly on them.) For example:

   - Imagine you are resigning from your job. Design a job description for the person replacing you.

   - Design a syllabus to teach people how to do your job.

   - Write a newspaper article in which you discuss the goals of your organization and what the organization has achieved.

4. Lead students in a "branching exercise" to help them to add detail and texture to their portfolio essays. In other words, ask them to write a preliminary paragraph describing what they do or what they know. Then, have each sentence in the paragraph serve as the first sentence for a separate paragraph, and ask students to write those paragraphs. Repeat the process for as long as it is fruitful.

5. Over a period of weeks, invite class members to share their portfolio narratives-in-progress. After individuals read their drafts aloud, ask the group to discuss what is strong and clear in the writing and what needs more work and detail.

6. Have students make oral presentations to the group concerning an aspect of their jobs or activities they know well. These may be prepared on notes or in writing beforehand. Alternatively, have students make spontaneous presentations while other students take notes. Those notes (which also give students practice in note-taking, oral communication, and organizing ideas—all important parts of their developing academic repertoire) can then be reconstructed into an outline for an essay.

7. Explore the idea of "academic skills" as one instance of the human skills of thinking and communication, such as:

   • Thinking clearly and systematically

   • Accessing information and ideas

   • Communicating with others

   • Finding and weighing evidence

   • Critically evaluating what we take for granted

   • Storing information

   Ask students to think about the ways in which they have gained and used these skills in their work and life activities. Discuss how these skills can be learned, honed, and used in a range of academic settings. (One useful book dealing specifically with the skills of critical thinking among adults is Michael Andolina, *Practical Guide to Critical Thinking,* 2002.)

8. Give writing assignments designed to tap the *conceptual knowledge* concerning their workplace, community, or organization that many students have gained. For example, you can ask students to think about, research, and/or write about:

   • The social structure of their workplace

   • The history of technology in a given industry

   • The changing economic and social environment of an industry

- The relationship between an organization and the community
- The changing demographics of a neighborhood and its social/political/cultural implications
- The history of a specific social or economic problem, and the movements that have been developed to address it

9. As another way to help students think about and identify some of the conceptual bases of what they know or do, assign readings that provide overviews of the social and psychological dynamics of workplaces and organizations. Ask students to use their own experiences as the basis for responding to these ideas, for discussing the strengths and/or weaknesses of a specific approach, and for applying these ideas to the workplace or organization they know best. Possible topics and resources include:

- Organizational change (Rosabeth Moss-Kanter, *Evolve! Succeeding in the Digital Culture of Tomorrow,* 2001)
- Technological change (Jeremy Rifkin, *The End of Work,* 1995)
- New approaches to management (Sumantra Ghoshal and Christopher Bartlett, *The Individualized Corporation,* 1999)

10. Introduce students to the idea of academically "transferable" skills. Identify those skills that adults often develop on the job and in their family and community lives: listening skills, note-taking, organizing information, managing time, and debating a point of view. Give them the opportunity to identify how and where they gained and now use those skills and how those skills can help them in the academic environment.

11. Starting with the premise that there is no such thing as an "unskilled worker," help students identify the conceptual and problem-solving skills that are required to do their jobs. Explore these skills for the purposes of confidence-building, transferability of learning to an academic environment, and credit for prior learning.

12. Use readings about contemporary culture as a way to provide students with opportunities to practice their skills in description and critical analysis. Ask students to use these readings as take-off points for their own written reflections on such issues as family, education, gender, opportunity, and justice. Class discussions of such readings also provide students with a model of how one approaches a problem or question academically. (Two possible readers for students in the United States are Gary Colombo et al. eds., *Rereading America: Cultural Contexts for Critical Thinking and Writing,* 2001; and David Bartholomae, *Ways of Reading,* 1998.)

13. Students often associate "academic skills" with skills in reading and writing. The Academic Orientation approach can also respond to other areas, such as those concerned with quantitative thinking. For example, ask students to collect current newspaper or journal articles that use graphs, statistics, or numerical data. Use discussion of these materials to identify the use of quantitative methods in research and analysis (whatever the specific field) as well as in our everyday understanding of things.

14. Help students gain experience as public speakers in an academic environment by asking them to deliver a talk on changes in their workplace, discuss the challenges of their current position, or give a demonstration of a skill or task they know well. Use this exercise to give practice in organizing ideas, note-taking, and effective presentation—and to prepare for that part of prior learning assessment that will take place through interviews and demonstrations. Simultaneously use it to recognize and celebrate the oral traditions of learning and teaching that are the hallmark of many of the communities and workplaces from which students come.

15. Choose a number of current social issues and ask students to research them. Assign student roles in a series of debates, in which they present and support arguments and respond to the points of view of others. Use these activities to give students experience in:

   • Developing and articulating their own ideas

   • Making arguments and developing evidence

   • Gaining comfort working with ideas and interpretations

   • Researching topics

   • Critically evaluating what they read and hear

   • Speaking publicly

   • Sharing ideas with others

16. Ask students to identify two of their most important learning experiences, one in which they learned in a formal setting (i.e., in a course or a training) and one in which the learning was unstructured and more experiential (i.e., work they have done in the community or skills gained on the job). As a first exercise, ask them to describe:

   • What they learned in each context

   • How they learned it

   • The ways in which the two learning experiences were similar

   • The ways in which the two learning experiences differed

   • Their understanding of the advantages and disadvantages of each method

Use this activity as a way for students to think about how their college-learning might be similar and different from the way in which they learned on the job, and as an opportunity for students to begin to talk with one another about what "learning" is.

17. Arrange a library orientation with follow-up assignments, in which students identify and locate books, articles, and other scholarly materials in an area of their experience/expertise. Use this as an opportunity to introduce students to the range of resources available in a library, and to the art of research, bibliography building, academic referencing, and scholarly writing. This kind of activity can also be important as a way for students to gain first experiences as online researchers and as explorers of databases relevant to what they know and to their future studies. (Among many useful texts and handbooks in this area are Wayne C. Booth et al. *The Craft of Research*, 2003; and Diana Hacker, *Research and Documentation in the Electronic Age*, 2002.)

18. Using the college catalogue, ask students to identify a specific course whose content they believe they have mastered experientially. Ask students to:

   • Obtain a copy of the syllabus, reading list, and other course requirements;
   • review one or more of the key readings in the course;
   • if possible, audit a session of the class; and/or
   • interview the professor or a student who is taking (or has taken) the course; and
   • write about what they have done and learned about the relationship between what they know about the subject and the content of the course.

   Use this exercise to help students familiarize themselves with formal academic coursework (including the names of courses, how they are described, and the departments or disciplines within which they fall), and to explore the similarities and differences between experiential and academic learning. Especially in programs that evaluate prior learning on a course-analogue basis, also use this exercise to help students begin to identify possible sources of credit.

19. Select an issue relevant to students' lives and work to serve as the basis for exploring how scholars from different disciplines view the same issue. Through readings; library, online, and museum assignments; and

presentations by academics and professionals, use this exploration to provide students with an introduction to the vocabulary of departments and disciplines, and to the basic ways of academic knowledge and of scholarly approaches to inquiry.

For example:

- Students with families might examine how psychologists, sociologists, historians, and policy analysts have thought about the experiences and roles of children, about the expectations of parents, and about the responsibilities of various governmental agencies;

- a group of students from a particular industry might examine its technological history, and the economic, social, and cultural effects of change on that industry; and

- students who have been involved in various political activities might examine the ways in which historians, political scientists, and statisticians have approached the study of politics and political action.

20. Ask students to read and/or view a series of works of literature and art on a topic of common interest. Appropriate topics may vary, but the assignment might include short stories and poems, a visit to a local museum, or the exploration of an online exhibit. Use this assignment as a basis for discussing the ways in which artists and writers see the world, and the ways in which the humanities help broaden our understanding of ourselves, one another, and the world.

21. Use an exploration of the nature and quality of students' lives as a means of addressing time-management issues that will surface for adults returning to school. Guide students through timeline and time-restructuring exercises. Use specific portfolio assignments as opportunities to think about schedules, planning, prioritizing, and meeting college deadlines.

22. Administer a learning-styles profile exercise and use the results to help students become more attentive to implications of their own learning styles and those of others. Encourage students to think about the ways in which they acquired their prior learning and the decisions they now face concerning new learning and alternative learning venues. (David Kolb's *The Learning Styles Inventory*, 1985, is an important and often-used resource here. Students might also find it provocative to look at various writings by Howard Gardner on the notion of "multiple intelligences." See his book, *Multiple Intelligences: The Theory in Practice*, 1993.)

Cheryl, John, and Maria: Applications of the Academic Orientation Approach

Like many adults who return to formal education, Cheryl, John, and Maria are knowledgeable, competent adults who draw upon knowledge gained in many settings. They have, moreover, developed sophisticated and effective communications skills. Cheryl's success as the owner of a small business and John's as a counselor and "big brother" have been predicated on the ability to communicate with clarity and sensitivity. Maria's work as a teacher's aide and especially as a union organizer and negotiator, in turn, is both cause and effect of an extremely wide range of public and interpersonal communicative strategies.

At the same time, there is a disjuncture between how Cheryl, John, and Maria communicate and utilize their knowledge and the ways of organizing and articulating knowledge that typify the academic environment. Maria is perhaps the clearest example. She is a highly effective public speaker who can muster evidence, present a nuanced argument, and combine factual and motivational presentation styles—orally and in Spanish. Thus, on the one hand, a curriculum that treated her as inarticulate would be an inappropriate and, no doubt, resented miscalculation. On the other hand, her skills in written English do not meet either academic expectations or her own felt needs, and Maria herself would be the first to insist on her need to improve them.

Each of these people has returned to formal education with an ambivalent relationship to academic knowledge. On the one hand, each has had experiences with "educated" people as both powerful and judgmental, at their expense. John has developed his extensive counseling skills the hard way—through years of battling his own addiction, through the "tough love" of recovery in a twelve-step program, and through years of helping other recovering addicts and, now, fatherless boys. Yet he has often been exposed to the arrogance of university-trained social workers who feel superior to those, like him, whose counseling skills developed in the trenches. Moreover, while he feels the need for credentials in preparation for a new career, he is uncomfortable with academic ways of knowing, which seem to him to have no basis in "real" life.

Cheryl's feelings and experiences in this regard are, if anything, more complex. At work in the garment industry, she had long resented being asked to train generations of college-educated "kids" just coming into the industry who were then promoted over her head. Now that the plant has closed, she finds herself without "a piece of paper" to demonstrate that she is even a skilled seamstress, let alone a valuable trainer and mentor in the industry. The promise that, through PLA, her skills will be recognized has, indeed, been a strong motive in returning for education. But, like John, she feels a bit as if she has been forced to, as she puts it, "join the enemy."

At the same time, for all their bravado and self-respect, these adults have internalized the message that experiential learning is not as "good as" academic knowledge and they thus struggle with their own sense of inferiority. The formal process of getting credit through PLA will help this, as will the demystification of academic structures and ways of knowing that Academic Orientation can provide. Thus, John can gain exposure to the ways in which academic knowledge is gathered, organized, and used in the scholarly disciplines related to substance abuse. Maria and Cheryl can make thoughtful and informed judgments if they are given the opportunity to explore what a number of academic fields can contribute to their future work possibilities.

Assignments that address a broad range of prior learning will be the most effective way both of honoring the knowledge these three adults possess and of giving them epistemological access to academe. Cheryl's knowledge of the effects of globalization on U.S. industries and workers, John's understanding of the psychology of addiction, and Maria's articulate understanding of the specific concerns of women workers all bear the marks of the contexts in which they were gained. But they overlap importantly with academic disciplines and theories, and they are the basis for an "academic orientation" in which these three can make their own decisions about what—and how—academic knowledge can be of use to them.

The Meaning of Education

Every viable program for adult students includes some attention to academic skills and, as the activities delineated above suggest, those skills can provide a focus for the portfolio-development course. At the same time, the issue may be broader than attention to specific skills; for many adult students, the entire higher educational arena could be rather alien terrain. Thus, it is crucial for us not to neglect the challenge of helping adults gain greater familiarity with, and more comfort in, what is for many a new learning environment—a world of attitudes, concerns, values, and orientations that they may experience as quite alien. The experience of learning is not new: adults learn in many ways and in myriad contexts. However, learning as a formal and self-conscious activity may be new to many.

No doubt, our students come to this course with many powerful and sometimes painful school experiences. Indeed, some of these have skewed their entire sense of themselves as learners. A focus on education in the portfolio-development course can bring such experiences and ideas into clearer view. Students can become aware of what philosophers and educators have said about knowledge, about the goals of schooling, and about the relationship between schools and other social institutions. In the process, they can be given an opportunity to examine their own often tacit assumptions about learning and their preconceived values about how it is acquired and how it is evaluated by others. Looking at the history of education, becoming more aware of the debates over the function and quality of schooling in America, or examining various theories of learning can help students gain familiarity with key academic terms. Importantly, such an exploration can help them realize that education itself is open to interpretation and thus subject to change.

Creating a portfolio using this approach helps students to reflect on their own learning and schooling experiences within a fuller philosophical, historical, and sociological context. As they explore how learning has been defined and how various educational institutions have organized knowledge in different historical and cultural periods, students can identify new ways to think about the significance of their own learning and about the relationship between what they know, how they learned it, and how that learning is valued—or not valued—in society.

Sample Activities

1. Assign readings by philosophers and educational theorists who represent different perspectives on the meaning of education. Among those to consider could be Plato, *The Republic* (1961); John Dewey, *Experience and Education* (1963); and Paulo Freire, *Teachers as Cultural*

Workers: Letters to Those Who Dare Teach (1998). Works representing a variety of perspectives include Neil Postman, *The End of Education* (1995); John Taylor Gatto, *Dumbing Us Down* (2002); E. D. Hirsch, *The Schools We Need and Why We Don't Have Them* (1999); and bell hooks, *Teaching to Transgress* (1994). Peter Jarvis's edited *The Age of Learning* (2001) includes useful readings. Use classroom discussions of and written responses to these readings to help students think about how others have defined education. These discussions can also be used to encourage students to explore their own values and feelings about learning and schooling, especially about how they and others define words like "knowledge," "expertise," "educated," "skilled," and "wisdom."

2. Focus discussion and readings on a critical issue in the history of education and on the contemporary debate about schools. The focus can be on issues of higher education or adult education, or students can be given the opportunity to revisit issues that influenced their own schooling as young people. Possible topics include:

- Standardized testing
- Liberal versus vocational education
- Segregation and schooling
- Schooling and social justice
- Schooling and upward mobility
- The expertise of teachers and professors

Encourage students to look at daily newspaper reports, scholarly articles, court decisions, texts on education, and popular books on schooling. In the current American context, Deborah Meier, *Will Standards Save Public Education?* (2000); Jonathan Kozol, *Savage Inequality* (1999); and Lisa Delpit, *Other People's Children* (1995) are all useful, critical, and provocative texts. Use these readings to raise questions about how schooling is connected to other social, cultural, and political realities, and how a student's own learning experiences have been shaped by a range of forces.

3. Ask students to think about the ways in which the experience of learning as an adult differs from that of children and adolescents. Help them examine the advantages and disadvantages of being an adult learner and link these qualities to their own experiences of schooling and to their plans for new learning. Interested students will find helpful introductions in Larry Daloz, *Mentor: Guiding the Journey of Adult Learners* (1999); and in Stephen Brookfield, *Understanding and Facilitating Adult Learning* (1986). Relate this directly to portfolio development by

assigning readings that focus on experiential learning as the heart of adult education. (Useful materials include selections from David Kolb, *Experiential Learning: Experience as a Source of Learning and Development,* 1984; Jack Mezirow and Associates, *Fostering Critical Reflection in Adulthood: A Guide to Transformative and Emancipatory Learning,* 1990; David Boud and Nod Miller, eds., *Working with Experience: Animating Learning,* 1996; and Kathleen Taylor et al., *Developing Adult Learners,* 2000.)

4. Assign students short autobiographical pieces on their school lives and on what they did (or didn't) learn in school. Ask them to think and write about the ways in which they later compensated for the limitations of their education by finding other sources of learning in their lives. Assign fictional or autobiographical readings that address the issue of schooling versus lifelong learning. (Helpful examples include *The Autobiography of Malcolm X,* 1999; Nelson Mandela, *Long Walk to Freedom,* 1995; Miles Horton, *The Long Haul,* 1990; Mike Rose, *Lives on the Boundary,* 1999; and bell hooks, *Salvation,* 2001.)

5. Ask students to identify a person they admire for the kinds of expertise and/or wisdom that person has attained. Use the persons so named to explore the various ways in which human beings develop knowledge, skills, and wisdom informally and experientially, as well as through formal schooling. Help students identify and describe the ways in which their own knowledge, skills, and insights about life have been attained. Encourage students to compare their learning experiences with those of others.

6. If a group of students is from a similar ethnic, racial, or religious background or is of the same gender—or if a number of different groups are represented in class—use readings and class discussions to explore the educational history of these groups and its social, cultural, and economic implications. Use this inquiry to help students to situate their own experiences within a broader historical context and to explore the relationship between a group's schooling experiences over time and that group's so-called life-chances.

7. If a number of students is from the same occupational or organizational background, ask them to work together to develop a picture of the "ideal practitioner" in their field. Ask them to identify the qualities that person has, as well as the specific skill areas and areas of knowledge he or she must possess. Use this picture of the ideal practitioner to help students identify their own areas of skill and knowledge, and use that as the basis

for organizing their writing about their skills and knowledge in
their field.

8. Ask students to write about their ideal school or learning situation.
Focus discussion on their values and assumptions and on the similarities
and differences among the ideas they articulate. Comparing these models
with other utopian educational designs and experiments throughout
history can help them wonder about what they and others take for
granted and about the different ways in which they might imagine
studying and thus thinking about themselves as learners. (Alfie Kohn,
The Schools Our Children Deserve, 1999; Nel Noddings, *The Challenge
to Care in Schools,* 1992; and Riane Eisler, *Tomorrow's Children:
A Blueprint for Partnership Education in the 21st Century,* 2001, are
all good starting points.)

9. Develop assignments that help students define and explain different
definitions of an "educated person" throughout history—the wider the
historical period, the better. For example, one interesting exercise is to
encourage students to examine various college mission statements and
analyze their ideas, their language, and their philosophical assumptions.
Students could also review a range of curricula from a variety of
institutions in order to think about *why* an institution chooses to include
a particular requirement, or why "majors" or "minors" are designed as
they are. Recent debates about "core curricula" or "general education
requirements" can also prompt discussion about the construction of an
education and about changing understanding of its goals.

Cheryl, John, and Maria: Applications of the Meaning of Education Approach

As we saw in the discussion of Academic Orientation, Cheryl, John, and
Maria all have a complex relationship to formal schooling. John is ambivalent about the academically trained social workers in his field, and Maria,
whose daughter is a social worker, has her own ambivalence. She is proud of
her university-trained children, but at the same time is equally proud of having sustained her family and made a life for them as an immigrant with limited formal education whose first language was not English. Like John, she
both desires and resents what formal education means to her.

Cheryl's understanding of the meaning of education is more communal
and historical; she grew up hearing stories of her parents' Jim Crow education
and of the struggle for the rights to an equal education in the civil rights movement. She knows how the denial of educational opportunity was an important

part of the historical denial of opportunity to African Americans. In this way, she connects her own desire for an education to the collective aspirations of her community. Exposure to more of that history and to the lives and ideas of those who were part of it will help Cheryl locate herself in the debate concerning the meaning of education in personal and societal change.

Reconciling the ambivalence these three students feel and their alienation from academic environments and ways of knowing is one possible goal of the portfolio-development course. Yet reconciliation may be less important than an open-ended exploration of the questions: What does it mean to know something? What is important to know? Exploring answers to these kinds of questions can both help students affirm the value of what they already know and encourage them to cultivate their curiosities and build on what they already know. This approach, moreover, can help to move students beyond the specifically vocational and organizational imperatives that bring many of them back into formal education. It can also help them ask themselves what they love for its own sake and what they want to know more about.

Finally, The Meaning of Education approach is one of the places in which ideas about experiential learning can be addressed. The notion of experience as the adult's "living classroom" and as the foundation for learning in adulthood can be introduced and linked to the exploration of the specific examples of experiential learning that is identified and described in a student's portfolio. Readings on the nature and importance of experiential learning itself can encourage a deeper understanding of the importance and legitimacy of experiential learning and give form and real legitimacy to the process of portfolio development.

Personal Exploration

As educators of adults, we often meet our students at turning points in their lives. Jobs are in flux, long-term personal relationships are beginning or ending, children are leaving home, financial stability is in jeopardy, and, for all these reasons, once-secure identities are often being questioned. Indeed, for these adults, the return to formal education is one more powerful imposition on their already complex lives.

These turning points, these critical junctures, may be ones of conflict or tension. They may also be ones of anticipation and exciting transition. But whatever their quality, it is *change* that defines these moments of college entrance. And change brings with it a host of new questions and concerns, a new self-awareness, and a new need to come to terms with one's past. It can also offer openings for wondering about possible futures.

The portfolio course can provide an opportunity for students to explore their own development as learners, as parents, as workers, and as members of their communities. Using personal exploration as a theme, students can use their own lives as the focal point of a self-reflective process that will help them gain a clearer and more meaningful appreciation of what they have done, what they are doing now, and how they might remold their lives in the future. In some cases, this may be a quite individual examination of the factors that make up each unique human life. In others, it may mean exploring how the shared experience of gender, class, ethnicity, sexual orientation, or nationality has influenced their lives and pushed them in a particular direction, led them to a certain social status or employment position—situated them in the world in a particular way.

Compiling a portfolio using this approach allows students to begin with their own lives and with the distinctive life histories that they bring to formal education. Such an orientation also provides opportunities for students to explore their interests, to more clearly articulate their personal and professional goals, and to become more aware of the patterns and idiosyncrasies of their own and other lives.

Sample Activities

1. Assign students an autobiography of someone whose life relates in some important way to theirs, or ask students to locate and read one. Based on this reading:
   - Ask students to write about and/or discuss the ways in which they identify with that person and the challenges that person faced, or the ways in which their lives have been similar or different to that person's life.

- Help students to explore how an individual life evolved within broader historical patterns, including the presence or absence of economic opportunity, the pressures of cultural expectations, the local and/or global political events of the day, and/or barriers to and opportunities for a fulfilling life.

- Tie this to prior learning assessment by focusing on the ways in which people develop skills and knowledge in response to specific life opportunities and challenges.

2. Ask students to write their own autobiographies. Encourage them to use these narratives as a starting point for the identification of key moments of their own experiential learning.

3. Assign books such as Mary Catherine Bateson, *Composing a Life* (1990) and *Full Circles, Overlapping Lives* (2000), which explore the multiple roles that adults play. Use these readings to help students focus on their life roles and on the skills and knowledge that grow out of each role and out of the need to "juggle" many roles. Discussions might also encourage students to examine the ways in which skills and knowledge developed in one area of life translate to other areas. A more demanding and theoretical book that deals with broad and relevant themes like parenting, working, healing, and learning is Robert Kegan's, *In over Our Heads: The Mental Demands of Modern Life* (1994).

4. Assign readings on the life cycle such as Helen Bee and Barbara Bjorklund's *The Journey of Adulthood* (1999); Daniel Levinson, *The Seasons of a Man's Life* (1986); Daniel Levinson and Judy D. Levinson, *The Seasons of a Woman's Life* (1997); Carolyn Heilbrun, *The Last Gift of Time* (1997); or Robert Sternberg, *Wisdom* (1990). Ask students to think about learning opportunities that were open or that were closed to them at different stages in their lives. Or ask them to write about key turning points in their lives—important moments in which they believe the way they approached or understood their lives shifted.

5. Use a book that deals with self-assessment and life-planning. A very accessible volume is Richard Bolles, *What Color Is Your Parachute?* (2003). Use such a reading (and the exercises that typically accompany such material) to help students identify creditable and/or transferable skills and to begin to make connections between what they already know and new areas of academic study or career exploration.

6. Focus on the concept of "transformation" and on the particular ways in which adults can identify and reflect on moments of change in their own lives. For example, ask students to write about questions such as: What

were key points of change in your life? What led up to them? What special knowledge or new learning emerged as a result of these experiences? Classic readings by authors like Carl Rogers (*The Carl Rogers Reader*, 1989) and Malcolm Knowles (*The Adult Learner*, 1998) are useful starting points. Jack Mezirow et al.'s *Learning as Transformation* (2000) includes a number of interesting articles on the notions of "transformative learning" and "perspective transformation," which might spur students to wonder about such moments in their own lives.

7. Ask students to write an extended letter to their unborn grandchildren (if they already have grandchildren, have them write it to their great-grandchildren, or to any child in a future generation) exploring the main events and lessons of their lives. Use this as a way to help students identify significant events and the learning (i.e., the insights, the new ideas, the change in perspective) that was tied to those events.

8. Work with students to explore possibilities for areas of assessment arising from their long-term interests, their personal reading, and/or their leisure activities. Typical topics might include Coaching Team Sports, Community Leadership, Quilting and Appliqué, The Birth and Significance of Jazz, Practical Politics, or Contemporary Fiction by Women. Opening up these kinds of areas to a more careful view is crucial, given the possibility that students might quickly put aside such learning by defining it as too idiosyncratic, too personal, or just too far away from what they assume to be "university learning." Students might also find it useful to read examples of more scholarly materials on these topics in order to begin to situate their learning within a broader context.

9. Assign a text such as Robert Coles, *The Call of Service: A Witness to Idealism* (1993); or Ram Dass and Paul Gorman's *How Can I Help?* (1985) as one way to encourage students to think about their core values concerning others and the ways in which they use their knowledge and skills to bring meaning into their lives. Larry Daloz et al., *Common Fire: Lives of Commitment in a Complex World* (1996); and Susan Shreve and Porter Shreve, eds., *How We Want to Live* (1998), offer good examples that can begin to help students relate the "personal" to the "social."

10. Focus on the theme of personal change within a broader socioeconomic and cultural context. For example, assign readings on the changes in social life over the past few generations. Ask students to write about the ways in which these changes have or haven't affected them. Possible topics include patterns of employment, family life and family roles,

assumptions about youth and aging, values and behavior, and popular culture.

- Use these readings as a way of exploring academic areas such as sociology, economics, and cultural studies. Explore the ways in which academic approaches do and do not capture people's (and the students') lived experience and what is gained and lost in the process.
- Based primarily on their own experience, help students to develop a "curriculum" that centers on the cultural and social history of their time.

11. Work with students to identify possible areas for the assessment of prior learning in cultural and social studies. Typical topics include Changing Patterns of Gender and the American Family; The African American Experience since World War II; Immigration, Assimilation, and Biculturalism; The Vietnam Generation; Religion and Politics in Today's America; The Experience of Children in Today's World; and The Role of the Arts in Encouraging Social Change. Help them broaden their understanding of "university-" and "college-level" learning and explore the overlap between idiosyncratic and personal interests and the curriculum.

Cheryl, John, and Maria: Applications of the Personal Exploration Approach

Personal Exploration will provide Cheryl, John, and Maria with the chance to view their lives holistically, not solely through the lens of a job or of schooling. Here, students can explore their values, interests, and skills; revisit the major events and issues in their lives; and begin to identify new areas of interest or reflect upon areas of real importance to them that may or may not have anything to do with paid employment.

It is in the Personal Exploration approach that portfolio development meets the liberal humanist tradition of adult learning: the exploration of learning styles, the examination of values and goals, the unraveling of assumptions about the world, and the examination of experience as a source of learning. As in the Meaning of Education approach, this one can help the portfolio-development process gain form through exposure to ideas of adult education (for example, Dewey on the centrality of experiential learning; Knowles, Maslow, and Rogers on the growth of psychic independence; Kolb on the learning cycle; Mezirow on "perspective transformation"; and Freire on "empowerment" and on education for "critical consciousness"). In this way, students can focus directly on the relationship between their experience and what they know, and between what they know and who they are.

Very importantly, the exploration of personal history and experiential learning is just that—highly personal. It pushes us to consider the ways in which our specific life experiences have offered us areas of interest and opportunities to learn. John is an example: His personal history as the child of an alcoholic father and as a recovering alcoholic himself has been a central learning experience. It has clearly contributed to forming his areas of interest and of work. His experience of growing up without a father and his understanding of how difficult life was for both him and his mother led him to work with young fatherless boys and to develop a specific understanding of their situation.

Maria, too, has just been through an experience in which what she learned as a union organizer (public speaking, for example) transformed her as a person. As a wife, mother, and teacher's aide, she has always defined herself as a woman in terms of children and child care, and thus had a great deal of trouble dealing with her own children leaving home. Now, she has begun to understand the possibilities for her life differently. She has gained self-confidence, leadership skills, and the ability to stand up for herself and for others. Importantly, the exploration of what she has learned in the way of "skills" necessary for the writing of her portfolio has been a way for her to understand her emotional and personal changes and growth.

In her mind, Cheryl's career skills are tied to her family history. All of the women in the rural communities where she grew up were skilled seamstresses. Her grandmother was a quilter, and her mother made all the dresses Cheryl wore as a child. She learned her sewing skills from her mother and her grandmother. Writing her portfolio became an occasion to tie the creditable professional skills she learned on the job to things she learned at home as a child and to connections with her grandmother, her family, and her community of origin.

The focus on the individual and the use of the personal exploration approach to portfolio development reflects our own Western liberal humanist predilections. As we design the portfolio-development course, it seems quite easy for faculty and students to slip into such an "individualistic" mode. While this approach is often quite effective in connecting our students to the portfolio-development process, our dependence on it sometimes makes us insufficiently attentive to the dimensions of selfhood that live in history and community. That is, we can neglect the ways in which the "personal" is shaped and embedded in the experience of a society and the ways in which students experience their lives as part of something beyond them as individuals. For example, Maria's empowerment as a person cannot be separated from that of other women, of Latina women, of immigrant workers, and of newly unionized workers. So, too, John has a sense of himself as part of a community of recovery in which people are deeply dependent on a shared experience, shared understandings, and interpersonal support. In a similar way, Cheryl is drawing upon a heritage of collective skill. All of these examples point to the fact that "personal exploration" is an occasion not only for claiming one's own hard-earned individual experiential learning but also for recognizing and celebrating the shared venues outside our formal educational structures in which groups of people pass on shared understandings and skills.

In their distinctive ways, Maria, John, and Cheryl embody the social history of their fields. As we work with them to identify what they know and the skills they have acquired as individuals, we are also helping them see and better understand the interconnections between their individual learnings and the broader social, political, ethnic, gender, and economic contexts in which they have lived.

Learning from the Outsider Within

The students with whom we work come to us with rich histories. As individuals, parents, workers, and members of organizations, they have lived and are living complex lives. Indeed, many of us are trying to meaningfully engage with students who are very different than the students we were as undergraduates. Part of our effort has to concern itself with how we truly "meet" these adults and help them (even as we help ourselves) make better sense of our world and of our place in that world.

Understanding the nature of the cultural, social, racial, and gendered world in which we live is an important goal of the portfolio course and an explicit aim of this approach. Here, students can directly explore the ways in which cultures frame our experience, inform our ways of thinking about ourselves, and place us in a specific social position faced with particular opportunities and with distinctive tensions and conflicts.

This approach to portfolio development can provide an important opportunity for students to reflect on their place as members of a broader world. Most importantly, it can encourage them to think about how their learning and their very identity as learners have been shaped by social and historical factors. By looking at this world and their place in it, students can begin to explore the ways in which what they have learned, where and how they have learned it, and the very qualities of their learning have distinctive origins and carry distinctive values. Students can thus situate themselves anew, become aware of the different forms of knowledge and understanding available outside the social mainstream, and begin to grapple with some of the difficult questions of how and why a group privileges a certain kind of knowledge and not another. Compiling a portfolio using this approach can thus help students think about the central question of "identity and difference"—of what it means to be "in" or "out," "mainstream" or "other"—as individuals and as members of a society.

Sample Activities

1. Read Patricia Hill Collins's essay, "Learning from the Outsider Within" (Collins, 1998). Use this reading as a way to encourage students to talk and make presentations about what they have learned as "outsiders." A number of important questions can follow: What insights did this learning provide to them? What value did it have? How did it affect the way in which they thought about themselves or how others thought about them? What connections or disconnections did they feel between this "outsider" knowledge and the "insider" knowledge that they had gained? How have they used this knowledge in their lives?

2. Assign the passages from W. E. B. DuBois on "double consciousness"—
   the basic "two-ness" of experience, ideas, and ideals described by the
   author in his *The Souls of Black Folk* (1986). Ask students to work in
   pairs or small groups to identify ways in which their consciousness is
   divided in DuBois's sense, and what they have learned as a result of these
   tensions and conflicts.

3. Bring a variety of "cultural objects" to class. For example, these objects
   can be photos of famous historical events, advertisements from the
   present and/or the past, household and other everyday objects, an article
   of clothing, or a piece of music. Ask each student to select an object.
   Explain to students that these objects have something to communicate to
   them about the experience of being an "outsider" or being "different" in
   society. Give students 3–4 minutes to examine their object. Then give
   them a few minutes to write down what the object has taught them.
   Follow this individual work with a class discussion about what they have
   learned from this "artifact" and how thinking about a specific example
   can help them reflect on important aspects of their lives and on the
   nature of the larger society.

4. Ask students to prepare a lesson on the experience of being an "outsider"
   (of the experience of "otherness") to be given to a "mainstream" class.
   For example, a Black student might be asked to teach an all-white class, a
   woman an all-male class, a gay or lesbian person a class of heterosexuals,
   a physically challenged student a group of students considered fully
   "abled" by society. Students should develop a list of the major objectives
   of their lesson, ideas that they want to convey, assignments they would
   develop, homework assignments they would give, and the form they
   would choose to communicate to their "students." Sharing their work
   will provide another opportunity for the students in the class to more
   vividly see the judgments we make about each other and about the
   complexity of seeing the world from another's vantage point.

5. Students can read materials that explicitly deal with an aspect of the
   experience of "otherness," such as discrimination, anger, rebellion, or
   internalized oppression. Whatever readings are chosen, students should
   have the chance to think and feel deeply about an experience different
   than the one they know, to think about how that new set of experiences
   molded the learning about being a self and being in a world of another
   person. The assigned reading could be a novel such as Toni Morrison,
   The Bluest Eye (2000); or Bharati Mukherjee, *The Middleman and
   Other Stories* (1988). It could also be a work of nonfiction, such as

Oliver Sachs, *The Man Who Mistook His Wife for a Hat* (1998). Autobiographical selections might include Nancy Mairs, *Waist-High in the World* (1998); Satish Kumar, *Path without Destination* (1999); or Fenton Johnson, *Geography of the Heart: A Memoir* (1996).

6. Assign students selections that deal with growing up in two cultures simultaneously. Possibilities include Maxine Hong Kingston, *The Woman Warrior* (2000); Richard Rodriguez, *The Hunger of Memory* (1984); Amin Maalouf, *In the Name of Identity* (2000); Eva Hoffman, *Lost in Translation: A Life in a New Language* (1990); or James McBride, *The Color of Water* (1996). Ask them to write an essay or make a presentation on the experience of children growing up in both the "old" and the "new" culture. What tensions and problems are faced by people in such situations? What is the range of decisions and accommodations made? And importantly, what are the kinds of *learning* one gains as a member of an "outsider" group who is seeking comfort in a new world of ideas, feelings, experiences, roles, and patterns of acceptance or discrimination?

7. Encourage students to develop a small project in their community in which they would interview people whose backgrounds are different from their own. Work with them to develop a set of questions that would focus on the distinctiveness of living in that "other" culture. What kinds of issues and problems does a person face? What are the basic values and attitudes sacred to that group? As a man, a woman, a parent, a child, an elder—what are the most important "learnings" that one is supposed to gain and internalize?

Cheryl, John, and Maria: Applications of the Learning from the Outsider Within Approach

As Cheryl's example suggests, different communities of expertise exist and interact with varying degrees of prominence and visibility. (There is no doubt, for example, that Cheryl is a part of a long tradition of seamstresses—of a distinctive culture—whose skills and artistry have been acknowledged in their communities but hold little weight outside of it.) In the main, PLA work has focused on how students' experiential learning overlaps (and is often indistinguishable from) mainstream knowledge represented in mainstream educational institutions and consistent with what we learn as members of the social mainstream (for example, through formal employment and business or as leaders of organizations). But here is an opportunity to work with Cheryl and adult students like her, to explore what we learn from aspects of experience that have been historically marginalized.

In this sense, all three of these students present a variety of forms of "otherness" and social marginalization that have given them qualities of experience different from that assumed by "dominant" groups. Thus, through years of training and work experience, John is by now a highly skilled counselor. But as a professional, he continues to draw deeply on what he has learned from the "outsider"—the child of an alcoholic father, the substance abuser now in recovery—"within." So, too, Maria's success as a union organizer was aided, in part, by the official training she received from the union. But she also depends upon a rich set of understandings about being an immigrant, struggling to learn English, and being a woman in a "man's world."

As representatives of academic institutions, we are regularly faced with adults like Cheryl, John, and Maria whose "outsider" knowledge is often easier to downplay or completely push to the side than to acknowledge, understand, and integrate into the ways of knowing and skills that are our scholarly currency. What does Cheryl know at the college level? Does John's family experience have any bearing on his counseling insights? Why is it important for Maria to concern herself at all with her earlier life in poverty? Isn't it more important to focus on what we take for granted as teachable and true? Working within this approach to portfolio development can help Cheryl, John, and Maria think about the multiple layers of influence upon what they think and know. At the same time, it can help the academy as a whole broaden our assumptions about the definition and the origins of valuable knowledge.

The World of Work and Careers

For many of our students, their lives at work have been the major source of their learning. They come to our colleges because of a belief that we will acknowledge the skills, the insights, and the knowledge they have gained on the job. Indeed, sometimes students have accumulated impressive amounts and great depths of knowledge in their area of expertise. At other times, such knowledge, even in its strength, may lack context. That is, students may be missing the social, political, historical, and cultural—in other words, the conceptual—grounding that would allow them to think about their experiences at work in a more all-encompassing and informed way.

The portfolio-development course offers an important opportunity to explore and carefully examine the broader circumstances, issues, and problems that have informed our students' work lives. The course can help students see the nature and quality of their work from new angles, can offer comparative contexts from which to understand what they do, and often can encourage students to rethink the skills they have learned using concepts and theories with which they are unfamiliar. Students can, for example, become more informed about the history of an industry to which they belong, more knowledgeable about the changing circumstances of work over time, more aware of the connections between communities and work, and more comfortable with the language social scientists use to analyze labor. Taken more broadly, the nature and quality of work itself and the role of work in human life can serve as a central theme of this course. In this way, students can be encouraged to identify and reflect upon their skills in a new light.

An adult student's academic life is often encased in the demands of careers and the immediate issues of finding a job, changing jobs, or gaining promotion in an industry. A portfolio course using this approach can also effectively include this most practical dimension. In fact, it uses what is often most vividly at hand—the work worlds from which our students come to us—to introduce them to social and humanistic studies that can respond to their immediate concerns about "jobs" while simultaneously encouraging them to stretch their perspectives. Course activities can help students place themselves within a broader social-historical constellation and to become more cognizant of the factors (and the debates about the factors) that have affected people's work lives. Such an approach may be particularly significant for those students with a great deal of technical/professional expertise but relatively little experience dealing with the questions and the approaches of the liberal arts and sciences.

Sample Activities

1. Ask students to review descriptions of various jobs and work situations different from their own. For example, students can use the descriptions Studs Terkel provides in his classic book, *Working* (1974), or they can refer to the narratives provided in a more recent book on work in America, J. Bowe et al.'s *Gig: Americans Talk about Their Jobs at the Turn of the Millennium* (2000). Ask students to write their own "contribution" to such a book as one way to encourage them to write about their jobs and about the similarities and differences among jobs and between their work and the examples they find in their readings. This kind of exercise could serve as a first step as they begin to outline and describe what they have done, learned, and most cared about on the jobs they have held.

2. Create an assignment in which students interview each other about their work lives and about their career choices. In such an exercise, preparing for the interview (i.e., developing questions and areas for exploration as interviewers) and carrying it out will help students identify the kinds of questions they need to ask *themselves* as they describe their own experiences and prior learning and as they perhaps contemplate a job change. Another variation of this model is to ask students to find someone in their own field or line of work outside of their class and interview them. Distancing themselves from the immediacy of their own work experiences is one important outcome of these kinds of activities. Small projects like these also raise important issues about "objectivity" and about what we learn (or claim to learn) from any kind of research.

3. Examine the area of worker satisfaction and alienation. This can be done by asking students to list what they most like and most dislike about various jobs they have held, then share their responses with each other. An interesting and often useful addition to this focus would be to ask students to read more theoretically from the literature on the sociology of work. How have sociologists and other workplace analysts evaluated the everyday experience of work? What aspects of work life or forms of working provide us with more or less satisfaction? And how do students think about their own work experiences given these ideas and concepts? Richard Sennett and Jonathan Cobb, *The Hidden Injuries of Class* (1993); Juliet Schor, *The Overworked American* (1991); Barbara Ehrenreich, *Nickel and Dimed* (2001); and Arlie Hochschild, *The Second Shift* (2003), are useful sources that help students contextualize their own feelings and experiences, and get a glimpse of how different social scientists with different points of view think about a key social issue.

4. Focus on the changing face of the workplace and on the future of work. This is another way to help students see and understand their own work experiences within a broader social, historical, and comparative context. It could begin to encourage them to imagine how new institutional and technological forms could affect their work lives and those of the next generations of workers or to consider the changes to the workplace brought about by globalization and immigration. They might consider this latter theme, for example, through Avtar Brah's *Cartographies of Diaspora* (1997); or through Louise Lamphere, ed., *Newcomers in the Workplace* (1994).

5. Help students think about what they do at work and what they have learned on the job through the reading of fiction. Here again is an opportunity to give students experience in college-level reading and analysis, familiarity with a genre and with authors who could be new to them, and awareness of another context and a very different angle from which they can reflect on their work lives. For example, Rebecca Harding Davis's novel, *Life in the Iron Mills* (1985); Charles Dickens's *Hard Times* (1991); or Herman Melville's "Bartleby, The Scrivener" (1995), can offer students a historical vantage point and an opportunity to read materials new to them. Films such as *The Man in the Gray Flannel Suit, Modern Times, Norma Rae,* or *Metropolis* could provide another approach that offers students different ways to think about—to vividly "see"—the experience of work.

6. Ask students to write a history of their occupations during their own working lifetimes, mentioning the changes and events they have seen, participated in, and been affected by directly. Have them use themselves as examples of how one occupation, its workers, its technology, its products and services, and its customers and clients have changed. Ask students to think about how specific trends such as downsizing and outsourcing, globalization, and computerization have affected their industries and working lives. In group discussion, use these experiences to paint a broad portrait of change across industries and the economy as a whole and of the old and new kinds of skills students have developed in response to changing realities. (The fact that these issues are often contested and characterized by a range of viewpoints and strong feelings gives students a good opportunity to gain experience in developing arguments, offering evidence to support their ideas, and evaluating ideas that differ from their own.)

7. Pose a provocative and very specific idea such as "There is no such thing as an unskilled worker." Ask students to analyze this thesis about work

and to explore the ways in which all work requires skill, the ways in which skills are rendered invisible, or the social functions of "job ghettoes." Also use that discussion as a way to tease out and more carefully describe areas of skills and knowledge that may not be readily identified and that, in some cases, may not be specifically identified in job descriptions, vocational curricular, or other "formal" lists of job skills.

8. Guide students through the process of educational and career planning using one of the myriad books in the field. Some possible titles include Richard Bolles, *What Color Is Your Parachute?* (2003); Laurence Boldt, *Zen and the Art of Making a Living: A Practical Guide to Creative Career Design* (1999); and Stephan Pollan and Mark Levine, *Second Acts* (2002). Students can work through much of this material on their own. However, hearing and questioning other students about their ideas, dilemmas, and fantasies is often a very useful experience. It provides students with a glimpse of different experiences of work, different career goals, and a glimpse into the dilemmas that others have faced in their work lives.

9. While a good deal of the material on career planning is necessarily concrete and practical, many students would be helped by the opportunity to think about their past and future learning within the context of broader goals and strongly felt value commitments. (Indeed, some students might be returning to school exactly because their present work does not seem consistent with their sense of what they most care about.) One book mentioned earlier, Robert Coles, *The Call of Service: A Witness to Idealism* (1993), can aid students in raising some of these questions. From a very different perspective, so does Michael Novak, *Business as a Calling: Work and the Examined Life* (1996); and Milton Mayerhoff, *On Caring* (1990). Sara Lawrence-Lightfoot's *Respect: An Exploration* (1999); and Howard Gardner et al., *Good Work: When Excellence and Ethics Meet* (2002), might also provoke this kind of reflection on values and on the ethical context of career choices.

10. Assign readings and/or schedule speakers on the current job market and on projected employment trends. Students can regularly consult documents such as the *Monthly Labor Review* and the *Occupational Outlook Handbook* and gain important experience reading the business page of their local newspaper. Assignments can focus on the kinds of skills, training, and credentials needed for new employment opportunities; on job titles; and on comparative earnings. Job search activities can also offer students a good opportunity to gain more

comfort and facility using online sources. So-called electronic job hunting is a useful skill to gain, and a book like *Adams Job Almanac* (2000) is one of a growing number of useful guides to electronic employer databases and to locating job-hunting sites on the Web.

11. Ask students to describe the "perfect" job. Work with students to identify those qualities or components that make the job attractive to them. Students then can research the range of jobs and careers that possess similar qualities and components.

12. Help students write a detailed skills resume. This exercise (which demands identifying, ordering, grouping, and describing skills) is an excellent parallel activity to the writing of the student's portfolio. Thus, this resume can help the student see what he or she has done and learned (that student's areas of competency) and how those skill areas are at the heart of both the portfolio and the job resume.

13. Create the opportunity for students to carry out mock job interviews. Students can interview each other based on questions they have devised and job descriptions they have found or developed. Students can thus gain practice in presentational skills and in thinking about the kinds of qualities a potential worker should possess.

Cheryl, John, and Maria: Applications of the World of Work and Careers Approach

All three students, Cheryl, John, and Maria, are in job transition. Cheryl needs either to develop a skills resume and/or get a formal credential for a new job in the garment industry or to develop her part-time business into a full-time job, or else she needs to focus on a new career. If she chooses the former, she will have to more thoroughly investigate the legal and financial steps she would have to take to create a small business of her own. If the latter, she will have to identify her current transferable skills, explore her work interests and her values, and get reliable and up-to-date information about the job market (including gathering information on career paths, necessary skills and training requirements, and salary and benefit levels).

John has longer-term questions, since he will still be employed for a number of years and is not faced with layoff. He can explore venues for remaining in substance abuse counseling outside of the police department (such as getting a master's degree in social work and working professionally in that field), or he can pursue other paths of interest without having to worry about his current livelihood. Both John and Cheryl, though, may do well to explore a range of work options, searching for connections between available careers and their own preferences and possibilities. Hearing other students talk about their ideas, their conflicts (including how their personal desires impact those around them), and their fantasies will be useful to both of these students. Such discussions can give them a framework within which to think about the skills they have, the interests that motivate them, and the barriers they face in doing the kind of work they believe will give them real satisfaction.

Maria needs a number of things that this approach can provide. First, while she is in a program that will lead to teacher certification and thus provide her with the teaching job she so covets, her experience has been in only one school and she has never really had an opportunity to explore how her talents might be used in other educational arenas. The portfolio course will thus be Maria's opportunity (as it could be Cheryl's) to think about her skills, talents, strengths, and real interests. Secondly, although Maria has been involved in her union and begins with some experience in thinking about the conditions of work and the quality of a person's work life, this approach will provide her with new and more systematic opportunities to look at the history of her chosen profession and to compare it to the history of other kinds of work. (Thus, the very practical work of job preparation will be effectively linked to new learning in history and the social sciences.)

Finally, while John feels great trepidation about actually leaving the police department, Maria and Cheryl are clearly frightened about their work situations. Like many adult women students, issues of job security and day-to-day finances are paramount. Maria is also very worried about her age and about completing her "training" at an age when no one will hire her. The process of identifying what they know, having their skills and learnings acknowledged and assessed, and developing a portfolio that makes public their life of work can give them important confidence and new sources of information.

Dimensions of Expertise

It is not unusual for adult students who come to our institutions to be confused about what they think they know, what others think they know, and what any number of authorities (including our colleges and universities) assume they need to know. That is, the question of expertise is never far away.

In a most basic way, portfolio work, the project of PLA, is necessarily about expertise, and this approach makes the question explicit and tries to engage the student in serious consideration of it. Here is an opportunity for students to grapple with expertise not as something solid and the easy arbiter of all truth claims, but as a problematic and changing notion. Thus, students can be encouraged to place what they know within a more complex and socially constructed context, and to learn more about the history of expertise as it presents itself in their professional fields. This approach also encourages students to look ahead and to find out how expertise (and thus educational expectations) may continue to change in the area of study they are pursuing.

Our students come to us trying to make sense of competing notions of what is important to know. Often, adults have a clear sense of what has been personally important to them. They also often find themselves in work hierarchies in which there are clear markers between who knows and who doesn't. And students are entering academic territory with its own rules and assumptions of knowledge and authority. The very existence of the PLA process has already made the line between the academic and the experiential more permeable. In this approach, students will be thinking about what they know, about what others know, and about the new learning their professional and academic goals demand. Students will also have an important opportunity to think about what knowledge is valued, by whom, and under what circumstances. Here, then, is another bridge between the portfolio process and any new learning experiences: Students are seeing how learning is created and communicated, and how it changes over time.

Sample Activities

1. Help students develop a detailed "skills resume" in their field. Use that resume as the basis for fuller descriptions of areas of skill, how these skills were learned, and how students acquired new skills or upgraded the ones they already possessed. (Here again, a clear and full resume "exercise" is a logical and very useful stepping stone to the identification and description of a student's prior experiential learning.)

2. Introduce and explore the range of assessment forms and evaluation tools (for example, essays, demonstration projects, product assessment, interviews, and standardized exams). Work with students to identify the specific methods they feel will best allow them to present their skills and knowledge. Within the range of evaluative opportunities allowed in your institution, help students to make reasonable choices about how best to present their knowledge. In this way, students will be thinking about two things: First, they will be introduced to the issues and problems of any kind of "evaluation" of what someone knows or learns; second, students will be encouraged to think not only about *what* they know, but also about how they can best express and show what they know to someone else. (Thus, this is a good opening to a discussion of learning styles.)

3. Help students explore the similarities and differences between workplace-based and academic organizations of knowledge, using a variety of activities.

   • Using students' skills resumes as a basis, identify the ways in which skills and knowledge are organized and understood in students' own fields of expertise. Using your institution's curriculum as a basis, identify the ways in which skills and knowledge of those same fields are organized and understood academically. Discuss the similarities and differences and the implications of these for the meaning of "expertise" as well as possibilities for prior learning assessment.

   • Focus on specific examples of individual courses offered in your institution in order to explore the differences between workplace-based and academy-based organizations of knowledge and value systems concerning knowledge.

   • Invite experts from the workplace and from the academic faculty in a given field to make presentations to the class about what kinds of knowledge are required at various levels in the field. (Alternately, you may wish to ask students to interview such experts and to share what they have learned with the class.) Use those discussions to compare and contrast assumptions concerning such issues as the differences between foundational (introductory) and advanced knowledge, theory and practice, and liberal studies and professional/technical skills.

4. Explore the issue of theoretical and practical knowledge and individual versus collective learning, as they appear both in academic and workplace cultures of knowledge. Assign selections from such texts as Donald Schon, *The Reflexive Practitioner: How Professionals Think in Action* (1983) and *Educating the Reflective Practitioner* (1990); or

Jean Lave and Etienne Wenger, *Situated Learning* (1991) as the basis for discussion. Ask students to think about and write essays exploring their own theories about what they do, and the ideas that they believe underlie their professional practices. Help them to articulate their own sense of the relationship between theory, practice, and experience, as well as their own experience of individual versus group learning.

5. Examine the most basic question: What is "expertise"? Focus on both the students' understanding of what it means to be an "expert" and on various theoretical investigations of this topic. Texts such as Robert Chi et al., eds., *The Nature of Expertise* (1988); Steven Brint, *In an Age of Experts* (1996); and Frank Fischer, *Citizens, Experts and the Environment* (2000), are all helpful starting points for faculty to look for ways to help their students think about their assumptions about what an "expert" is and how such expertise is connected to both the individual and to what Clifford Geertz (2000) has described as "local knowledge." Such a direction is also useful as an important opportunity for students to read work of a more *theoretical* nature, to see how academic language seeks to capture some of what they know through their observations and practices, and to gain some confidence in their role as "theorists."

6. Through readings, interviews with older and more experienced workers, and the students' own memories, construct a history of the student's field of work and the changing skills and educational requirements within it. This kind of exercise often helps students to locate themselves, their current skill levels, and their educational needs within that history. The focus on the "changing" nature of skill requirements also provides an opportunity to think about the issue of "relative" and "absolute" knowledge. Does what we mean by knowledge ever stand still? Who judges it?

7. Explore the specific skills in communication and analysis required in the students' fields. What skills have students already gained in these areas? Have these skill requirements changed? (Because communications and computerization are often linked, this activity could be connected to a discussion and readings about the ways in which new technologies have altered the way people work and communicate with each other at work. In this way, too, this approach is intimately tied to the discussion of the changing nature of work life and of the work environment described earlier.)

8. Identify the educational paths that enable job mobility in students' fields. Help students to place and measure themselves in those terms. This kind

of activity can be used as the basis for portfolio development (what do I already know that will be expected of me?) and for educational planning (how can such external expectations offer me a plan for new studies?).

9. Examine a textbook from the past and a textbook of recent vintage in the same field. Identify the similarities and differences between areas of knowledge and skill that were accepted as "essential" to the field in the earlier text and those that are deemed "necessary" today. This kind of research and discussion of it also help students begin to think about the "construction" of knowledge, and about the ways in which the definition of knowledge is influenced by the social, historical, and technological context in which it exists.

10. Help students raise questions about the current academic curriculum in their fields through a number of activities.

    • Lead students in a critical examination of the curriculum offered in their field and about current debates concerning that curriculum. Identify what is included in the curriculum, what is missing (and why they think it might be missing), what is and isn't relevant, and the meaning(s) of "relevance" itself.

    • Ask students to design the *perfect* curriculum to meet their professional and personal needs.

    • Have students design a lesson plan and/or a curriculum to teach *new workers* in their field. (What would it include? How would they go about teaching it?)

    • Have students design a lesson to teach a group of *teachers* in the field what they should know—and don't seem to know—about the field.

    (Each of these activities can be directly tied to helping students identify and describe what they already know and why they think that knowledge and those skills are important to them.)

11. In company- or organization-sponsored programs, take class time for a three-way meeting between company/organizational representatives, academics, and the students to discuss the educational needs in the field. A number of questions can serve as the take-off point: What does "expertise" in this field now mean? What do "experts" need to know to be successful in the field? What will such experts need to know in ten years? And how do representatives from these different constituencies think that the curriculum should be structured or restructured to meet these changing definitions? Then, have students identify similarities and differences in approaches and make curriculum recommendations.

Cheryl, John, and Maria: Applications of the Dimensions of Expertise Approach

Cheryl, John, and Maria are highly skilled in areas that are regularly taught in tertiary education, but they have acquired their knowledge through life experiences, work, and community and organizational activities. Their skills range from interpersonal competencies in organizing and counseling, to job skills such as sewing and dress design, policing, and teaching, and to areas of knowledge such as the causes of and therapeutic approaches to substance abuse, fluency in foreign languages, and knowledge of culture.

However, now they are meeting these areas of knowledge as understood, organized, and taught academically for the first time. For them, portfolio development provides a chance to investigate the academic aspects of and approaches to the field, and to compare those approaches to their own. In this course, they are invited to identify the intersections, the meetings, between academic knowledge and their own experiential learning and to reflect on the different dimensions of the knowledge and skills in a field, some gained best through direct experience and application, some gained best through more theoretical approaches.

This is not an easy meeting on either side. The very point of the approach is, in effect, to level the playing field so that cultures of knowledge come together with mutual interrogation and mutual respect. John's resentment of academically trained social workers, for example, is not misplaced. He has real reason to understand how limited a purely theoretical or "thirdhand" knowledge of substance abuse can be and, based on his own experiences, he understands aspects of the field that cannot be taught in a classroom or through a book. But if his knowledge and skill can be given respect and visibility through PLA, it will be easier for him to investigate those areas of his field of interest that are better learned through academic study.

Maria's knowledge of labor-management is an example of the ways in which the growth in understanding and knowledge is mutual. The Dimensions of Expertise approach gives her a chance to explore what can be learned about labor-management relations through, for example, the study of law, management, labor history, and occupational safety and health. Yet, what she is learning is that she can contribute to the field. For example, many conventional ways of analyzing and teaching U.S. labor-management relations take native-born male industrial workers as the norm. An exploration of Maria's experiential learning touches on areas of significant learning such as labor studies, women's studies, and Latino studies and provides new opportunities to examine what she can gain from and contribute to each.

Finally, because this approach explores how communities of expertise evolve and how traditions of mentoring and apprenticeship exist outside of formal institutions, Cheryl's own experience as a daughter and granddaughter who comes from such a tradition gains legitimacy and publicness. At a time at which her self-worth and her pride in her professional skills are being undermined by job loss, she can revisit other communities of memory and expertise in which her skills are given value. And, too, by reading work by Patricia Hill Collins (1998) and Alice Walker (1983)—materials that will be new to her—Cheryl will be exploring in an academic environment many dimensions of expertise of which her own skills are an integral part.

RESOURCES FOR
PORTFOLIO DEVELOPMENT
FOR CHAPTER 2

What follows are those texts mentioned in Chapter 2, Approaches to Portfolio Development. As noted earlier, they are given in the spirit of offering examples of the kinds of resources that can be used by faculty who are planning a portfolio course. Given the range of areas, topics, and questions typically raised in such a course, and the fact that the context in which the course is given will necessarily influence the choices that are made, any list can only be suggestive. Our hope is that the materials listed here can at least provide background information and the identification of useful titles for perusal and evaluation.

Adams Job Almanac. (2000). 8th edition. Avon, MA: Adams Media Corporation.

Andolina, M. (2002). *Practical Guide to Critical Thinking.* Albany, NY: Delmar Publishers.

Bartholomae, D. (1998). *Ways of Reading* (4th ed.). Boston: St. Martin's Press.

Bateson, C. (1990). *Composing a Life.* New York: Plume Books.

————. (2000). *Full Circles, Overlapping Lives.* New York: Ballantine Books.

Bee, H., and Bjorklund, B. (1999). *The Journey of Adulthood* (4th ed.). Upper Saddle River, NJ: Prentice Hall.

Boldt, L. G. (1999). *Zen and the Art of Making a Living: A Practical Guide to Creative Career Design.* New York: Penguin.

Bolles, R. N. (2004). *What Color Is Your Parachute? A Practical Manual for Job-Hunters and Career-Changers.* Berkeley, CA: Ten Speed Press.

Booth, W. C., et al. (2003). *The Craft of Research.* Chicago: University of Chicago Press.

Boud, D., and Miller, N., eds. (1996). *Working with Experience: Animating Learning.* London: Routledge.

Bowe, J., et al., eds. (2000). *Gig: Americans Talk about Their Jobs at the Turn of the Millennium.* New York: Crown Publishers.

Brah, A. (1997). *Cartographies of Diaspora: Contesting Identities.* London: Routledge.

Brint, S. (1996). *In an Age of Experts.* Princeton, NJ: Princeton University Press.

Brookfield, S. D. (1986). *Understanding and Facilitating Adult Learning.* San Francisco: Jossey-Bass.

Chi, M. T. H., Glaser, R., and Farr, M. J. (1988). *The Nature of Expertise.* Hillsdale, NJ: Erlbaum.

Coles, R. (1993). *The Call of Service: A Witness to Idealism.* Boston: Houghton Mifflin.

Collins, P. H. (1998). *Fighting Words: Black Women and the Search for Justice.* Minneapolis: University of Minnesota Press.

Colombo, G., et al. (2001). *Rereading America: Cultural Contexts for Critical Thinking and Writing* (5th ed.). Boston: St. Martin's Press.

Daloz, L. A. (1999). *Mentor: Guiding the Journey of Adult Learners.* San Francisco: Jossey-Bass.

Daloz, L. A., et al. (1996). *Common Fire: Lives of Commitment in a Complex World.* Boston: Beacon Press.

Dass, R., and Gorman, P. (1985). *How Can I Help? Stories and Reflections on Service.* New York: Knopf.

Davis, R. H. (1985). *Life in the Iron Mills and Other Stories.* New York: Feminist Press.

Delpit, L. (1995). *Other People's Children.* New York: New Press.

Dewey, J. (1963). *Experience and Education.* New York: Collier.

Dickens, C. (1991). *Four Complete Novels.* New York: Doubleday.

DuBois, W. E. B. (1986). *The Souls of Black Folk.* New York: Library of America.

Ehrenreich, B. (2001). *Nickel and Dimed: On (Not) Getting By in America.* New York: Henry Holt.

Eisler, R. (2001). *Tomorrow's Children: A Blueprint for Partnership Education for the 21st Century.* Boulder, CO: Westview Press.

Elbow, P. (1998). *Writing with Power: Techniques for Mastering the Writing Process.* New York: Oxford University Press.

———. (2000). *Everyone Can Write: Toward a Hopeful Theory of Writing and Teaching Writing.* New York: Oxford University Press.

Fischer, F. (2000). *Citizens, Experts and the Environment: The Politics of Local Knowledge.* Durham, NC: Duke University Press.

Freire, P. (1998). *Teachers as Cultural Workers: Letters to Those Who Dare Teach.* Boulder, CO: Westview.

Gardner, H. (1993). *Multiple Intelligence: The Theory in Practice.* New York: Basic Books.

Gardner, H., et al. (2002). *Good Work: When Excellence and Ethics Meet.* New York: Basic Books.

Gatto, J. (2002). *Dumbing Us Down: The Hidden Curriculum of Compulsory Schooling.* Gabriola Island, BC: New Society Publishers.

Geertz, C. (2000). *Local Knowledge: Further Essays in Interpretive Anthropology.* New York: Basic Books.

Ghoshal, S., and Bartlett, C. A. (1999). *The Individualized Corporation: A Fundamentally New Approach to Management.* New York: HarperBusiness.

Hacker, D. (2002). *Research and Documentation in the Electronic Age* (3rd ed.). Boston: St. Martin's Press.

Heilbrun, C. (1997). *The Last Gift of Time: Life beyond Sixty.* New York: Dial Press.

Hirsch, E. D. (1999). *The Schools We Need and Why We Don't Have Them.* New York: Anchor Books.

Hochschild, A. (2003). *The Second Shift.* New York: Penguin.

Hoffman, E. (1990). *Lost in Translation: A Life in a New Language.* New York: Penguin.

Hong Kingston, M. (2000). *The Woman Warrior.* New York: McGraw-Hill Humanties.

hooks, b. (1994). *Learning to Transgress: Education as the Practice of Freedom.* New York: Routledge.

———. (2001). *Salvation.* New York: Perennial.

Horton, M. (1990). *The Long Haul.* New York: Anchor Books.

Jarvis, P., ed. (2001). *The Age of Learning: Education and the Knowledge Society.* London: Kogan Page.

Johnson, F. (1996). *Geography of the Heart.* New York: Scribner.

Kegan, R. (1994). *In over Our Heads: The Mental Demands of Modern Life.* Cambridge, MA: Harvard University Press.

Knowles, M. S., Holton, E. F., and Swanson, R. A. (1998). *The Adult Learner: The Definitive Classic in Adult Education* (5th ed.) Houston, TX: Gulf Professional Publishing.

Kohn, A. (1999). *The Schools Our Children Deserve: Moving Beyond Traditional Classrooms and "Tougher Standards."* Boston: Houghton-Mifflin.

Kolb, D. (1984). *Experiential Learning: Experience as the Source of Learning and Development.* Englewood Cliffs, NJ: Prentice-Hall.

———. (1985). *The Learning Style Inventory.* Boston: McBer.

Kozol, J. (1992). *Savage Inequality: Children in America's School.* New York: Perennial.

Kumar, S. (1999). *Path without Destination: The Long Walk of a Gentle Hero.* New York: William Morrow.

Lamphere, L., ed. (1994). *Newcomers in the Workplace: Immigrants and the Restructuring of the U.S. Economy.* Philadelphia: Temple University Press.

Lave, J., and Wenger, E. (1991). *Situated Learning: Legitimate Peripheral Participation.* New York: Cambridge University Press.

Lawrence-Lightfoot, S. *Respect: An Exploration.* Reading, MA: Perseus Publishing.

Levinson, D. (1986). *The Seasons of a Man's Life.* New York: Ballantine Books.

Levinson, D., and Levinson, J. D. (1997). *The Seasons of a Woman's Life.* New York: Ballantine Books.

Maalouf, A. (2000). *In the Name of Identity.* New York: Penguin-Putnam.

Mairs, N. (1998). *Waist-High in the World: A Life among the Nondisabled.* Boston: Beacon Press.

Malcolm X. (1999). *The Autobiography of Malcolm X.* New York: Chelsea House Publishing.

Mandela, N. (1995). *Long Walk to Freedom.* New York: Little Brown and Company.

Mayeroff, M. (1990). *On Caring.* New York: Perennial.

McBride, J. (1996). *The Color of Water: A Black Man's Tribute to His White Mother.* New York: Riverhead Books.

Meier, D. (2000). *Will Standards Save the Public Schools?* Boston: Beacon Press.

Melville, H. (1995). *Bartleby.* New York: Viking-Penguin.

Mezirow, J. (1990). *Fostering Critical Reflection in Adulthood: A Guide to Transformative and Emancipatory Learning.* San Francisco: Jossey-Bass.

Mezirow, J., and Associates. (2000). *Learning as Transformation: Critical Perspectives on a Theory in Progress.* San Francisco: Jossey-Bass.

Morrison, T. (2000). *The Bluest Eye.* New York: Penguin.

Moss-Kanter, R. (2001). *Evolve! Succeeding in the Digital Culture of Tomorrow.* Cambridge, MA: Harvard Business School Press.

Mukherjee, B. (1988). *The Middleman and Other Stories.* New York: Fawcett Crest.

Noddings, N. (1992). *The Challenge to Care in Schools: An Alternative Approach to Education.* New York: Teachers College Press.

Novak, M. (1996). *Business as a Calling: Work and the Examined Life.* New York: Free Press.

Plato. (1961). *The Collected Dialogues of Plato.* Edited by E. Hamilton and H. Cairns. Princeton, NJ: Princeton University Press.

Pollan, S. M., and Levine, M. (2002). *Second Acts: Creating the Life You Really Want, Building the Career You Really Desire.* New York: Harper Resource.

Postman, N. (1995). *The End of Education: Redefining the Value of School.* New York: Knopf.

Rifkin, J. (1995). *The End of Work: The Decline of the Global Labor Force and the Dawn of the Post-Market Era.* New York: Tarcher Putnam.

Rodriguez, R. (1984). *Hunger of Memory: The Autobiography of Richard Rodriguez.* New York: Bantam Books.

Rogers, C. (1989) *The Carl Rogers Reader.* Edited by H. Kirschenbaum and V. L. Henderson. New York: Houghton Mifflin.

Rose, M. (1999). *Lives on the Boundary: The Struggles and Achievements of America's Underprepared.* New York: Free Press.

Sachs, O. (1998). *The Man Who Mistook His Wife for a Hat and Other Clinical Tales.* New York: Touchstone Books.

Schon, D. A. (1983). *The Reflective Practitioner: How Professionals Think in Action.* New York: Basic Books.

Schon, D. A. (1990). *Educating the Reflective Practitioner: Toward a New Design for Teaching and Learning in the Professions.* San Francisco: Jossey-Bass.

Schor, J. B. (1991). *The Overworked American.* New York: Basic Books.

Sennett, R., and Cobb, J. (1993). *The Hidden Injuries of Class.* New York: W.W. Norton.

Shreve, S., and Shreve, P., eds. (1998). *How We Want to Live: Narratives on Progress.* Boston: Beacon Press.

Sizer, T., and Sizer, N. (1999). *The Students Are Watching: Schools and the Moral Contract.* Boston: Beacon Press.

Sternberg, R., ed. (1990). *Wisdom: Its Nature, Origins and Development.* New York: Cambridge University Press.

Taylor, K., et al. (2000). *Developing Adult Learners: Strategies for Teachers and Trainers.* San Francisco: Jossey-Bass.

Terkel, S. (1974). *Working.* New York: New Press.

Walker, A. (1983). *In Search of Our Mothers' Gardens: Womanist Prose.* New York: Harcourt.

3

MODEL STUDIES IN
PORTFOLIO DEVELOPMENT

AN INTRODUCTION

There are intricate relationships between educational philosophies and the practice of those philosophies. Sometimes, the most cherished principles and concepts are clearly reflected in the daily practices of teachers and students. At other times, there are obvious tensions (and, at points, direct contradictions) between what has been espoused and what is done. And there are times in which the practice pushes the theory, that is, in which experiments in learning force us to expand the way in which we have imagined what we can or should do.

Certainly, there are gaps between the purposes and strategies of the portfolio. As we described in the introduction to this volume, high ideals and deeply felt educational values as well as the exigencies of social and economic change informed the development of the assessment of prior learning and the use of the portfolio in the first place. But what is striking about the practices that have emerged in the last thirty years and that are reflected in the sampling of cases that have been gathered here are the diverse ways in which educators from across the world have used the portfolio to respond to the academic, professional, and individual needs of adults in higher education. Faculty and administrators have indeed experimented with alternative structures, created and revised syllabi, and integrated ideas from a range of disciplines. In so doing, they have created a fascinating, distinctive, and ever-evolving arena of academic practice. We can now imagine ways of working with our students that were not part of the repertoire of practice thirty, or even ten, years ago. Indeed, this body of practice is a testament to our own experiential learning as adult educators.

The ideas presented thus far about the use of the portfolio course were hypothetical in nature. Our goal was to offer a glimpse of the kinds of approaches, organizational frameworks, and learning activities from which one could draw in the development of the portfolio course. We wanted to show how, in this course, students like Cheryl, John, and Maria could find meaningful ways to organize what they have done, identify the skills and knowledge they have gained, and reflect on significant learning they are bringing to the academy. We now present models from twelve institutions in which the portfolio course has been used. These are intended not as formulae to be followed exactly but as occasions to explore what faculty and administrators in a variety of contexts have created and how portfolio-development continues to evolve in interaction with changing and challenging environments.

The programs and institutions represented here were chosen for a variety of reasons. First, while we have neither focused on nor systematically evaluated the procedures used for assessment, each of the programs follows the basic principles of good practice formulated by the Council for Adult and Experiential Learning (CAEL; see Whitaker, 1989). Second, we wanted to present a range of programs from around the world that used the kinds of approaches identified thus far in effective and imaginative ways, that is, that sought to use the portfolio-development course to respond to a particular institutional setting, to a particular sociocultural context, and to a distinctive population of learners. The fact that the examples represent current work being done by both private and public institutions in the United States, the United Kingdom, South Africa, Australia, and Canada attests not only to the growth of a significant movement for educational change but also to the multiple uses of rich educational tools, the portfolio and the portfolio course, to respond to the needs of adult learners.

As you will see, each model begins with a short introduction to the institution and to the particular ways in which that institution has adapted the portfolio course to its own program. What we hope emerges in the following pages is an invitation to experiment—to meld various approaches and activities into unique course designs suited to an institutional situation. Indeed, examples of such serious and exciting practice should provoke us not only to continue to ask what else we can do but also to be mindful about why we are doing it in the first place.

Reference

Whitaker U. (1989). *Assessing Learning: Standards, Principles, and Procedures.* Chicago: CAEL.

THE OFFSPRING OF DOING

FRAMING EXPERIENCE
AT ALVERNO COLLEGE

James Roth, Georgine Loacker, Bernardin Deutsch,
Suzann Gardner, and Barbara Nevers

Alverno College, a private liberal arts college for women in Milwaukee, Wisconsin, organizes its curriculum around areas of "ability" in which students work through six increasingly advanced levels of development. In both its approach to education and in its assessment of prior learning, the emphasis is on performance, that is, on the relationship between understanding and action. Alverno's complexly structured and thoughtful model of teaching, assessment, and learning brings to life John Dewey's insistence that "there is no such thing as genuine knowledge and fruitful understanding except as the offspring of doing" (1916, p. 275).

Alverno's model of portfolio development is especially interesting for its use of a competency-based framework in which the criteria for assessment, while formally articulated, emphasize broad abilities rather than highly specific areas of knowledge and skill. Adult students are thus able to map their own developmental trajectory, using the "ability" framework to explore both current levels of performance and future learning goals.

The curriculum of Alverno College offers women of all ages a liberal arts education, with majors in the traditional arts and sciences as well as in professional areas that include management, education, nursing, and communication. In subject matter, the various courses of study are similar to those of other liberal arts colleges. Since the early 1970s, however, the Alverno faculty has worked to transform the liberal arts curriculum to focus on student development of ability integrated with knowledge (Alverno College Faculty, 1992). Instead of assuming that abilities develop naturally as a by-product of mastery of subject matter, we explicitly teach students to develop abilities that facilitate the "doing" of what they know. This curriculum, including a mode of assessing student performance that assists students to develop frameworks for reflecting on and taking responsibility for their learning, is also a powerful means for turning life experience into learning.

Key Components of the Alverno Curriculum

The Alverno faculty has identified eight broad areas of ability that we believe characterize the liberally educated adult: communication, analysis, problem solving, valuing in decision making, social interaction, developing a global perspective, effective citizenship, and aesthetic engagement. In doing this, we have not just named these abilities as hoped-for outcomes of a liberal arts education. We have also carefully considered what it means to communicate effectively, to solve problems, and the rest, and we have determined how those abilities can be developed through instruction, practice and coaching, and reflection. From our experience of observing effective student performance, we have specified developmental levels for each ability and described each level in behavioral terms so that it can be taught and assessed in courses across the curriculum. The descriptive criteria for each ability constitute what we call "ability frameworks" (ways of visualizing the ability, ways of constructing one's own performance of the ability), which assist students in demonstrating mastery of the abilities at progressive levels of complexity as they move through the curriculum. (See the box, "Abilities and Developmental Levels.")

Our explicit emphasis on student development of abilities in the context of the disciplines has led to a shift in the way we specify the requirements for our degrees. As in most collegiate programs, students must successfully complete general education courses in the liberal arts as well as the required and elective courses specified by their majors and minors. But the actual determination of degree progress at Alverno College comes through the validations that represent the demonstration of all eight abilities. Within the general education courses required by the college and the courses required by major and minor fields of study, students must demonstrate the first four levels of all eight abilities through course-based and comprehensive assessments. Then, in their major and minor programs of study, they must demonstrate the advanced levels of those abilities that their departments have incorporated into outcomes reflecting the knowledge bases, intellectual skills, and dispositions expected of baccalaureate graduates in those fields. One of the outcomes for a major in business and management, for example, is that she "uses organizational and management theory to interact effectively in organizational contexts that require leadership of groups or other types of interpersonal interactions."

Abilities and Developmental Levels

Develop communication abilities by connecting with everything involved in communication: people, ideas, texts, media, and technology

Level 1—Identify own strengths and weaknesses as communicator

Level 2—Demonstrate the interactive nature of communication in a variety of situations that involve combinations of speaking, writing, listening, reading, quantitative literacy, and computer literacy

Level 3—Effectively and purposefully make meaning using a variety of communication modes (speaking, writing, listening, reading, quantitative literacy, media literacy, and computer literacy) in a given communication situation

Level 4—Communicate creatively in ways that demonstrate integration using disciplinary frameworks

In majors and areas of specialization:

Level 5—Communicate with habitual effectiveness in relation to disciplinary/professional positions or theories

Level 6—Communicate with creativity and habitual effectiveness using strategies, theories, and technology that reflect engagement in a discipline or profession

Develop analytical abilities

Level 1—Show observational skills

Level 2—Draw reasonable inferences from observations

Level 3—Perceive and make relationships

Level 4—Analyze structure and organization

In majors and areas of specialization:

Level 5—Establish ability to employ frameworks from area of concentration or support area discipline in order to analyze

Level 6—Master ability to employ independently the frameworks from area of concentration or support area discipline in order to analyze

Develop facility in using problem solving processes

Level 1—Articulate own problem solving process, making explicit the steps taken to approach the problem(s)

Level 2—Analyze the structure of discipline- or profession-based problem solving frameworks

Level 3—Use discipline- or profession-based problem solving frameworks and strategies

Level 4—Independently examine, select, use, and evaluate various approaches to develop solutions

In majors and areas of specialization:

Level 5—Collaborate in designing and implementing a problem solving process

Level 6—Solve problems in a variety of professional settings and advanced disciplinary applications

Develop facility in making value judgments and independent decisions

Level 1—Identify own values

Level 2—Infer and analyze values in artistic and humanistic works

Level 3—Relate values to scientific and technological developments

Level 4—Engage in valuing in decision making in multiple contexts

In majors and areas of specialization:

Level 5—Analyze and formulate the value foundation/framework of a specific area of knowledge in its theory and practice

Level 6—Apply own theory of value and the value foundation of an area of knowledge in a professional context

Develop facility for social interaction

Level 1—Identify own interaction behaviors utilized in a group problem solving situation

Level 2—Analyze behavior of others within various theoretical frameworks

Level 3—Evaluate behavior of self within various theoretical frameworks

Level 4—Demonstrate effective social interaction behavior in a variety of situations and circumstances

In majors and areas of specialization:

Level 5—Demonstrate effective interpersonal and intergroup behaviors in cross-cultural interactions

Level 6—Facilitate effective interpersonal and intergroup relationships in one's professional situation

Develop global perspectives

Level 1—Assess and articulate own knowledge about the world and identify useful strategies for developing awareness of others

Level 2—Use course concepts to describe the world's diversity and interconnections

Level 3—Apply disciplinary concepts and frameworks to understand the influences and implications of diversity and global interconnectedness

Level 4—Articulate understanding of globalization and international relationships drawing on varied perspectives and personal reflection

In majors and areas of specialization:

Level 5—Integrate own global perspective with theoretical approaches to generate a pragmatic response to topics with global dimensions

Level 6—Independently generate theoretical and pragmatic approaches to global problems within and across disciplinary and professional contexts

Develop effective citizenship

Level 1—Assess own knowledge and skills in thinking about and acting on community issues

Level 2—Identify community issues and strategies to address them

Level 3—Examine organizational and community characteristics and identify strategies that facilitate accomplishment of mutual goals

Level 4—Apply developing citizenship skills in a community setting

In majors and areas of specialization:

Level 5—Show ability to plan for effective change in social or professional areas

Level 6—Exercise leadership in addressing social or professional issues

Develop aesthetic engagement

Level 1—Articulate a personal response to various works of art

Level 2—Explain how personal and formal factors shape own responses to works of art

Level 3—Connect art and own responses to art to broader contexts

Level 4—Take a position on the merits of specific artistic works and reconsider own judgments about specific works as knowledge and experience change

In majors and areas of specialization:

Level 5—Choose and discuss artistic works that reflect personal vision of what it means to be human

Level 6—Demonstrate the impact of the arts on one's life to this point and project their role in one's personal future

Each course in the curriculum provides assessment opportunities for selected levels of selected abilities. The abilities and levels are chosen by the faculty of each department for their appropriateness to the discipline and to the level of the course. We monitor the distribution of assessment opportunities among all courses so that by the time a student has completed all course requirements for the degree, she will also have had multiple opportunities to demonstrate all of the abilities. And since each course beyond the introductory level carries ability prerequisites as well as content prerequisites, the student is assured of encountering those assessment opportunities at developmentally appropriate places in her program of study.

Alverno's Curriculum and the Challenge of Serving Adults

The educational philosophy underlying the Alverno curriculum includes three major assumptions. The first of these is that effective education requires active participation on the part of the learner. Education goes beyond mastery of knowledge to the application of that knowledge, not only for students in advanced-level seminars, independent studies, and research courses but also for all students at all stages of the curriculum. As early as 1916, John Dewey lamented the separation of knowing and doing as a contradiction of his principle "that there is no such thing as genuine knowledge and fruitful understanding except as the offspring of doing" (p. 275). We believe, as Howard Gardner (1999) has recently written, that "understanding should be construed as a performance, a public exhibition of what one knows and is able to do" (p. 128). Second, we maintain that learning increases when students have a clear sense of what they are setting out to learn and what standards they must meet. As a result of these first two assumptions, what we call performance assessment, which includes both public criteria and self-assessment, is a required part of both classroom instruction and of the integrative experiences external to individual courses. Finally, we believe it is essential to teach students how to transfer abilities to new situations. Our challenge as a faculty is to help students use our ability and disciplinary frameworks to develop frameworks of their own in order to organize what they already know and apply that learning independently. Through focused, analytic reflection on both formal and informal educational experiences, they gradually transform their experience into learning.

New students of traditional college age who enter directly from high school are introduced to the principles and assumptions of the Alverno curriculum through introductory courses in a wide variety of disciplines. In all introductory courses in the natural sciences, social sciences, humanities, and fine arts, we explicitly teach students to be aware of the ability frameworks and the ways they use them to organize their interpretation and communication of ideas. One such framework, for example, is the valuing process by which one makes decisions with awareness of the values underlying them. By the time students reach their intermediate- and advanced-level courses, the habit of searching out underlying constructs and assumptions is a regular part of their approach to learning.

But what happens when nearly half of our entering classes consist not of new students but of older students *new to Alverno?* Most transfer students and graduates of two-year colleges have already completed some or all introductory courses by the time they arrive at Alverno. Other returning adult students, those who interrupted their studies years earlier for marriage, family, and/or work, may have less formal education but a rich set of life and work experiences that, if carefully reflected upon, might constitute the equivalent of college work. All of these students may already have the knowledge required for course work, but not all may possess the particular abilities integral to the Alverno curriculum or may not be aware of the abilities they possess. To assist them in identifying and demonstrating this learning, we have designed a required, six-credit transition course, Transfer of Learning: Approaches and Strategies, that enables them to draw on their prior learning experiences in a focused way.

Transfer of Learning: The Introductory Course

Transfer of Learning has three major objectives. First, it assists students to identify and demonstrate in the present what they have learned from prior experience, both formal education and life experience. Second, it immerses students in the principles of the Alverno curriculum—active and reflective classroom participation, ongoing demonstration of learning through assessment and self-assessment, the role of criteria in guiding learning, and ways of applying learning independently in new situations by focusing on the abilities. Third, it works to develop students' identity as learners confident in their ability to learn independently.

Students with previous college experience have already been granted transfer credits through the admissions process. For them, the course is an opportunity to familiarize themselves with the eight broad abilities required for graduation, identify abilities implicit in their previous college courses, and demonstrate them in performance-based assessments. Returning adult students with life and work experience also have opportunities to demonstrate abilities through various assessments, but in addition the course provides a vehicle for them to earn course credit by demonstrating learning equivalent to formal college courses.

The Prior Learning Portfolio

Over the course of the semester, students in Transfer of Learning gradually develop a portfolio of prior learning that verifies past performance. The course is designed as a recursive process of examining prior experiences in the light of new theoretical and conceptual ideas that help students to frame their experience and understand the learning potential contained within it. Assignments and activities go back and forth between the ongoing development of portfolios and the introduction, week by week, of the eight ability frameworks that define the Alverno degree. Our emphases on abilities as frameworks for learning and on active learning and assessment are keys to this transformation of experience into learning.

The course begins with an exercise in writing, a series of portraits of prior experiences that provide a basis for the portfolio. Students are asked to describe and reflect on their experiences in six categories: Paid Employment, Family Responsibilities, Formal Educational Experiences, Volunteer Activities, Experiences with the Arts, and Critical Experiences that Led to the Selection of the Major Area of Study. In their first drafts, almost all of these portraits are lists or narrative descriptions of experiences, not demonstrations of learning. Even when students reflect on what they learned in previous college courses, they usually enumerate accomplishments (writing papers, passing tests with high marks) rather than characterizing the learning that they took from these courses.

But throughout the semester, students are assisted in revising and developing these portraits so that they become a prior learning portfolio that can be used for the assessment of both abilities and knowledge. That is, they can be used by the instructor in combination with other in-class assessments as evidence to credential the level that each student has demonstrated in each of the eight abilities. Students are also encouraged to bring their portfolio of reflection and evidence to department heads as well for the purpose of requesting credit for courses. In this second case, credit may then be granted by the departments based on review of the portfolio, additional prior learning interviews with the student, or performance assessments grounded in the content of the disciplines.

Abilities as Frameworks for Learning

In addition to the ongoing writing and revising of the prior experience portraits, Transfer of Learning is organized around the introduction, week by week, of the eight ability frameworks. Students examine the logic of progressively more complex levels of each ability and infer the relationships to their own learning as they study the specific criteria that define each level. In the same way that faculty learn to use criteria to discern the level of a student's performance, students learn how criteria can be used as a guide for constructing their own effective performances at progressively advanced levels. The levels themselves are generic in the sense that they are not tied to specific assignments or disciplines. Working simultaneously with the ability frameworks and their own experience helps students to ground the levels of the abilities and make them more meaningful by placing them in a concrete context. Being able to identify the abilities students have developed in the context of their prior experience is at the heart of turning into learning the experience they have documented in their developing portraits.

When students work with problem solving, for example, instructors ask them to look to their portraits for critical incidents where they were engaged in problem solving. This might be a personnel issue affecting productivity in the workplace or perhaps a challenge to a neighborhood's integrity posed by industrial development or city planning and viewed from the perspective of the student's membership in a church organization or a neighborhood watch committee. Being asked specifically to connect the ability framework to the portfolio portraits gives students the opportunity—in the context of familiar experiences—to explore the new language and principles they are learning. Some students recognize at this point that their portraits are not well enough developed to enable them to analyze their learning and that they need to recall more detail and rewrite them in a more reflective way, focusing on what they have done that requires specific complex skills.

Since not every student's initial set of portraits includes equally rich experiences for exploring all of the ability frameworks, instructors also provide collections of readings from disciplines such as environmental science and political science. One such assignment concerns the classic problem of the pollution at Love Canal, New York, and asks students to apply the same formal problem solving principles to these larger issues in structured exercises. As students examine the analysis of these problems by other writers, they discover ways to deepen their reflection on their own experience.

The process of exploring Alverno's framework in valuing and decision making is another example of where a series of formal classroom experiences—centered on Shirley Jackson's short story, "The Lottery" (1992)—helps to connect the ability framework to students' own past experiences and even to prompt student recognition of additional significant experiences. Some students are not aware of the many public moral dilemmas that touch their lives. When reading "The Lottery," they use our valuing framework in written worksheets to infer the values represented in the characters and the value conflict that drives the plot. Then they represent the point of view of different characters in small-group discussions that extend the situation of the story. This helps them to experience the reality of multiple perspectives and the absence of a single right answer. Finally, asked by their instructors to turn their attention back to their own experience and prior learning portraits, students bring an increased awareness of "lotteries" in their own experience such as welfare reform, tax reform, and campaign finance reform, and they reflect on the values inherent in their own attitudes toward such issues.

Transfer of Learning incorporates articles and taped presentations from specific disciplines in the humanities, fine arts, and social and natural sciences that most transfer students have already studied and that form the core of Alverno's general education requirements. These articles and tapes serve as stimuli for teaching frameworks of analytical reading and listening and as sources for developing arguments in effective speaking and writing. The readings serve as models to assist students to become more metacognitive in their approaches to the experiences in their prior learning portraits.

In this case, the course instructors choose readings and presentations that self-consciously emphasize the methods and epistemological perspectives of the disciplines. Some examples include excerpts from Thomas Kuhn's (1996) work on paradigm shifts and scientific discovery, a text by Barbara Tuchman (1978) that clarifies the difference between the past and the historical interpretation of the past, and a survey of brain research by Carol Gilligan (1982). In response to each of these articles and taped presentations, students complete detailed process worksheets in which they identify theses and underlying authorial assumptions and analyze the structure of generalization and supporting evidence. As students learn to appreciate an intentional, discovery-based approach to making meaning of experience on the part of these scholars, they are directed by their instructors to return to their prior experience portraits to apply some of the same standards to their reflections on their own experiences.

In both these personal and academic contexts, students actively practice applying the ability frameworks to realistic situations—writing and speaking to simulated audiences, collaborating in groups to analyze readings and solve problems, and producing educational resources such as posters and brochures. All of these application assignments are performance assessments as Alverno describes them because they include observable examples of student behavior, performed with conscious reference to explicit criteria; they are self-assessed in terms of specific strengths and weaknesses and are evaluated, with improvement-oriented feedback, by classroom instructors or other expert assessors in terms of those same criteria (Alverno College Faculty, 1994).

Thus, as students become familiar with each ability framework, both in theory and in practice, they go back to the prior experience portraits they created at the beginning of the semester. In revising their reflections (or in some cases beginning to reflect on lists of experiences), students are encouraged by instructor feedback on the original drafts to look for criterion-based evidence of the abilities in their prior experiences. How, for example, did a student make decisions about the quality of works of art offered to her as the volunteer organizer of a fundraising auction at her church? What problem-solving strategies did another student choose in order to resolve personnel conflicts at her workplace? How might yet another student's analytical insights from course readings on topics in psychology or economics help her to place her prior experiences in context?

Throughout the semester, assessments of individual abilities connect back to the portfolio as a work in progress. For example, one assessment of effective writing employs the rhetorical device of preparing a letter to the faculty members on a committee for assessment of prior learning, explaining how roles students have played in their personal and work lives reflect strengths they bring to their current learning. This simulated assessment may later take on very real meaning when students bring their portfolios to departments to make a case for earning course credit for learning that is grounded in life experience. In another assessment focused on aesthetic engagement and prompted by attendance at a live theater performance on campus, students are asked to reflect on prior aesthetic experiences such as theatrical performances, poetry readings, or musical concerts that had significance for them and to discuss how those experiences helped shape their judgments about the artistic merit of the current performance. As students become more adept at using the language of learning in relation to the eight abilities and to the disciplines, they are better able to unlock the learning potential of their prior experience.

Student Assessment-as-Learning

The way we define performance assessment—what we call student assessment-as-learning—and practice it throughout our entire program provides several means of assisting a student to identify and demonstrate what she has learned from experience. First, we make public criteria essential to any assessment for students. Our definition of *criteria* as "components that constitute *a picture of the ability*" means that students have available to them our best definition of any outcome they are required to demonstrate. Therefore, students can use the criteria as a very detailed framework for their analysis of what they have learned from experience. For example, a woman who worked for years as an executive assistant finds in our criteria for effective writing a way of analyzing whether the samples she can provide of her written work constitute college learning. Are her writings organized coherently around principles or concepts? Has she validated her conclusions with substantiated thinking? She gradually internalizes those criteria by applying them, receiving feedback on them, and using them to assess both her peers' and her own performances. Then she is ready to analyze the specifics of her own style and refine the definitions of the ability that the criteria represent. She can set her own criteria for individual performance in varied contexts.

Second, self-assessment of the student's performance is an essential part of every assessment, whether of present or prior learning (Loacker, 2000). In the same way that faculty learn to discern the level of a student's performance, students learn how criteria can be used as a guide for constructing their own effective performances at progressively advanced levels. Through practice in self-assessment, students learn what it means to develop judgment based on criteria and how criteria define the essential nature of an ability. They also learn to provide evidence for their judgment. One effect of this is to encourage students more and more toward the kind of independent learning that makes future—in fact, lifelong—learning possible.

Self-assessment is at the heart of all of the work in the Transfer of Learning course. In effect, students develop the ability to make more informed judgments about their learning *while* they are making them. Through feedback from instructors and peers and their gradual recognition that they are developing a better understanding of the criteria they are trying to apply, students feel increasingly secure about the judgments they are making and become increasingly self-confident as learners who can understand that evaluating their own learning is an essential part of that learning (Mentkowski & Associates, 2000).

In addition to judgment, our self-assessment process includes analysis/interpretation as essential, thus creating a focus on self-reflection. In the ongoing development of her portfolio in Transfer of Learning, each student receives prompts that are designed to teach her how to reflect and to take the time to do so as part of the process. For example, in preparation for a demonstration of one component of effective citizenship, she is given an assignment that focuses on preparatory thinking. The situation involves assessing her knowledge and skills in thinking about and acting upon local issues—in this case, her stance regarding some aspect of mass media and the role she is playing, or is considering playing, in addressing it. The assignment asks her questions such as "What generally have been your experiences and attitudes toward the mass media? What factors have actually influenced your thinking in this area? How has your reading expanded your attitudes and awareness regarding the media?" Such questions are designed to assist a student to reflect on her experience and probe it in a way that assists her to make meaningful inferences about her own learning and its development. As she forms a habit of reflecting in this manner, she becomes more and more adept at independently understanding her own learning and when and how it occurs.

The Completed Portfolio

By the time a portfolio developed from the early portraits is ready to go to disciplinary department heads and instructors of general education courses, the content has been translated and expanded. Built from a slender folder into a thick binder, it is still basically organized around the original categories, though some may have been eliminated or changed. For example, students who see their education as preparing them for a specific career might realize that experiences listed under "Family Responsibilities" are relevant to that career and therefore change the category to "Career Potential." Within these categories, the student has translated former experience lists into skills integrated with content that can be transferred and substantiated. She has added evidence for each claim of learning. One student's training of teenagers in volunteer catechism classes or Junior Achievement might lead to some level of the outcomes for a teacher education major. For her evidence, she would accumulate lesson plans, notes from readings done in preparation, and/or a statement of her philosophy of education. Another student's membership on a village board might be the source of her development of the outcomes of a sociology course. Her portfolio would have everything from meeting agendas and minutes to resolutions she had written and had passed, and to the scripts of political speeches. Accompanying each portfolio are letters to the persons—department heads and instructors of general education courses—from whom the student seeks approval of credit.

Assessment as a Work in Progress

Conducted in such a way as to make the transfer of course credit possible, prior learning assessment in higher education may actually fragment the experience that returning adult students bring with them to college. Work experience that unifies, say, analysis of economic trends, sensitive report writing, and understanding of how local governments and businesses work together is often driven apart by the organization of academic life into discrete Carnegie units, thus requiring students to meet with multiple instructors and challenge for a series of individual course credits in Economics, English, and Political Science. Given the hurdles that such a system sets up for adult learners, it is little wonder that the average credit award via prior learning assessment is only about nine credits (Lamdin, Keeton, & Whitaker, 1999).

We need to find a better way to help students take advantage of experience that was not neatly organized into course units. At Alverno, we have the potential for such a breakthrough in that our overall approach to assessment is integrated. For any student to earn credit for a course taken in our curriculum, she must demonstrate through performance the appropriate abilities integrated with the appropriate knowledge bases for that course. If we can integrate assessments of course content and abilities, we should be able to assess students on liberal arts and disciplinary outcomes that are broader than a single course and are more relevant to the personal and professional contexts where students will use their learning.

Such assessment seems achievable because all departments have gradually articulated for their majors learning outcomes that integrate the subject matter and methods of the disciplines with the abilities. We are working on what it means to use those outcomes literally as frameworks for assessing prior learning toward a major. This would move us away from course-by-course assessments and at the same time could be a valid, rigorous way of assessing the level of a student's understanding and use of the theories of a discipline, meaningfully revealing learning gaps that additional course work might address. Our extensive experience with designing assessments has prepared us to tackle the kind of complex, comprehensive assessments that would validly assess the outcomes of a discipline.

The assessments that instructors have begun to use in Transfer of Learning have focused on the demonstration of abilities and the achievement of them in multidisciplinary contexts, thus also eliminating the need, in these contexts, to tie validations to specific general education courses. We are also in the midst of articulating a set of comprehensive liberal arts outcomes incorporating required content that is not tied to specific texts or syllabi.

The instructors for Transfer of Learning already see the outcomes for majors as ways that students who have selected a major or show inclinations toward a particular one can frame their experience. For example, the woman who organized community art shows, contributing to the criteria used in judging pieces for display and communicating with the artists seeking selection, might have a start in "verbally communicating an analytic understanding of the nature and principles of visual art as they pertain to both her visual work and the contemporary art world." This is one of the outcomes that art majors are required to demonstrate for their degree.

In our efforts to focus on a more holistic, integrated approach to validations of ability, we have recently put into operation a concept of "comprehensive validations," applicable to transferred courses, by which a student is placed in a course at the level of ability that matches where she *would* be in our curriculum. If she passes that course, she is consequently awarded validations for all the levels of ability that precede the level she demonstrates. For example, a student might be enrolled in an advanced writing course. If she demonstrates that she can communicate complex relationships from varied perspectives to a variety of audiences, then we also grant her credit for all of the writing skills that are involved in that advanced ability. The multiplicity of contexts that we require for demonstration of any level of the ability is inherent in the assessments within the course.

We find that the process of understanding how to assist students in developing learning out of their experience and how to assess it is ongoing. Several phenomena support our commitment to keep improving. One is the fact that we are constantly learning more about how students learn. Another is that we are bombarded by multiple claims that technology can make learning more accessible. Finally, complex abilities have become more and more necessary for persons to function in society. Thus, our challenge to rethink and refine what we already do is increasingly greater. We realize that we need to keep requiring of ourselves one of the major skills we encourage from our students—raising questions that lead to more profound thinking and improved action. If we can do that, our learning from our experience with our students and from our colleagues throughout the world who are interested in student learning can keep our process dynamic and focused on improvement.

References

Alverno College Faculty. (1992). *Liberal Learning at Alverno College.* Milwaukee, WI: Alverno College Institute.

———. (1994). *Student Assessment-as-Learning at Alverno College.* Milwaukee, WI: Alverno College Institute.

Dewey, J. (1916). *Democracy and Education: An Introduction to the Philosophy of Education.* New York: Macmillan.

Gardner, H. (1999). *The Disciplined Mind.* New York: Simon & Schuster.

Gilligan, C. (1982). *Psychological Theory and Women's Development.* Cambridge: Harvard University Press.

Jackson, S. (1992). *The Lottery and Other Stories.* New York: Noonday Press.

Lamdin, L., Keeton, M., and Whitaker, U. (1999, November). Lessons Learned in a Quarter Century of CAEL Experience. Panel discussion at the Third National Forum on Prior Learning Assessment and Recognition, Vancouver, BC, Canada.

Kuhn, T. (1996). *The Structure of Scientific Revolutions,* 3rd edition. Chicago: University of Chicago Press.

Loacker, G., ed. (2000). *Self Assessment at Alverno College.* Milwaukee, WI: Alverno College Institute.

Mentkowski, M., and Associates (2000). *Learning that Lasts: Integrating Learning, Performance, and Development.* San Francisco: Jossey-Bass.

Tuchman, B. (1978). *A Distant Mirror.* New York: Knopf.

LEARNING FROM OUR EXPERIENCE

PORTFOLIO DEVELOPMENT AT SINCLAIR COMMUNITY COLLEGE

Carolyn M. Mann

The portfolio-development process at Sinclair Community College rests on a long tradition of serving the professional and academic needs of adult learners. Taking both experiential learning and academic preparedness seriously, SCC uses the portfolio-development process as a way to help students explore career options, become more comfortable in an academic environment, and explore how their experiential learning relates to academic study.

This model, an example of portfolio development at a two-year public institution, shows how to practice the assessment of prior learning imaginatively within the constraints of a "course match" model. It also describes how, over time, an institution can continue to rethink and improve portfolio development in order to respond to the combination of structure and flexibility that adult learners need. Recognizing the Credit for Lifelong Learning Program as a work in progress, says Carolyn Mann, "The staff have themselves been true experiential learners as they have grown in their abilities to guide students through the portfolio-development process."

Introduction

Sinclair Community College (SCC) is a comprehensive community college located in Dayton, Ohio, offering over 2,000 different credit courses with over eighty associate and certificate degree programs. Currently 20,000 full- and part-time students attend SCC with an additional 40,000 individuals involved in training activities through the Division of Corporate and Community Services. SCC has a long history of serving the needs of adult learners since its beginning in 1887 as a YMCA college offering evening courses. The average age of our students is 32 years, and 53 percent of the student population is 25 years or older.

Twenty-five years ago, SCC embarked on the exciting journey of assisting learners with the portfolio-assisted evaluation of their prior learning. The college had previously recognized college credit for standardized examinations (i.e., College Level Examination Program and Advanced Placement Program) and internal proficiency examinations as early as 1972, and a substantial emphasis on the assessment of prior learning had begun in the mid-1970s with the development of the Credit for Lifelong Learning Program (CLLP). Under the leadership of Dr. Barry Heermann, the momentum to implement prior learning assessment as an educational program was spurred by the following factors: (a) faculty's interest in serving the needs of their adult students, (b) recognition that learning is a lifelong process, and (c) the growth of learning activities taking place outside of direct college sponsorship. In the early 1980s, with the portfolio process established, the college revised its procedures for assessment based on examinations and program evaluations, consolidating procedures and linking them to the portfolio process. The Academic Credit Assessment Information Center (ACAIC) was established in 1983 to oversee the policies and procedures and provide a full range of assessment options. The use of different assessment options now enables both the faculty and the student to select the method of assessment that accommodates both the subject matter and the student's learning style.

The college acknowledged early in its journey that the assessment of prior learning was only one component necessary to serve the needs of adult learners. Adult learners were interested in completing their academic degrees; after the assessment of their prior learning, they needed to be able to finish course requirements in a way that allowed them to juggle their multiple responsibilities of work and family. They needed an alternative beyond the offering of evening courses. In conjunction with the development of the Credit for Lifelong Learning Program, the Experience Based Education (EBE) department implemented the College Without Walls Program. This is an external study option available in over thirty degree programs, enabling learners to complete course requirements using learning contracts.

Over the years, additional degree programs have been added as the college placed more emphasis on access and flexibility for all learners. For example, the Associate of Technical Study and the Associate of Individualized Study degrees provide learners with the ability to tailor degree plans to their specific educational and career goals. This provides learners with the opportunity to be actively involved in designing their degrees, linking prior learning and academic goals, and taking ownership of the entire process in a way that more traditional degrees have not accommodated. SCC has grown from offering a few courses on local television to a division offering numerous courses in a variety of formats: video, print-based, and audio courses; Internet courses; and courses delivered by satellite. The creation of a new academic division, the Distance Learning Division, has enabled the college to commit increased resources to and emphasis on the use of technology to reach students, eliminating barriers of time and place.

The strength of SCC's prior learning assessment program is grounded in four factors: (a) the involvement of academic faculty in the award of academic credit, (b) the number of assessment options available, (c) the integration of prior learning assessment into the academic institution, and (d) the college's commitment to expanding access to all learners. The college gave a great deal of effort to developing faculty support for the concept of assessing prior learning, actively involving faculty from all divisions in early discussions and implementation decisions. While the EBE department oversees the assessment of prior learning, SCC faculty determine the award of credit and have the autonomy to determine assessment methods. Prior *learning,* and not prior *experience,* was firmly established as the basis for the award of credit. Guided by academic faculty, the EBE department has ensured that the emphasis on learning from experience is the guiding principle.

The fact that the EBE department is part of the instructional arm of the college established prior learning assessment as part of SCC's basic educational process. Indeed, EBE has worked diligently to establish linkages with all academic departments. The faculty we refer to as "portfolio faculty" have academic rank and the same kinds of qualifications as any other community college faculty. That is, these members of the faculty both teach the portfolio-development course and determine what credit should be awarded. Two full-time faculty members in Experience Based Education serve as portfolio facilitators, teaching the Portfolio Development course (EBE 100). There is also a close and important association between EBE portfolio facilitators and the faculty evaluators.

EBE 100: The Portfolio-Development Course

EBE 100, the Prior Learning Portfolio Development course, has served as an anchor for the Credit for Lifelong Learning Program since the program's inception. While the three-credit-hour course has grown and evolved over the years, its basic objective has always been to help adults identify their learning from experience, match their learning to college-level courses, and develop a portfolio that articulates and documents their request for SCC course credit.

SCC's program is a course-match process. This means that with the assistance of a member of the faculty, students will identify specific courses for which they will prepare a portfolio, articulating and documenting how their learning from experience matches the course competencies.

At SCC, the term "portfolio" represents both the document *and* the process. A portfolio is a written document or record used as a vehicle for organizing and distilling prior learning experiences and accomplishments into a manageable form for assessment of college-level learning. Portfolio is also a term that has come to represent the entire process by which learning from prior experiences can be translated into educational outcomes or competencies, documented, and assessed for academic credit. It is not unusual to hear a faculty member tell a student, "You should portfolio that course."

Looking Back

Interestingly, the Credit for Lifelong Learning Program (CLLP) staff have themselves been true experiential learners as they have grown in their abilities to guide students through the portfolio-development process. As we reflect over the past twenty-four years, we can identify three stages of the course's evolution. The first stage was grounded in the assumption that all adults were self-directed learners. The course met as a group for the first three weeks of the quarter only, and for the rest of the course students met individually with their portfolio facilitator (the EBE 100 faculty). While many students liked the flexibility of this approach, attrition was a very real concern. As we were struggling with how to improve the course, a key faculty member became seriously ill, forcing the remaining staff to meet her students as a group for the entire quarter. Much to our surprise, most of the students completed portfolios. We learned three important lessons during this phase: (a) Not all adults are self-directed, and many needed assistance in developing these skills; (b) most learners benefited from more structure as they juggled the multiple responsibilities of work, family, community involvement, and school; and (c) we were asking students to tackle learning from a very different perspective than they had ever encountered. Adult learners knew what it meant to go to school: You came to class and did what the teacher told you to do in a time frame the teacher had established. The assessment of prior learning requires something different: Students had to refocus and explore their experiences from the viewpoint of what they had already learned, not what they were going to learn. This was a new process for many learners and required more input and guidance from the portfolio facilitator (EBE 100 faculty), as well as more opportunity to share and dialogue with other learners.

Building upon what we learned from this early experience, in the second stage of the course's evolution, we moved to regular weekly meetings with the students, allowing for both group and individual interaction. Drawing on literature from the humanistic approach to adult learning, the faculty focused on values clarification and goal-setting exercises and developed methods to build student confidence in their role as learners. As a result of our efforts, the percentage of students completing EBE 100 increased to a 72 percent completion rate from Fall 1980 to Spring 1986, compared to a 54.3 percent rate from Fall 1978 to Summer 1980.

The components of the portfolio itself also changed during this second stage of the course's evolution. Up to this point, portfolios had consisted of the following components:

1. Chronological Record, a year-by-year account of a learner's experiences since high school;

2. a Goals Paper listing personal, career, and educational goals;

3. a series of Competencies, which provides a concise statement of experience and details what the student has learned, as it relates to a particular course; and

4. documentation of the learning experiences that support the competencies.

During this stage, we added the Life History Paper, a 4–5-page paper detailing important events, turning points, and insights, to add what we felt was a missing piece in the process. We discovered that as students listed events in their Chronological Record, they would reflect on these experiences and would need an opportunity to share them in a way that the Chronological Record and Goals Paper could not capture. Preparing the Life History Paper enabled learners to reflect upon *how* they have grown and changed. This assignment provided adult learners with the opportunity to review their goals, decisions, and areas of learning and to explore how these would impact future goals. Importantly, the Life History Paper also allowed students to explore personal insights and learning that could not be reflected in the course competencies. The opportunity to review their lives in a more holistic manner was a powerful process for many students, enhancing both their self-confidence and their ability to set goals. As one student reported: "This really helped me find new things or new angles that I had not considered about myself." Another concluded: "I found this to be a very valuable process. Due to my lifestyle and my job, I had never taken the time to reflect on what all had taken place in my life."

However, the "competency" has always been the heart of the portfolio. Using a specific three-column format, students outline the experiences that have been significant in their learning about the objectives for a specific course and discuss what they have learned about the course objectives. Documentation is provided to verify and support students' credit request. Once a portfolio is submitted to the appropriate faculty for evaluation, the faculty member reads the document and has the option of interviewing the student. The faculty evaluator can ask the student to provide additional work or participate in other types of assessment techniques that they deem necessary to help them decide *if* the student should receive credit and *what grade* should be recorded.

Moving Forward

As the college developed more options to serve the needs of the adult learner, the Portfolio Development course has evolved into its third stage. Students take the course to help them achieve an academic degree in an efficient, timely manner and focus on accumulating credit toward their degree. Yet, the accumulation of college credit, while a significant focus of the course, has proved to be not the only one. Many students enroll in the course to explore where they have been and where they want to go, using the course primarily as a goal-setting process that focuses on planning for a career or career change. Some students take the course because they need recognition of college credit for their learning from experience for job advancement. In some cases, the students have a baccalaureate degree or even a master's degree, but their work experience is in a totally different area and they need college credit in a specific field for job advancement in that field. Students value the course as an educational planning process, helping them to explore how their prior learning experiences link to both career and educational goals.

The diverse reasons why students enroll in Portfolio Development are tied, understandably, to the economic realities of Dayton and similar cities. The assessment of prior learning at SCC began evolving at a time when there was increased pressure for a college degree as the credential for both job entry and advancement. Many workers facing layoffs sought associate degrees to make them more employable in the new economy of office work and high-tech industries. As the Dayton economy has shifted from heavy emphasis on manufacturing to service and technology, adult students are again finding it imperative to look at their credentials and to build and expand the skills that they possess. The associate's degree has become what one student referred to as an "insurance policy."

Due to these very different reasons for enrolling in the Portfolio Development course and the many demands adults have on their time, we felt a need to address how we could better assist learners. We have therefore made two changes, one a procedural change and one a course change. Previously, students were required to complete as many competencies as they could in the eleven weeks that the Portfolio Development course was offered. After the initial course, if they had additional courses that they wanted to write portfolios for, they were required to take another three-credit-hour course. As we assessed this policy, we discovered that, due to a student's financial and time constraints, the second course was not often used. What adult learners needed was *more time* to work on their portfolios, not another course. Thus, we implemented a new policy, allowing students two years after taking the Portfolio Development course to submit all portfolios. During these two years, faculty are available for advising, answering questions, and reviewing portfolios. A one-credit-hour course was created, called Portfolio Update, for students who wished to continue after their two-year period. An educational planning component was added to the course to help students create a road map to guide them toward the completion of their academic goals and to direct this activity after the portfolio course.

The Portfolio Development Course Today

Typically, the Portfolio Development course meets one evening a week. Students in a given class have varied backgrounds, areas of expertise, learning styles, goals, and reasons for participating in the course. The faculty have developed a process to allow for both group work and individual meetings, guiding learners in a way that enables them to define where they want to place their emphasis. Assignments and activities are structured around the course goals and the completion of the five major components of a portfolio. Methods of instruction include a combination of mini-lectures, large and small group activities, as well as individual meetings.

During the eleven weeks, the students focus on the following course goals:

- Identify their learning from experience
- Identify their academic goals, which build upon the student's prior learning
- Match their learning to specific SCC courses
- Examine all the prior learning assessment options available and identify any other assessment options that they want to use for specific courses

- Learn how to write[1] a portfolio
- Develop an educational plan, detailing how they are going to complete their academic goals, taking advantage of the numerous learning options at SCC and elsewhere

The process of portfolio development begins with the Chronological Record and Life History Paper. A simple Time Line exercise, in which students are asked to identify major events across a time line as an in-class process, helps students get started. Another class exercise asks students to quickly list the five most important events in their life and to form small groups of two or three in order to share why they consider the events important, how these events have affected their lives, and what they have learned from them.

Once the process is underway, preparing the Chronological Record helps students begin to list and organize all their experiences in a way that can be used for further reflection. Class discussion of different theories of adult development, such as those of Levinson (1978), Hudson (1991), and Sheehy (1976, 1981, 1995), are used as a means to help students reflect on their development. These kinds of activities assist students in deciding how they want to write their Life History Paper. Class discussions and sharing help students examine patterns in their lives and explore options from a broader perspective.

After reflecting on their past experiences, the students' next step is to prepare a draft of their Goals Paper. As stated in the student guide, *Credit for Lifelong Learning:*

> Your life/career goals are the starting point for this sorting process. This is how the process works: Once you have your life/career goals in mind, you can select the college degree that is most likely to help you achieve them. With this degree goal established, you can examine the courses required for the degree, and decide which ones cover topics that match your learning from experience. Then you can sort through your experiences and focus on the ones that yielded relevant learning, applicable to the courses you have selected. (Mann, 1998, p. 31)

---

[1]There are no prerequisites that must be completed before students can take the Portfolio Development course. Since the course requires a great deal of written work, reflection, and the gathering of information, however, students are advised to take SCC's English and Reading entry-level assessment and take remedial courses if that is indicated before taking the portfolio course. Faculty review drafts of assignments during the quarter. Students are encouraged to share assignments with each other for additional feedback on their writing. Students who are having difficulty with writing during the course can seek assistance from the Tutorial Office or the Writing Center.

Goal setting is a significant component of the entire portfolio-development process. Drawing upon Richard Bolles's (1981, 1999) work on life work planning, students are encouraged to examine goals in work, education, and their everyday lives, and to explore how goals in one area impact the other areas. Faculty discuss the importance of goals, criteria for goals, and the link between goal and planning, drawing on materials from Steven Covey's *Seven Habits of Highly Effective People* (1989) and Anthony Robbins's *Unlimited Power* (1987). A variety of different small-group exercises are used at this point. In one, for example, students are asked to take a few minutes to think about one of the following questions:

1. If you could do anything you wanted for one year and be guaranteed success, what would you do?
2. If you could have the ideal job, what would it be like? What would you be doing? Where would you be? Would you be working with people or by yourself?

We have found that using these questions helps stimulate discussion and expands thinking about possibilities. Students are encouraged to explore additional resources available at the college, such as consulting with academic advisors, using the Career Planning and Placement Office, and meeting with professionals in the Office of Counseling and Student Services.

The next step in the course is to help students understand college-level learning. We begin this process by reviewing the course catalog. As one member of the faculty tells students, "This is a boring but necessary discussion." Since students have such a diverse background, some with previous college experience and others with no formal education since graduating from high school, this review ensures that all students understand academic vocabulary and institutional structure. This discussion includes a review of such questions as "What is an academic credit? What is the difference between quarter hours and semester hours? What programs does SCC offer? What is the difference between a certificate program and an associate's degree? How do you transfer credits to Sinclair, and how do SCC credits transfer to other institutions?" We also make sure students understand all the options for translating learning into college credit at SCC.

Next, we discuss the difference between experience and learning, using a student's Chronological Record and syllabi from related courses to illustrate differences. Using the Learning from Experience Worksheet (see the box, "Learning from Experience Worksheet"), students start to move from merely listing their experiences to exploring what they have learned.

Learning from Experience Worksheet

Experience	Time Spent in Activity	Description of Duties, Tasks, and Activities	Description of Learning Outcomes and Competencies	Documentation: Can You Suggest Ways an Evaluator Can Judge You?

Students are asked to complete the chart using their chronological record as a guide, or using larger categories, such as education, work experience, and volunteer experiences. The more detailed the reflection that students conduct, the more useful the Worksheet can be. Working in small groups, students use the college catalog and course syllabi to begin to identify college-level learning and specific courses that match with their learning. At this point in the course, we schedule individual meetings with students to focus on their particular backgrounds, goals, and concerns. During the individual meetings, we make suggestions of programs and courses for students to consider.

As students explore how their learning from experience matches academic courses, they develop a much clearer understanding that while all experiences are the source of learning, not all learning matches academic courses. Much learning from experience is job specific, and more applied or vocational learning sometimes lacks the theoretical component considered central to most academic courses. In effect, the portfolio process helps students develop a broader perspective on what an academic degree is all about. They identify courses of which they may know *parts,* but are not competent in large segments of the course objectives. Alternatively, students may have strong applied knowledge of an area, but are not knowledgeable in the theories and concepts of the course objective. SCC does provide an option for very applied knowledge. We have a long-standing Cooperative Education program in which students can earn credit for the learning from participating in co-op work experiences.

Credit for learning acquired through cooperative work experiences can be used to fulfill degree requirements as electives in many of Sinclair Community College's occupational and technical programs. The ability to request internship credit enables students to advance toward completing degree requirements while avoiding requesting credit for courses for which they did not have the theoretical understanding. Special Topics courses allow students to request credit for learning in an area that SCC does not teach.

At this point in the course, students are ready to begin to draft their competency statements. The purpose of the competency is to provide the faculty evaluator with: (a) an explanation of the experiences that have helped students learn about competencies of a specific course, (b) an overview of their knowledge of the course competencies, and (c) documentation to verify and support

Competency Statement		
Description of Experience	Learning from Experience	Documentation

their request. Students are required to write a competency for each course. The competency is prepared using the format seen in the following box:

How to help learners write the competency requesting credit for a specific SCC course has always been a significant concern of the faculty. Preparing the Learning from Experience Worksheet helps students begin to think about the kinds of information they will need to write their competencies. The competency format does this as well, in a form that emphasizes the distinction between experience and learning and enables them to present a more focused request for credit for a specific course. Still, students struggle with how to approach this project and how to distinguish between their experience and their learning. We have therefore developed a worksheet that takes students through a six-step process that includes the following:

1. Identify major learning objectives for the course in which you want to be assessed.

2. Identify experience(s) relating to those learning objectives.

3. Organize Step 1 and Step 2 into an outline that links learning to specific learning objectives, and details in what order you want to discuss experience and learning.

4. Write the first draft of the Competency, using the three-column format.

5. Identify and provide appropriate documentation.

6. Revise draft.

Steps 1 and 2 require students to gather key information for the competency. Step 3 is necessary to create a way to link the two steps in a manner that presents a competency that is clear and comprehensive, focusing on the objectives for the course. As the student guide explains:

> The most common way to merge the two lists is to use your chronological order of experiences, fitting the objective to the experience. Usually you will not be able to make an exact match with your experiences and the course objectives. You will need to decide which experiences will enable you to discuss your learning to its best advantage. (Mann, 1998, p. 60)

After students prepare their first draft, a class exercise reviewing a "poor" and "good" competency provides a practical example to clarify students' understanding of how to write this crucial part of their portfolio. Students receive feedback on their first drafts from the faculty as well as from their fellow students. Using this feedback, they then revise their competency using the following set of questions to guide this process:

1. Have I covered the course objectives?

2. Have I explained my experiences clearly enough for the faculty evaluator to understand the situation?

3. Have I organized my experiences and learning so that the faculty evaluator can easily follow along?

4. Have I separated my learning from my experience?

5. Am I being clear and concise?

6. Am I leaving too much for the evaluator to assume?

7. Am I repeating myself too much? (Mann, 1998, p. 61)

The last part of the process is to assemble documentation to support the competency. Class time is spent on discussing the importance of documentation, what documents to use, and how to obtain documentation. Initially, we thought students needed to begin collecting documentation as soon as the course began, but we have learned that documentation makes more sense once the students have a better understanding of the course(s) they are going to submit for evaluation. In this way, students are more likely to gather documents focused on the course topics and supporting their specific request for credit, rather than present a random collection of documents.

Up to this point in the course, students have been gathering a great deal of information about themselves, their past experiences and learning, and SCC programs and courses. The next step in the process is to revisit their Goals Paper and to develop their educational plan. As the student guide explains:

> However, goal setting, in and of itself is not the answer to our growing and being successful. Growth comes only when all the parts of the process are combined: setting goals, making plans and taking action to carry out the plan. (Mann, 1998, p. 31)

The plan allows them to explore all the assessment options, delivery options, and degree and certificate programs and to create a plan that is optimal to accomplish their goals. This process also helps students to organize and make sense of all the information they have been collecting.

There are a number of class activities that center on developing an educational plan. In addition to the traditional on-site classes, Sinclair has a variety of ways that students can take courses: video, satellite, Internet, and College Without Walls. We therefore spend one class session discussing differences in learning styles and use different inventories, such as David Kolb's (1999) "Learning Styles Inventory," to help learners assess their own styles. Understanding the concept of learning styles is useful. Gaining comfort with the concept allows students to explore all the learning options available to them and how to select those that support their particular learning styles. For students who are planning to earn a baccalaureate degree, we encourage them to research and decide what school they will be attending, so that they can plan the best course of action at SCC for transfer to the four-year institution. Finally, the student guide has a series of educational planning worksheets, where students can outline what degree or goals they are pursuing and list courses they have completed at SCC or transferred, courses for which they are going to prepare competency statements, courses they are going to challenge using other prior learning assessment options, and courses they need to complete and how they are going to do so. Students are encouraged to set time lines for completing each activity of their plan.

At the end of the course, we review each student's completed portfolio. This is not the same as a full portfolio evaluation, but an important part of the overall process. Throughout the course the faculty member works with his or her students, reading drafts, making comments, advising, encouraging, and supporting. At the end of the course, another faculty member reviews each student's work, thus providing another perspective. Written comments are submitted, and students have the opportunity to make revisions before the portfolios are submitted for evaluation. The review process provides feedback that helps students strengthen their requests for college credit.

We have offered EBE 100 at numerous locations both on campus and off campus, taking the course to where the students are by offering the course at work sites and neighborhood centers, using employer classrooms, boardrooms, the corner of the cafeteria, a church basement, and even a trailer in the middle of a manufacturing plant. With the growing advancement of technology, the course is now being offered as a video course and as an Internet course. There are ten half-hour lectures on videotape to guide students through the process. The use of technology has allowed us to provide more flexibility to our students and expand our outreach. The use of the Internet and e-mail has benefited students taking the course on campus as well. They ask questions and submit drafts of their work via e-mail. Master course syllabi are now accessible on the Web through the college's homepage.

Conclusions

In the past twenty-five years, we have worked with thousands of students, expanding their access to higher education. Participation in the portfolio-preparation course has helped individuals in countless ways. They have been able to build their self-confidence, broaden their understanding of themselves as learners, expand their abilities to clearly articulate their skills and competencies, earn an academic degree from SCC and move on to a four-year college or university, enter new careers, or advance in their current jobs. Very significantly, too, our learners have helped us grow and shape the Portfolio Development course. We have surely learned from our experiences. As we celebrate our silver anniversary, we are honored to be part of this exciting journey and look forward to growing and learning along with our students.

References

Bolles, R. N. (1981). *The Three Boxes of Life and How to Get Out of Them: An Introduction to Life/Work Planning.* Berkeley, CA: Ten Speed Press.

Bolles, R. N. (1999). *What Color is Your Parachute? A Practical Manual for Job Hunters and Career Changers.* Berkeley, CA: Ten Speed Press.

Covey, S. R. (1989). *The Seven Habits of Highly Effective People: Restoring the Character Ethic.* New York: Simon & Schuster.

Hudson, F. (1991). *The Adult Years: Mastering the Art of Self Renewal.* San Francisco: Jossey-Bass.

Kolb, D. A. (1999). *Learning Styles Inventory, Version 3.* Boston: Hay/McBer Training Resources.

Levinson, D. J. (1978). *The Seasons of a Man's Life.* New York: Ballantine Books.

Mann, C. M. (1998). *Credit for Lifelong Learning* (5th ed.). Bloomington, IN: Tichenor Publishing.

Robbins, A. (1987). *Unlimited Power.* New York: Fawcett.

Sheehy, G. (1976). *Passages: Predictable Crises of Adult Life.* New York: Bantam Books.

Sheehy, G. (1981). *Pathfinders.* New York: Morrow.

Sheehy, G. (1995). *New Passages: Mapping Your Life across Time.* New York: Random House.

LOVE TALK

EDUCATIONAL PLANNING AT EMPIRE STATE COLLEGE, STATE UNIVERSITY OF NEW YORK

Lee Herman

Empire State College, SUNY's liberal arts college for adults, was founded on the principles of access, individualized learning, and the assessment of prior learning. For thirty years it has rooted its educational model on a highly individualized process of Educational Planning in which a student working closely with a faculty "mentor" designs a program that includes both prior and future learning and that can be adapted quite specifically to students' professional, academic, and personal goals.

Because many of the "courses" students take have been individually designed for them and because the primary pedagogical mode is one-on-one mentoring, ESC's Educational Planning course can be an intensely personal academic interaction, in which life imperatives, values, and the question of what is worth knowing surface often. This requires openness on the mentor's part no less than that of the student. As Lee Herman says, "When Educational Planning takes students and mentors beyond academic custom, the results can be controversial and politically significant. We are challenged to critically inspect our intellectual routines."

> If our skeptic, with his somewhat crude science, means to reduce every one of them to the standard of probability, he'll need a deal of time for it. I myself have certainly no time for the business, and I'll tell you why, my friend. I can't as yet "know myself," as the inscription at Delphi enjoins, and so long as that ignorance remains it seems to me ridiculous to inquire into extraneous matters.
> —Plato, *Phaedrus* (229e–230a)

Empire State College and Individualized Curriculum Planning

Committed from its inception in 1971 to individualized, student-centered education, SUNY–Empire State College requires that all matriculated students design their own curricula, or "degree programs." These degrees include a "concentration" (i.e., a major) as well as general studies. The college is also committed to recognizing college-level learning whenever, wherever, and however it occurs. Thus, students' degree programs typically combine prior experiential and academic learning with a plan for individualized "contract" studies. Empire State expects that, for every student, designing an individual degree program will be an intellectually rich activity, one that combines complex research, reflection, and design.

Educational Planning is the name given to Empire State's only required course, a 4–8-credit guided individualized tutorial in which students learn to recognize learning, to plan it, and to achieve academic credit for it. In every part of this process, students work closely with a faculty "mentor" in a collaborative relationship that reflects the College's approach to all tutorial studies. Successfully completing this Educational Planning study means that a student has designed a degree program that is formally approved by Empire State College and the State University of New York system of which it is a part.

One of the required outcomes of Educational Planning is a portfolio compiled by the student documenting prior learning through a range of assessment methods. These include transcripts from other colleges; records of standardized assessment instruments, such as CLEP exams and generic evaluations; and documents prepared by qualified evaluators, who assess, name, and quantify students' individual experiential learning. Credits from all of these sources, along with credits students propose to earn through learning contracts, are included in each student's degree program. Most important, all students write a "degree program rationale," in which they explain in detail how the programs they've designed suit and support the purposes for which they are seeking degrees. A review committee of faculty members, which formally assesses each student's degree program and its accompanying documentation, uses this rationale in order to determine that students understand the education they have created.

Learning the Student

Rick and I meet for the first time when he's ready to reenroll in college to complete a bachelor's degree. He's finished an associate's degree at a community college. He'll want to transfer those credits and continue to concentrate in business studies. Nervously jiggling his left leg, he tells me that he's in his mid-30s, married, has three kids, and wants to own a business.

"What kind?"

"A car wash. I managed several; now I want to own one, to provide a good life for my family and me. I want to get on with it."

Like most of my colleagues at Empire State, I've seen all kinds of career holders and seekers walk into my office to plan their educations: accountants, social workers, ministers, managers, park rangers, bakers, ship captains, software developers, woodworkers, philosophers, pilots, child caretakers, firefighters, historians, state troopers, wrestling coaches, lawyers, poets, and even a professional skydiver. Rick is my first auto-wash entrepreneur.

"Have you learned a lot from managing small businesses?"

"I think so. And I've heard that at Empire you can get credit for life experience learning."

"That's right. While you're planning your whole degree, you and I can look at your experiences, find the college-level learning there, and have it evaluated for credit. Empire State has a course in which you do all that, our only required course, Educational Planning."

"Sounds good. I need to get on with it."

"We can start right away. But, if you don't mind my asking, what's the rush?"

"Well, I'm kinda pressed for time." Rick's leg vibrates more rapidly as he turns to gaze out my office window into the gray late winter light.

"You want some of that American Dream, eh?" I ask with a professionally amiable smile.

"Yeah, I need to get things set up. I have MS."

Then I remember uncomfortably that Rick's application indicates he has financial support from the NYS Office of Vocational Rehabilitation. And I remember that he'd dragged his left leg a bit, the shaking one, while walking into my office.

"Okay. Okay. We can do this," I try to calm both of us. "You can design your degree to suit your goals, and you'll get academic credit towards your degree for doing so. Educational Planning is usually four credits, a big learning project. You'll figure out what you already know and what you need or want to learn, then put together a whole degree program plan that'll be approved by the College. We'll work on it together."

"Let's do it. Great!" He turns toward me from the window, his leg quiet for now.

What Have I Learned? What Shall I Learn? Why?

During the following weeks, Rick, like most students in Educational Planning, studies the catalogues of other colleges offering majors related to his interest. And he interviews people working in the type of position he wants to have: owners of car washes and other labor-intensive services. This is normal background research for the *prospective* part of Educational Planning. It provides information for one of the questions Rick needs to answer for himself: "What shall I learn that I don't already know or could usefully learn more about?" But this prospective orientation also highlights Rick's *retrospective* research question: "What have I learned already, in and outside of the classroom, that I can include in my program?" Looking at the descriptions of courses commonly required and listening to the advice of successful practitioners familiarizes Rick with the normal learning content of his field. He thereby also learns to describe the experiential learning both of us are sure he has but which he's never named.

In Educational Planning, these prospective and retrospective views support and influence one another. Students decide what to value in their prior learning, partly with regard for what they want or need to learn; they decide what future learning to value for their degree plans, with regard for what they have already learned. Then, they learn to integrate these perspectives, creating an entire, coherent degree program plan.

Similarly, students learn to consider and synthesize contemporary practical and traditionally academic perspectives. For example, the course descriptions available in published college catalogues offer a useful guide to normal academic expectations. However, sometimes those published offerings, having made their way through the deliberations of curriculum committees, lag behind innovations in a field. For example, another student, Joe, a steel production designer, casually mentioned during one of our planning conversations that he had invented a promising new alloy made from production waste. This alloy didn't even have a public name yet, though Joe was about to present a paper about it at a metallurgical conference. He was wondering if he could get some experiential learning credit for that!

The practical or experiential perspective can also correct the condescension academics sometimes affect toward the "real" world. Ruth, for example, had wanted to teach photography to poor grade-school children. The Education Department of the college she was then attending told her to wait until after she'd completed the proper credentials. Instead, Ruth got a small grant, created a community camera club, and taught kids to make and use the camera obscura, a pinhole and sheet of film inserted into the emptied cardboard cylinders of Quaker Oats. The knowledge she gained of resourceful teaching, program development, and community action found its way into the experiential learning portion of her Empire State degree program.

Interviews with practitioners offer a window into currency, tricks of the trade, and sometimes unsettling wisdom about what a career is really like. Rick discovered from the five or six car wash owners he interviewed that, hard as he had worked as a manager, he'd have to work even harder as an owner and should expect to wait at least several years before he saw much net profit for his efforts. He began to worry about reaching his goals and to wonder if they were best for him.

The Mentor's Role

As with all students for whom I am the assigned mentor, I listen to Rick's interests and for his educational needs. I suggest how he might find relevant academic and occupational information. Complementing his ideas, I indicate areas of potential experiential and relevant future learning. And I ask Rick questions that I hope will help him look carefully at the contexts, academic and professional, in which he hopes to thrive. I encourage him to evaluate his research and his interests in light of the purposes—about which he is becoming ever more explicit—that have brought him back to college.

Every two weeks, Rick and I discuss the information he has collected. We discuss and refine possible topics for experiential learning and for future study. The latter doesn't present any surprises. His "concentration" will be similar to those of most business administration students. Why bother, then, asking Rick to discover what is customary? I might give him a list of normal course requirements and an array of electives. However, through his research and reflection, Rick is making the field his own. He is making his own intellectual place in a public context of knowledge and practice. It is a context for which he is constructing his own coherence and meaning. Moreover, he is learning to test his dream against his own increasingly informed sense of the challenges to fulfilling it. For example, though he has managed the payroll and other "local" finances of the car wash, he learns that as an owner on a probably shoestring budget, he'll have to become much more adept at accountancy and business math—for him, not a pleasing prospect.

The prospect darkens more when Rick looks at the problem of time. It will be years before he can earn enough to provide the sort of life he wants to enjoy with his family and that he wants his family to enjoy "later on." This "later" remains, for a couple of months, an unspoken topic in our conversations. The issues are clear enough: How long will the MS allow Rick to work as a car wash owner? Will the stress of accelerated learning (both in school and afterwards) also accelerate the disease? If so much of his limited time is to be fiercely concentrated on making his way to his ultimate goals—pride of ownership, prosperity, and, especially, savoring life with his family—will he risk those ends for the sake of the means? I fear to raise these questions, worried that I'll intrude on his privacy.

By longstanding tradition, Empire State faculty do not presume to judge students' ultimate purposes. To be sure, we raise questions in Educational Planning: "Why are you here? What are your educational purposes?" By and large, we do so because we expect students to clarify their answers for themselves. It is one of the fundamental assumptions of this inquiry that we, the faculty, are not wise or knowledgeable enough to provide or preach such answers. This is a sound, Socratic principle of education: It is better to examine one's own claims to know and to encourage others to the same, than to presume one knows what is best, especially for another. Another fundamental assumption is that our students, adults who by and large already adeptly inhabit the lives they are here to develop, do possess and will develop their own wisdom about ultimate ends. Rick's ambitions seem a little crazy to me, fraught with risk for self-defeat. Yet who am I to pass judgment on his hopes? I know simply that the spirit that elevated his learning should not be clouded, not by his ignorance and not by mine.

It's fair to ask what mentors actually know. When so much educational autonomy and instructional responsibility are left to the student, what skills do we practice in Educational Planning and other tutorials? We are indeed often working with students who pull us beyond the traditionally understood boundaries of our disciplinary expertise. (My formal academic background is in literature and philosophy, not business management.) Thus, all of us, faculty and students, learn to "stretch." Often, we enlist other mentors and hire tutors to supply expertise we lack. Always, we are learning, from each other, from tutors and people in our communities, and from our students. This "experiential learning" gradually makes us generalists and unabashedly curious about whatever our students want to learn. Finding themselves so often consulted by their mentors, students learn to teach themselves; they learn to regard their questions as authoritative, to find answers, and to regard their answers as worthy of serious reckoning.

To be sure, mentors have information and ideas. I know that it will be useful for Rick to talk with successful entrepreneurs, especially ones he already knows and others to whom they would refer him. And I know that Rick and I can trust the messages about the learning he needs to acquire, messages that are gathering implicitly in the information and advice he collects from those interviews, and from trade journals and academic catalogs. Having learned something about Rick, I know that I can rely on his rationality, on his ability to adjust means and ends reciprocally as he learns more about each. That is, I know that Rick will use his learning, the learning he is acquiring through research and reflection, to shape a life he desires and an education suited to it. Perhaps what my colleagues and I know best is how to shape an inquiry, how to seed an environment in which our learning and our students' learning grow symbiotically. For that nurturing to occur, mentors have to know at least this: not to presume to know that which we do not. And that includes not presuming to know with what meaning and value each student inspires his or her education. Thus, above all, mentors must know how to take care to examine themselves.

How crisp, though, is the distinction between the clarification and the *evaluation* of values? Educational Planning requires students to engage in prospective and retrospective research. It also requires that they, like their mentors, engage in critical *self-reflection*. Students must decide what learning—both past and future—to include in their degree programs. They decide according to their own purposes, but, inevitably, when they begin to decide reflectively, they also begin to examine those purposes.

Practical Purposes and Academic Requirements

Like most adult students, the obvious primary purpose for which Rick has returned to college to complete a bachelor's degree is practical: He wants a prosperous career and for that he needs the kind of practical knowledge typically offered in a business degree. As he plans his degree program, Rick reads college manuals and consults with me to learn Empire State's requirements for all bachelor's degrees: 128 credits (of which at least forty-five must be "advanced") distributed between "concentration" and "general" learning and including studies in the liberal arts and sciences. By interviewing successful practitioners in his field, reading trade and professional journals, and examining business majors offered at other colleges, Rick learns what studies the variety of business degrees usually contain.

Some of these typical expectations are arbitrary: They are the historical accretions of institutions and professions. One wonders, for example, why colleges so commonly require all business majors, whatever their goals, to take a year's worth of accounting courses; and why required courses in management principles will often emphasize the dominant academic and consultant discourse about managerial "philosophy," regardless of its tenuous relationship to actual practice or its demonstrable influence on business performance and cycles. And of course some typically required studies are probably useful but intensely distasteful or fearsome to the individual student. Sometimes crude but not unfounded stereotypes come into play: For example, many students, no matter what their field of interest, shrivel at the mention of math; and many computer-absorbed students are loath to improve their skills in mainstream written and spoken English.

Despite these challenges to rationality and desire with which Rick was becoming familiar, the pragmatism that brings so many adult students to college will afford them the prudence to manage whatever seems necessary to reach their goals. If someone wants to go on to graduate school in, say, clinical psychology or social work, and the department advises that successful applicants know some human biology, then the prudent student will include it, no matter how leery he or she may be of science studies or how devoted he or she is to "humanistic" understandings of behavior and experience. Rick knows, through prior college experience, that it will be difficult for him to learn the math associated with finance and investment studies. He has also learned, through his planning research, that those studies, including their quantitative skills, will significantly help him become the successful businessperson he hopes to be.

Such requirements, and the practical student purposes that bring them to bear, can easily fill the greater part of an Empire State degree program. Even so, every Empire degree contains huge possibilities for student autonomy. This is a virtue we faculty must vigilantly school ourselves to respect, and one students discover, sooner or later. It is part of the learning in Educational Planning.

In fact, it is rare that Empire State students create curricula that are unique or remarkably idiosyncratic. The list of studies on an Empire State business degree, as mentioned, will usually look quite like the studies found in the management or business administration degrees of other colleges. In what sense, then, can it be said that Empire State students design their own degree programs? It is this: During Educational Planning, students are investigating both the commonly understood expectations associated with their individual purposes and the personal meanings and values associated with their purposes. Students learn to understand the rationale (however questionable) for the coherence and requirements of a discipline or profession; they also learn to understand what they care for and to what they are willing (or unwilling) to devote their learning. Then, they are in a position to decide for themselves what personal and public expectations to embrace. They are in a position to develop their own arguments to the College for being excepted from some of those external expectations, and to take advantage of the wriggle room often found in those requirements. Indeed, students can even create their own "concentration" titles to describe precisely how their academic plans express their particular purposes. Rick will eventually call his concentration "Business and Small Business Management."

The list of studies on an Empire State degree program, which is the tangible product of Educational Planning, may not appear to be very unusual. But the learning that gives rise to that list, the learning contained in the Educational Planning study, could not be more different from the imposition of curricular requirements many institutions prescribe. So much of commonly practiced higher education assumes that the degreed "we," the faculty, possess the knowledge most worth having. It also assumes that, like medical doctors protecting public health, we are to prescribe and administer that knowledge to the undegreed "others," as though we were to create healthily educated persons from ones who are cognitively and contagiously impaired. By contrast, at Empire State, Educational Planning is a collaborative inquiry among mentors and students. For every mentor, the first principle of that collaboration is that we respect and serve every student's purposes. The list of studies on Rick's degree program might well look like many others. But that convergence only came about because of thoroughly informed decisions Rick made about what learning would serve him, decisions I also participated in making and that my colleagues who finally assess his degree will honor.

Unfolding Purposes

But something more happens when students, even the most anxiously and strenuously practical-minded of them, are respected in this way. Other purposes usually emerge during Educational Planning. As students relax into trusting that their practical educational needs will be served, other interests and more meanings of learning unfold. More and more confidently and deliberately, students discover and present themselves as centers of widening circles of curiosity and aspiration: areas of intimacy and leisure, of purely intellectual achievement, of social status, civic commitment, and spiritual quest. Mentors keep an eye out for the unfolding of those previously implicit purposes. At first with light questions and, perhaps later on, with suggestions for provocative reading, we encourage students to embrace this creation of a broadening self.

Thus, as Rick looks in ever-greater detail at the learning he will need to do to have the career he believes he wants to have, he also becomes more occupied with wondering why. The "why" question calls him to examine the sort of life he will be creating, for himself and for his family.

I notice signs of Rick's wonder: casual comments about the many hours a week, for many years, he realizes it will take him to build a business; about attending more closely to his medical condition; about starting off working in a large, well-established business so that he does not overtax himself; about reviving former participation in the local volunteer fire department.

Eventually, I ask, "What do you enjoy, for its own sake, aside from school and work? Do you want to make time for those pleasures while you are still earning your degree and building your business?" We've been talking, not for the first time, about the intensity of the academic and work plan he was creating.

"I like off-road bike riding. I meditate and read about Zen. I enjoy just being with my wife and kids, especially traveling around."

"Do you want to make time for those things while you are still a student and while you are learning the ropes of being a car wash owner?" Rick's left leg, which has been quiet during our recent meetings, begins to vibrate.

"I'd like to," he says.

As nervous as he, I ask, "Please tell me if it's none of my business, but may I ask you a more personal question?"

"Okay, go ahead."

"It's about your health. Will the study and work you plan to do, at the pace you plan to do it, affect your MS? Will they deplete or damage the time you want with your family and the other things?"

"Maybe. Probably. But I want to get my degree and I need to provide for my family. I haven't worked in more than two years. I don't know." Rick looks down at his shaking leg.

I respond: "These are tough decisions. Big ones. I know they're not really my business or the College's. The faculty will approve any degree program you design so long as it meets the formal requirements we've discussed and the purposes you say you have. But do you want to look at those decisions, sort them out, in Ed Planning?"

"Seems like a good idea. I probably should. How?"

"Well, part of your research could be to speak your family and your doctor about these things. There'd be no need to tell me about those conversations, just the results that are relevant to your degree program design."

"Okay." Rick takes a deep breath, and as he exhales his leg quiets. "I think I just might do that."

Later, I also ask him to read some things about leisure and about entrepreneurship in a "24/7" world: Juliet Schor's *The Overworked American* (1993) and William Greider's (1998) *One World, Ready or Not*.

More than a month passes. When Rick comes in next, he brings along a draft of a complete bachelor's degree program. It contains a large block of proposed experiential learning credit for "Supervisory and Small Business Management," the customary advanced-level studies for a business concentration, and proposed studies in "Zen Philosophy," "Adaptive Trail Riding" and "Fire Investigation." He has read the books I had suggested. He has talked with his family, some friends, and his doctor. He has renewed his membership in the volunteer fire department and has discovered that if he trains to investigate a fire's causes, he can participate in this public service without straining his health. His wife and friends, though worried, want to support whatever decision he'll make. The doctor warns him that high-pressure activity might well accelerate the disease. "I still want that degree and that car wash as soon as possible. But my doctor admitted that neither she nor anyone else knew exactly how fast a course my MS would take. I can go a little slower. Maybe instead of jumping into my own business right away, I'll get some more experience and earn some money helping out the owners I already know. And in the meantime, I'll have more time for my family, myself, and for the fire department. That'll be okay, for now."

Rick and I polish his degree program and prepare it for formal Empire State assessment and approval (as described in the first section, above, "Empire State College and Individualized Curriculum Planning"). The final program contains fewer business studies in the concentration than Rick and I had originally anticipated. And overall, the increased diversity of learning suits the multi-intentional life Rick has decided to lead. His written degree program rationale nicely describes the student he was and the creative learner he is becoming. Such an accomplishment takes time—time for research and planning, time to reflect, and time for emergence. Rick completes Educational Planning nearly a year after he began. Mentors make suggestions, we help our students assess their research and discoveries, and, though we might guess what would emerge, we must wait for the unfoldings as they happen.

Lifelong Learning: Revising the Plan

The pace, rhythm, and continuity of these developments can vary widely among students. In fact, planning one's education can, at Empire State, continue long after Educational Planning, long after the student has designed and achieved formal approval of the degree program plan. This remarkable phenomenon, perhaps unsettling to those of us who like closure, occurs because something not at all surprising happens: Once students have become successful independent learners, once they have learned to create their own educations and thus to learn about their own learning, they continue to do so. The self-examination continues. Our students become very sophisticated "lifelong learners."

For example, Astrid, a veteran nurse, is well into a new career in hospital administration. She is cool, sophisticated, certain. Making maximum use of substantial prior academic and experiential learning, she quickly puts together a professionally useful bachelor's degree in health care administration. The degree plan is approved and, as a full-time student with a family and full-time job, she grinds out credits toward graduation. But something changes about a year after Astrid has completed Educational Planning and is preparing to do the final twelve credits before graduation. Her husband, a very successful industrial businessperson, transfers to a new job, out of state. With unusual urgency, Astrid asks to see me. We'd not done much direct academic work together since she'd planned her program, my areas of knowledge being different from those of most of her studies. But we still keep in touch so that I can help arrange tutorials for her with other faculty.

"Something's missing in my education," she announces. "I have to fix it."

"What's missing?"

This exchange opens an intense, hours-long conversation. We are searching for the missing piece. She says it has to do with her "soul"; and that, she tells me, has increasingly little to do with her profession. I wonder if this concern—a surprise to me, given what I'd known of Astrid so far—is about her feeling an upsurge of freedom in the absence of her success-driven husband. But I don't ask.

Our discussion leads to mythology, the myths of the ancient Greeks, and eventually to Homer. As thorough and pragmatic as always, Astrid decides that it wouldn't do to study Homer in anything but the original Greek, a language of which she knows nothing. So, for her final credits, she studies Homeric Greek. This addendum to her education means that Astrid must gain approval from the College for changing her degree program. She does. Upon finishing the twelve credits and thus her degree, she buys herself a present: the supremely erudite (all notes to the Greek text are written in Latin) Oxford Classical Texts edition of the *Iliad* and *Odyssey*. Astrid continued "educational planning" up through graduation, and, I imagine, well beyond.

Sometimes continuing, introspective educational planning can lead to a career change. Like Astrid, Henry had formally completed Educational Planning early on in his Empire State studies. A veteran corrections officer, he'd designed a program concentrating in sociology. Remarkably, he sought no experiential learning credit for his knowledge of corrections, nor did he plan any contract studies on crime or penology. Expressing no particular postgraduation career ambitions, Henry told me that he'd just serve out his "25" in corrections, retire, and then "do something else." During the many tutorial studies we did together, he wanted to understand the larger society, the moral and civic culture, which generated, depended upon, and cozily ignored the brutal, contained environment in which he worked. He tried to embed and diffuse his daily experience of prison by studying the U.S. Constitution and classical concepts of justice and honor. His inquiries brought him to the moral influence of families, to wonder how children learn virtue and civility; he wondered, as well, how he sustained his own. The more Henry followed his insistent, groping curiosity, the more he changed what he wanted to learn and the more he learned what he wanted to do with his learning. We discovered together that the bachelor's degree plan he'd originally designed was obsolete.

Gradually and informally, as Empire State allows, we changed the individual studies Henry had planned to do. Only when his final several studies and his final years of working as a corrections officer approached did Henry decide what he wanted to do after he graduated and after he retired from the Department of Corrections. He decided to become a public school social studies teacher. He was convinced this was the best way he could help kids not to wind up living or working in prison, the savage, hopeless place where he had spent the majority of his waking hours for so many years. Having made this decision, Henry did the intensive career research that students have typically already finished during the Educational Planning tutorial. He found out how he could get a public school teaching certificate through a master's program; he learned the changes he'd have to make in his undergraduate program in order to qualify. He altered his degree plan accordingly, and then sought and received formal approval from Empire State for those significant curricular changes. Henry was accepted into a master's program just as he completed his final undergraduate studies. For him, "educational planning" lasted almost ten years. He and I learned that "lifelong learning" can mean that one might change both the content and the purposes of one's education.

From Experiential to Academic Learning

Just as educational planning often continues after students design their programs, it often begins well before they formally begin the Educational Planning study. Before coming to Empire State, Melanie, Sheri, and Wally had never been in a college. But they'd been busy, working and learning. Melanie, in her mid-20s, was a parent and bookkeeper; Sheri, somewhat older, was also a parent and worked as a Headstart teaching assistant. And Wally, in his late 40s, was a construction worker, as well as a gadfly to the rural public school his children attended. Each of these adult students was an energetic learner. But, to all of them, "the academy" was a formidable if vague obstacle they figured they'd have to "get through" in order to "get on" with their lives.

It seemed to me that I'd only be adding confusion to their wariness if we began their formal educations by dealing directly with such academic arcana as "concentrations," "liberal studies," "experiential versus academic learning," and credit hours. Of course I told them about the Educational Planning requirement during their orientations to Empire State College. I assured them that, when they felt ready, I'd help them design their own programs, including getting credit for life experience learning. I suggested that the "up side" to not having college credits to transfer was that they had plenty of time and room to explore and to become used to college. When each asked, somewhat anxiously, "What do I have to take?" I replied, "What are you curious about?"

It emerged that each of the three had strong and quite specific intellectual passions. Moreover, none of those interests neatly fit the traditional course packages that introduce the academic disciplines. A generic "Introduction to College" course would have missed the quite different and individually intense curiosities of these students. So, with each of them, I collaborated in designing a first independent study tutorial about her or his interests. Melanie loved Beethoven and was curious about his "life and times." Sheri wanted to understand more about "poor kids and learning." And Wally was interested in citizens frustrated with bureaucrats and politicians. Each student designed with me a broad, diverse study on her or his topic—or, as we academics might say, "a transdisciplinary thematic study."

Melanie made a list of her favorite pieces and picked out a recent Beethoven biography. I suggested a short book on music appreciation and the Durants' popular omnibus history of the late eighteenth and early nineteenth centuries. Sheri wrote about the memories and diary she'd kept of her Headstart experiences. I asked her to read some of Jonathan Kozol's books and Deborah Meier's *The Power of Their Ideas* (2002). Wally read Orwell, Kafka, and some selections from Weber and bell hooks, among others; and he drew upon successful efforts he and one of his daughters had made to buck the local school administration. In this way, each became used to college, to independent academic study, and to planning learning while doing it. After several of these experiences, all of them told me, without prompting, when they were ready to do formal Educational Planning. They designed associate degrees as "platforms" for eventual bachelor degrees. And, now successful with formal college-level learning, they found it easy to identify, articulate, and be evaluated for their substantial "experiential learning." Indeed, each had more than enough potential experiential learning credits to save some to include in the bachelor's degrees they'd design.

For most matriculating students, "getting credit for life experience" is a major attraction of Empire State. Prior learning assessment (PLA) or, as we call it, "credit by evaluation" occurs during Educational Planning. Making PLA part of degree program design rests on the assumption that learning takes on meaning, particularly as quantified credits, only in relation to a context: a degree program, an intellectual passion or career goal, a life. "How much credit can I get for running a car wash?" Rick asked. Or "For doing heavy construction?" (Wally), "For raising and teaching kids?" (Sheri), "For doing accounting and running the office of a small CPA firm?" (Melanie). Answering such questions depends upon the student and mentor exploring two more questions: "What do you believe you *know* from these experiences?" and "How much does that knowledge matter to you?" Both questions imply and point to a context, often several layered contexts: to experience and plans, to domestic and social relations, to working for money and status, and to taking journeys of the soul.

Within each context, I ask students similar questions: "What can you do now, what do you understand now that you could not do, did not understand before?" "Can you do as much as/more than what other people with similar experiences do?" "How important is this knowledge in comparison to the other things you already know or want/need to learn?" Addressing these questions is often a long process. It requires that students learn to make subtle, often exquisite distinctions between "experience" and "knowledge"— distinctions that academics may neatly refer to but rarely examine rigorously. It requires that we, both students and faculty, look inside. We learn to bring to consciousness material we surely but inchoately possess, and then to give it order and names.

What Is "Learning"? Expanding the Academy

The Educational Planning study, especially when students and mentors look back, trying to name the learning implicit in experience, stirs and disturbs our unexamined assumptions about what learning "really" is. We'd love to fall in love with a rule that sharply divides "learning" from "experience." What is the learned part and what is the unlearned part of any experience, even an academic one? We'd love to know just exactly where in running a car wash, raising children, or constructing a building, and, for that matter, reading a book, the intellect listens and speaks while the rest of us (whatever we might call that!) remains deaf and mute. The Educational Planning study asks us, both mentors and students, to resist this seduction. Scraping at our comforting assumptions, Educational Planning asks us to explore this very question: "What is 'learning'?"

We must begin somewhere, with something that, at least provisionally, looks like knowledge. So, mentors often ask students to make lists of what they think they've learned outside of school. At first, these lists usually fuse experience and learning: "I raised my children." "I built factories." And the topics are very general: "I read books about American history." Then, considering these taxonomies of their lives, students refine their topic lists and then write brief descriptions of the experiences and the learning suited to each topic. "Raising children" might become "Maternal Skills and Thought Processes." "Building factories" might become "Industrial Construction Techniques"; and "reading American history," "The American Civil War."

The portfolio made up of these "learning descriptions" will be given to appropriately expert college faculty and others we sometimes recruit from our communities. The written learning descriptions provide these evaluators with the preparatory memoranda for interviewing the students. It's on the basis of those interviews that the evaluators verify the students' knowledge claims and make credit recommendations. The evaluators, the students, and the Educational Planning mentors all assess how much learning might be "in" the experiences. We do so by making connections with and understanding relationships between the individual's experiential learning, what others have learned, and what's in the degree program this particular student is creating. During the PLA part of Educational Planning, all of us pass back and forth through the membranes separating "constructing" and "uncovering" knowledge. We straddle experience remembered and experience understood. It is no wonder that nearly every student who begins Educational Planning, expecting to be "given credit for experience," exclaims proudly at the end, "I didn't realize I'd have to learn so much to do this. I didn't know I knew so much."

As with degree planning as a whole, PLA occurs within contexts of institutional standards, received ideas, and customary expectations. Thus, as they do in planning future learning, students make use of standard course descriptions to identify, sort, and name learning they've already achieved through experience. However, they are not limited to those. Educational Planning, including PLA, not only opens the academy to "nontraditional" students; it also opens the academy to nontraditional learning.

For example, Ellen, a production manager for a high-pressure and "hitech" manufacturer, was concerned about the well-being of her production teams. She was troubled by the ethical tension between respecting her workers and demanding from them very high production quotas. We discussed this issue at length during Educational Planning. We provisionally understood that, within the broad topic of "business ethics," Ellen must have thought a lot, for example, about conflicts between the "family environment" the company claimed to provide and the grueling productivity it required. As I interviewed her about her experiences, Ellen looked back at purchases she'd made of expensive machinery her teams used. She realized that an important criterion she used to choose among closely competitive products was "beauty" (as she called it) in both appearance and functional design. Her experiences convinced her that this aesthetic standard added both to the excellence of work and the happiness of work life. Neither my colleagues nor I knew of a ready-made course on this theme. Having some expertise in philosophy, I helped Ellen remember and improvise, write and speak what she knew about this fascinating combination of aesthetics and ethics. The "Moral Aesthetics of Production and Work-life" became a credit-bearing topic in the PLA section of her Empire State bachelor's degree program.

When Educational Planning takes students and mentors beyond academic custom, the results can be controversial and politically significant. We are challenged to critically inspect our intellectual routines. For example, it is common and easy for students to seek credit for their prior experiential learning in the business world. These students are mostly men. It is much less common and much rougher for Empire State students to seek credit for their learning experiences in the domestic world. These students are mostly women. The academically recognized skills and information collected under "strategic planning" or "supervisory management" are, from habit, easy to see, name, and evaluate. Not so for "maternal thinking and practice" or "household management." But, can we say with the same intellectual rigor we faculty demand of students that the cognitive demands of raising children and managing a home are any less than those of supervising employees or leading a business? Educational Planning can confront us, the faculty, with our own ignorance. Educational Planning requires that we, the mentors, examine what we believe we already know. Every time we do Educational Planning, a Delphic voice, like Socrates', calls us to know ourselves better.

Discovery and creation occur at the margins between the familiar and unfamiliar. Those are also tense places, where liberation and oppression are experienced. When students and mentors do Educational Planning well, we visit those liminal places. The visit is an elaborate and delicate experience, but when that experience is apprehended, it too becomes part of the learning achieved in Educational Planning. Further, student and mentor often discover that they learn in quite different topographies, that they have very different notions of "real" learning. These differences, potent with conflict, can become occasions for mentor and student to inquire further.

Conflict: Authority Shared, Authority Imposed

When tensions rise over these differences in liminal places, who and what should wield authority? The student's expectations of what should be counted as real learning? The mentor's? The layers of questioning and conflict can be even more complex than that. At the individual level, both student and mentor can each be separately conflicted. Students might defiantly desire to receive academic credit for almost anything they've done or wish to do, and at the same time deeply fear that they really know nothing. Faculty might pride themselves on their commitment to critical inquiry, yet, confronted with their own uncertainties and with demanding students, find comforting clarity in customary academic expectations. And an institution (in the case of Empire State, both the College and the entire university system of which it is part) can be driven from exploration, as will be discussed below, by the seductive politics of "accountable standards" and "productivity." As these pressures mount beneath the terrain elaborately fractured between the desire to learn and the desire to be certain, the resolving release can often only be found in waiting, in slowing the time devoted to Educational Planning. We wait, in order to become clear, carefully and caringly.

Liz, for example, has worked for twenty years in low-level, often part-time, human service jobs. She wants to get as much credit as possible, a lot, and as quickly as possible. To her, this seems simple, a kind of cashing in on her years of dedicated, poorly paid, and little honored service to others. To me, it is problematic, because Liz seems a very unreflective student, unable and unwilling, for now, to do the work of identifying, ordering, and describing the learning she may have acquired through her experiences. Our expectations clash. Moreover, I'm not at all sure how or when to help her learn to do what I'm certain she must and what she's equally certain she need not do. I strongly urge—eventually, I insist—that she wait, until she becomes more adept, through her other studies, at doing the sort of advanced-level learning, the careful analysis and reflection, PLA requires. She agrees, suspiciously, and our relations remain tense. After a time, during which Liz works successfully with other faculty on other subjects, our expectations change and our relations ease. Liz is now more practiced with analysis and exposition. And I'm more certain, as I now listen to her talk about her human services experiences, that she's acquired substantial learning from them and that she can successfully articulate it. Did she know these things in the first place, as she had believed, and was I thus too impatient with her demands? Or did she become a stronger student, more capable of meeting the expectations that I had been so certain were correct? I don't know. I do know that, while both of us waited, both us became better at speaking with one another and collaboratively discovering learning.

Sometimes, this distribution of initial expectations is reversed. Kathy, in her early 50s and a recent summa cum laude graduate of a community college, wants to become an English teacher. She'd frequently tutored weaker writing students while earning her associate degree and was certain she'd found her calling. But she's not sure she can do it, fearing she's too old. I suggest that as part of Educational Planning she learn about the current public school and college teaching shortages. Skeptically, she agrees and discovers a vacuum so strong and persistent that even New York State—infamous for its rigid teacher education machinery—is working on alternative, more flexible methods of certification. Further, I encourage Kathy to consider some substantial PLA. She's even more skeptical about that, although experiential learning credits will get her all the more quickly to a degree and a teaching career. Exhilarated by the experience and prospect of "the higher learning," like Hardy's Jude, she sees the academy as an august place to fulfill her long-postponed dreams. At first, experiential learning strikes her as not quite the real thing and as something irrelevant to the academic career she desires.

Eventually, I ask, "What have you been doing instead of going to school?"

"Just keeping house, managing the farm, and, you know, raising kids. Four of them. They've all gone to college now. I've loved raising my kids."

After more conversation, I ask her, "Are there any similarities between nurturing children and teaching?"

Kathy thinks about this question for several weeks. She returns eager to write an experiential learning description on "Parenting and Teaching."

She says, "I didn't know *that* was *learning*. I thought it was just something I *did*."

Her learning description eventually becomes a fine, searching essay on meanings of parental and academic nurturing. Given slow, leisurely time, Educational Planning can allow a student to discover that she already had known what she believed she had yet to learn.

However, institutional pressures, as suggested above, can sometimes damage this leisure. Sometimes contexts of inexorable academic expectation can be pernicious to learning itself. Within and around the State University to which Empire State College belongs, the cultural and economic politics of education have squeezed the leisurely freedom of Educational Planning. New York State amply manifests national cravings for certainty and stability in a changing, multiplicitous world where, as Marx long ago observed, "all that's solid melts into air." In response to these fears of difference and change, the Trustees of the State University have paradoxically chosen both to disinvest in public higher education and to demand from the university system "higher" standards, more efficiency, and a greater yield of more skilled, productive, and responsible citizens. The University Trustees have therefore devised and imposed a set of very specific "general education" liberal arts requirements. In the name of intellectual rigor and democratic citizenship, the faculty, including the faculty of Empire State College, are now required to administer monitored and testable doses of "a foreign language," "a narrative history of the United States," "natural science," and other subjects. It's doubtful that most students will remember much of these things after they've passed the tests. But what memorable lessons will the Trustees and faculty have modeled for the diverse citizens of this democratic society? That a privileged few will use their power to make "the others" become comfortingly like themselves? That higher degrees and the higher status they purchase perforce contain a higher wisdom? Where, under this regime, will the room for inquiry go? When will students and their teachers have time to explore and to examine what they assume they know and need to learn?

Conclusion: What Mentors Learn from Educational Planning

During its some thirty years of existence, Empire State has successfully practiced, especially in Educational Planning, two principles of learning: When people follow their curiosity, they learn well. And, when their curiosity is nurtured, it expands indefinitely, beyond "getting credits" credentialed for a career. Thus honored, curiosity not only achieves those necessary practical goals; it also transcends them, embracing questions about the meaning of personal and civic life, and even more. Astrid discovers Homer; Wally, De Tocqueville. Rick wants to run a car wash; and he wants to think about satori and nature, perhaps while tracing a bike trail or the cause of a fire. While she manages production quotas, Ellen thinks about improving the beauty and civility of her workplace. When students like these discover that the state has prescribed for them small injections of this science or that math, this history or that language, what will happen to the beauty and happiness of their intellectual lives? Perhaps following the example of higher education policy-makers, they will plan their learning with the cynical and intellectually shallow acquisitiveness too commonly attributed to "adult" students.

However, such students may be less dispirited, feckless, and complicit than the State University faculty and administration have been in immunizing themselves against arrogant prescriptions. During Educational Planning, we discover how extraordinarily adept our students can be at managing and comprehending complexities of their lives. They learn how to transform the clamor of their multitudinous experiences into diverse, coherent, and liberating educations. They are experts at finding freedom and creating expanding selves amidst the seemingly intractable constrictions of their obligations and circumstances. Perhaps they will help mentors do the same.

When adult students return to or begin college, they commit an intrinsically revolutionary act. Consciously or not, they have decided to overturn their routines. They do so at an age when things are supposed to be "settled." And even when they seem merely prudent and practical, driven by force of circumstance and convention, they are also choosing to challenge the suppositions of their families or partners, their colleagues and bosses. Even more deeply, they are questioning the habitual views they have had of themselves. This churning critique bursts into view during Educational Planning. Even so methodical and practical a matter as learning self-directed academic time management becomes, for people with lives already filled with affiliations and commitments, a passionate struggle to create the freedom to savor reading, writing, and inquiry. Marriages and workplaces become objects of contemplation and overtly political territories. So often, students begin Educational Planning by fearfully wondering what they have really learned and have yet to learn. They emerge confident that their learning experiences matter and that they can learn whatever it is to which their curiosity leads them. They become able to question the seemingly unquestionable. Mentors who nurture and bear witness to these passages are awed. And, if we are lucky and shrewd enough to be inspired as well, we wonder, "If they can do it, why can't I?"

This essay opens with an epigraph from Plato's *Phaedrus*. It is a dialogue about "love talk," about patiently and slowly understanding words and ideas—*logoi*—of love. Before Phaedrus begins to recite the speech he's been eager to give about love, Socrates recommends that they turn their minds away from speculations about the stories people tell about goings-on in the world. In this case, it is a story he and Phaedrus briefly discuss about the seemingly inexorable power of Boreas, god of the north wind, who had supposedly stolen away Pharmacea (the nymph of "healing remedies") from the riverbank along which Phaedrus and Socrates are walking. Instead, Socrates recommends that they converse in a quieter place, in the soft grass next to a plane tree overlooking the river. He suggests that if they are to learn from one another about love or any other precious thing, they should turn their attention from "extraneous matters" toward knowing themselves. Phaedrus agrees; the inquiry begins. Rick feels the power of his wasting illness and considers how to respond and to make his way in the world. Gradually, he turns his attention to discovering what he loves most of all, at any risk. Should I, should any educator, do any less?

References

Greider, W. (1998). *One World, Ready or Not: The Manic Logic of Global Capitalism*. New York: Simon & Schuster.

Meier, D. (2002). *The Power of Their Ideas: Lessons from America from a Small School in Harlem*. Boston: Beacon Press.

Plato. (1966). *Phaedrus*. Translated by F. N. Fowler. Cambridge, MA: Harvard University Press.

Schor, J. (1993). *The Overworked American: The Unexpected Decline of Leisure*. New York: Basic Books.

I AM A WRITER

WRITING FROM LIFE
AT THE EVERGREEN STATE COLLEGE

Kate Crowe

The Writing from Life course at the Evergreen State College is an example of a portfolio-development process that uses the articulation of students' prior learning as a vehicle for developing academic writing skills. The goal is not only to make visible the students' experiential learning and its transferability to the academic setting but also, more broadly, to help students find their "voice." Drawing on the Evergreen's foundational principles of collaboration, engagement, and respect for difference, Writing from Life takes students through the all-important process of empowering them to succeed in the academic environment. "By writing from their lives," Kate Crowe explains, "students have some familiar ground from which to begin to learn or build upon writing skills. . . . In effect, prior learning writing becomes an opportunity to combine reflective personal essay writing with various rhetorical modes."

Introduction: The Context of Prior Learning

The Evergreen State College is a public, liberal arts college serving students in Washington State. Since 1970, its mission has been to help students realize their potential through innovative, coordinated studies programs that address a problem, theme, or question. In addition to preparing students within their academic fields, Evergreen seeks to provide graduates with the fundamental skills to communicate, to solve problems, and to work collaboratively and independently in addressing real issues and concerns.

This mission is based on a set of principles that underlies the development of all Evergreen College programs and services. The principles, called the Five Foci, are interdisciplinary learning, collaboration with faculty and peers, personal engagement in learning, the integration of theory and practice, and learning across significant differences. Using these principles as a foundation, the goal of the faculty is to assist students in developing their own voices in order to participate effectively and responsibly, individually and collaboratively, in a diverse and complex world. In effect, everyone at Evergreen—faculty and staff—is engaged in supporting student learning and in working together to that end. Faculty team-teach, usually with different teams each year, and both faculty and qualified staff can sponsor individual learning contracts with students.

In the early years of the college, faculty established the Prior Learning from Experience program (PLE), reasoning that many students gain expertise from their work and life experiences and that granting credit for relevant college-level experience is a way to value that expertise. This has made particular sense for the student population that Evergreen has served in its three decades of operation, during which time the median age for students has been about 24. Currently, 24 percent of the student body is 30 years or older, and our PLE students are predominantly from this group.

Moreover, the PLE program seeks to actively acknowledge the rich background students bring to their academic studies. Our Tacoma site (about forty-five miles from Olympia) is an inner-city campus in which our students are predominantly Afro-Americans. At Grays Harbor College (a community college in an economically stressed rural area), Evergreen provides upper-division programs to place-bound and dislocated workers. Evergreen also has a presence at six tribal reservations in Western Washington. The PLE program has been particularly successful in attracting and enrolling people to reflect this rich diversity. There is no doubt that there is an intimate and critical link between our institutional mission, our diverse student population, and the goals of the PLE program. Many students at these locations take advantage of the PLE program, which gives them an opportunity to more effectively and efficiently complete their four-year degrees. In fact, approximately one third of the students enrolled each year in PLE are designated minorities or come to Evergreen from outside of the United States.

PLE Policies and Procedures

PLE at Evergreen recognizes learning that results not from formal academic study but from life experience. That is, Evergreen takes seriously learning derived from a wide variety of sources, including work-based training, knowledge gained at professional conferences, skills and competencies developed on the job, and learning gained as a result of community involvement. For example, it is not unusual for students to request credit for their knowledge gained through community service, small business endeavors, political activism, environmental projects, social work, and art or poetry projects at the community level or in the schools. The PLE program, however, does not evaluate vocational or craft skills, or self-improvement experience, unless the significance of this learning extends beyond the individual. For example, the college would likely not grant credit for learning a skill such as landscape gardening, but would take seriously the learning of a student who taught him or herself landscape gardening and went on to start a business in gardening or taught courses on gardening in the community. Whatever the source of learning, in keeping with CAEL standards, students learn quickly that credit is never awarded as a result of experience alone. The student must demonstrate college-level learning as a result of the experience by writing an extensive Prior Learning Document (a combination of personal and expository essays), which describes the experience and analyzes the knowledge the student has gained. These documents serve the practical purpose of components of a portfolio; they also provide the reader with an in-depth understanding of the student's approach to learning and to a student's learning development.

The Prior Learning Program also encourages students to become aware of how they learn and how to apply their knowledge and skills to new situations. Beginning with a personal essay about their experience, they write a document explaining what they have learned and link their practice to relevant theories. To do this, students regularly conduct research and literature reviews. Some prior learning essays include case studies and observations from the field. Almost all essays are expected to cite sources, consistent with the expectations of any academic paper.

Potential students are recruited into the PLE program through presentations, brochures, and a Web site as well as through referrals from faculty, staff, and former students. Students fill out a PLE application form, which consists of a description of the student's previous academic history, an extensive resume or work history, and an essay on why they think the PLE program may work for them. Eligibility is assessed based on the application materials, after which an advising interview takes place. We consider students good candidates for the program if they have an appropriate amount of college-level experience and a strong desire to write about their experience. Students who appear to be eligible are encouraged to enroll in "Writing from Life," Evergreen's portfolio-development course. Other students may be advised that the PLE program does not fit their academic plans. For example, if a student plans to be a teacher, he or she must complete a prescribed curriculum and specific courses necessary to fulfill State Teacher Certification requirements and so cannot take advantage of portfolio-based assessment. In other cases, overlap may present a problem. For example, a student may want to write his or her portfolio in photography, but has already taken several courses on photography in a formal college setting. Business students quite typically have to confront this problem because they sometimes believe they can continue to study business-related topics with which they are already familiar.

The Writing from Life Course

Writing from Life is a four-credit course offered each academic quarter and is designed to assist Prior Learning from Experience students in writing their prior learning documents and, by teaching academic writing through the personal essay, to improve the writing of every student in the class. During the course of the quarter, students write an autobiographical paper and create an extensive outline of their PLE project and a personal essay, the contents of which relate directly to their PLE document.

The goals of Writing for Life include the development of writing skills, the exploration of diversity, and the exploration of Evergreen's Five Foci. The main objective of Writing from Life is to help students become comfortable writing lengthy papers and to also help them find the "voice" that will best suit their prior learning work. An important related objective is for students to gain academic comfort and confidence, that is, to become self-motivated and directed toward completing the prior learning work. The course is also geared to aid students in dealing with the "fear" factor in writing that many bring to their academic work. By writing from their lives, students have some familiar ground from which to begin to learn or build upon writing skills that also foster PLE document writing. In effect, prior learning writing becomes an opportunity to combine reflective personal essay writing with various rhetorical modes such as exposition, argumentation, narration, and description. The work in Writing from Life is organized around reading an essay a week (essays taken from Lynda Barry's text, *The Good Times Are Killing Me,* and from *Across Cultures: A Reader for Writers,* edited by Sheena Gillespie and Robert Singleton), participating in in-class writing exercises, and collaboratively presenting a chapter out of Roger Garrison's *How a Writer Works.*

Assigned readings for Writing from Life promote the exploration of the diverse lives of our students. For example, Barry's *The Good Times Are Killing Me,* is categorized as "autobiographical fiction." Barry, a syndicated cartoonist, fiction writer, and artist, is a graduate of the Evergreen State College. Her book is written in the voice of a young girl who tells about growing up in a racially mixed neighborhood in South Seattle. Many students identify with her stories of class issues, racial conflicts, and broken families. This reading sets the stage for others, such as *Across Cultures* by Gillespie and Singleton (an anthology of essays), which encourage participants to think deeply about differences and diversity.

In addition to the choice of readings, however, it is the intriguing mix of students that encourages the attention to diversity and that is so central to the effectiveness of this writing/portfolio course. The class is typically composed of people from all walks of life. There are usually four to five conventionally aged undergraduates, many of them with the tattoos, body piercings, fishing lure, and hair color of their generation. The majority of the students in Writing from Life are older, nontraditional students, usually including several retired or active police officers as well as a number of people who work in state agencies doing social work, accounting, or management. There are usually one or two artists, business entrepreneurs, ex-hippies, ex-loggers, active environmentalists, and passionate "new age" psychologists. Many people live and communicate in two cultures; they are Hispanic American, African American, Native American, and Asian American. One of our hopes is that students benefit from the thought-provoking statements people unlike themselves make. Readings, writings, and discussions of life experiences offer many opportunities to reflect on differences and points of commonality. Thus, establishing a nonthreatening atmosphere is essential for supporting such a conversation. Students must feel that their opinions will be respectfully heard when they are encouraged to reflect individually and as a group on the experiences of and possibilities for learning across cultures and subcultures. Writing from Life offers a truly unique opportunity to do this.

Importantly, too, Writing from Life explicitly addresses all Evergreen's Five Foci. To encourage both personal participation and collaborative learning, for example, the environment of the class is purposefully student-centered. Students gain the experience of "being in charge" of their learning—a key element in all of their work at Evergreen. Thus, in collaboration with one or two others, students take responsibility for leading the seminar each week, collaboratively presenting a chapter out of Garrison's *How a Writer Works*. Students are told that they "cannot be boring" and that their presentation should teach their fellow students about what they learned in that particular chapter. Presenters are also encouraged to involve the entire class in some way and to use elaborate props such as music, food, creative posters, and theatrical games to engage their classmates. This kind of activity prepares them for future work at Evergreen and in their communities where presentations are a common component of work. Having them present to and teach the others what they have learned about writing also supports the student-centered approach to teaching and learning they will encounter throughout their studies at Evergreen.

Garrison's text, of course, also focuses students on the process of writing. He addresses common elements and problems in writing such as wordiness, revision, grammar and syntax, cliché usage, punctuation, and paragraphs. Another important element in this student-centered approach to writing is that students read and critique each other's papers before turning the paper in to me for my responses. Again, this puts the responsibility of editing and re-editing papers for grammatical, spelling, and syntax errors on the student and allows the instructor to focus on content, voice, direction, and on the academic strengths and limitations of student writing. Gaining practice in and strengthening skills in reading, writing, speaking, editing, and collaboration will serve these students well. Thus, while students enter this course with the quite practical aim of wanting to develop their documents for prior learning assessment, they are gaining important experience as college-level readers and writers and becoming better equipped with a range of academic skills.

Writing from Life: Initial Exercises and Assignments

There are many writing exercises and activities that serve as a basis for Writing from Life. The following examples are certainly not exhaustive; they are intended to provide a sense of the content, the spirit, and the emphasis on collaboration that serve as its foundation. The array of sample assignments is also intended to offer a glimpse of the overall trajectory of the course and its efforts to help students gain strength as writers and as effective presenters of their prior learning.

1. I Am a Writer: Each term, the Writing from Life class begins with this exercise. Participants need to think about themselves as writers because that is how they will be considered in the course. They are reassured, "I will work with you at any level, so don't worry. This is your assignment." Then they are asked: "Imagine you are a writer. You can be anywhere in the world, any time in the world—any decade or century. You can switch genders or be a different age. Describe yourself in your favorite writing space. Describe what you look like, your clothing, etc. Describe your surroundings. What is your view? What do you have in the room?" Many students claim they felt confidence as writers by

just doing this exercise, and that is exactly the goal. Many older students have not written anything creative or self-searching for many years, if ever, and they respond to the insistence that they are "writers." This activity is also a great icebreaker because it can be followed by a series of follow-up questions. But most importantly, nobody looks at anyone else's work. Instead, this is an in-class assignment of approximately 20–30 minutes, after which we discuss their reactions to the work and to the very process of writing.

2. Free Writing: In the early weeks of the quarter, each class starts with a free writing exercise. Students are told to write for fifteen minutes without stopping. They are not to pay attention to grammar, spelling, or punctuation. This is one of the most important exercises for getting to their "voice." They need to feel free to write whatever is on their minds. Students are often amazed at how helpful this exercise really is. Once again, nobody reads their work because it is the experience of "freedom" to get feelings and ideas on paper that is the critical goal here. However, sometimes students read aloud if they choose to do so. This is the beginning of a sharing process that is very important to the work of the course.

3. Map of My Life: In the first or second week of the quarter, students make a map of their lives using crayons (quite deliberately in order to stir early childhood memory by smell!) and large newsprint. They can use words as well as drawings. They are told to design the map however they please and to include significant events from their lives, starting with childhood. Some people work backwards, but the point is made that there is no right or wrong way to do this exercise. In effect, students can begin and move along any way they like. Students can work from a list of suggested categories from which they can draw, such as special events, emotional upheavals, places you have lived, your first love, your worst enemy, valuable learning situations, embarrassing scenes, travel, people who have influenced you, community work, books, music, and important jobs.

Because issues of identity and confidence are especially important to students new to the academic environment, participants can use this exercise to find validation of who they are. The point of this "mapping" exercise is to help them recognize that everyone has stories to tell and everyone has lived a life rich in experiences. Again they are free to keep their work private, but many wish to show what they have done, and they are asked to share their maps with one other person in the class for five to ten minutes. When given a safe opportunity, most people love to talk about themselves, and this work gives them a chance to meet another person and compare maps and experiences. Importantly, too, some of the key topics and areas of prior learning they might pursue later begin to emerge here.

4. Childhood Memories: In the second or third week of the quarter while the students are writing their first paper (which is autobiographical in content), they do what is called a "writing round." Each student gets a list of beginning phrases such as: The color blue . . . , When I was ten . . . , The smell of fresh mowed grass . . . , Grandma was so . . . , My shoes were . . . , I cried so much when . . . , That night I didn't know . . . , I hated the taste of . . . , and so on. They are told to choose an "entryway" that appeals to them and write for fifteen minutes. I stop them at that point and ask if anyone wants to read. Some always do, and then we resume writing for another fifteen minutes. Again there is a pause while people read and then there is one more round of writing and reading aloud. They can resume writing on the piece they started or choose a different statement. Students are both influenced and encouraged by the voices of other students. Many students share funny or particularly tragic stories, which in turn allows others to remember and begin to make sense of their own feelings and experiences.

   As in the other writing exercises, the goal here is for the student to develop confidence in his or her voice and to create an atmosphere of acceptance among students in the class. Students recognize how similar their backgrounds are, even though people may be from what are perceived as different cultures. Students also begin to see and think more carefully about how people who have been raised in a range of cultures and countries have been influenced by the distinctiveness of the worlds from which they came. Here again, the developing writer is dealing with issues of identity, commonality, and difference. This kind of exercise is offering students another opportunity to work with complex and vital matters.

5. The Senses: This is an exercise created to introduce students to the use of their senses in their writing. It also encourages students to work with random groups rather than to connect only with people they know.

   Students count off by four or five and divide into small groups. One group goes outside, finds a common area, and makes a list of all the things it sees. Then, members of the group have to collaborate and write a piece using their list. "Anything goes" as far as how they write it.

However, it is sometimes valuable to tell students that they can't use adjectives. The focus on verbs and adverbs helps them become more aware of how adjectives can be a crutch in writing and how strong verbs improve their descriptions.

A second group makes a list of everything it hears in a chosen area and writes its story. Still another group makes a list of everything it smells and works together on its writing. And then there are groups that focus on touch and taste. When they come back in the room, each group reads its list and then its story. We all listen for the differences in the writing, which are often quite remarkable.

This exercise comes early on in the term because students are constantly reminded to use their senses in writing. It makes for richer detail and description. But this new experience of collaborative writing is equally important. It is usually quite a stretch for students the first time they do it, but the vast majority soon learn to love and trust this process because they report that it frees them to be wild and zany and helps them find ways to express their perspective to others. Students are amazed at what other people contribute. They love the camaraderie that results from working in groups. Indeed, the diversity of the class makes this exercise a multicultural learning experience as well. Students are freeing up their writing, gaining experience in focusing and describing detail, and also finding the opportunity to work with others to see how they experience their surroundings and think about their lives.

Moving into Essay Writing

The next group of writing exercises in the class helps students to move into essay writing. By this time in the quarter, they have turned in an autobiographical essay and have also had an in-depth individual meeting to discuss the content of their Prior Learning document. In effect, up to this point in the course, writing exercises have been designed to build students' confidence in their voice and validation of who they are in relation to their classmates. Their next two papers are written in essay form and relate more directly to their prior learning work. For example, if a student is writing his or her document about a successful small business venture, a first essay at this point might explain how the student started a small business and what the student learned in that process. This is an important transition.

The first in-class writing exercise involving the essay form follows from the kinds of the more creative writing exercises they have been doing. The assignment still derives from the personal experience of the writer, in which students are writing about something they know and have experienced. At this point, however, students are encouraged to go beyond the description and narrative to probe and think more fully about what that experience can show about their lives, about what it means not only in personal terms but also in terms of how those experiences fit into the larger society. In addition, students need to begin to see connections between experience and ideas, to explore thinking about an idea, to compare it to other experiences, and to become more aware of central themes and patterns in their thinking. This exercise is designed so that students have a closer encounter with these concepts.

Again, because students can learn a new concept more quickly and forcefully by working together, they are organized into small groups and sent to find a place somewhere on campus to collaboratively write a "reflective essay." They are instructed to observe their natural surroundings attentively to come up with a common theme. When the class comes back together, each group reads its essay and we have a discussion about how successful each essay was and why. Students share work with each other and are often struck by the wide range of possibilities the reflective essay allows. Even when students are not completely successful at communicating the full range of their thinking, they are gaining important experience in listening carefully to the successes or limitations of a piece of writing in conveying themes, issues, and larger patterns of thinking. Conversations in class often provide a kind of openness and clarity that a one-on-one dialogue with the teacher does not always achieve.

The different "rhetorical modes" are introduced at this point in the course so that students can learn how to recognize them in essay writing and understand when it is appropriate to apply a particular mode in their prior learning document. In these initial exercises, I merely want students to recognize the differences. They receive a handout with a brief description of each mode and spend a few minutes working in small groups to choose one of the following modes: Description, Narration, Classification, Comparison and Contrast, Analogy, Definition, Process, Cause and Effect, and Induction and Deduction. They then have forty minutes to develop an 1–2-page essay collaboratively. When the class comes back together, each group reads its paper and the rest of the class tries to guess which mode was used and to discuss its strengths and weaknesses.

The next class exercise follows up with a closer look at the problem of relying on description in a student's first attempt at a Prior Learning essay. One or two students volunteer their first draft for a public feedback session in which the class tries to identify as many of the exposition types as possible and looks for places in the essay where more of a particular mode of writing could be included to attain additional clarity or necessary detail. Here again, this is a student-centered approach, which engages participants in the process of discovering what is already present in their papers and how to develop the pieces that are missing. Students are quick to see weaknesses in each other's work, and they are appreciative of the feedback they receive in this classroom environment. Very importantly, these kinds of discussions both further and depend on an atmosphere of trust in the classroom. Because students have already worked collaboratively on several earlier exercises, they have built a foundation of trust in each other's feedback responses. Here, too, students are learning to revise their writing, to work on finding words and an approach to communicating their prior learning. They are also being pushed to acknowledge and reflect on experiences that could differ from their own.

As they work on the chapters of their document, some students find that they need additional help with their writing skills. These students are able to find writing support through the campus Writing Resource Center in which trained people are available to read and discuss student writing in order to keep the development of the document progressing toward completion. Students are also advised, if at all possible, to join other PLE students to edit their writings. It has been our experience that actively working to make these connections for the student and helping to keep them on track by reading and commenting on writings-in-progress in an ongoing and timely way are significant components of any prior learning program.

In addition to accessing help with their writing, students are also strongly encouraged to work with content-area faculty who can help them identify and explore the theoretical foundations of their areas of prior learning. For example, science students are expected to discuss their potential credit with a science faculty member to ensure that the document they are preparing has included the necessary theoretical background. Faculty often give students advice on relevant texts to study. They may also guide the students toward new research they can do to better describe and validate their prior work and learning. It is not unusual for these faculty advisors to become the assessors who evaluate the student's final document.

There is an ongoing tension in the Writing from Life course, which is a result of the emphasis on autobiographical writing. Sometimes students get hooked on writing about their lives in an early autobiographical paper and find it extremely hard to make the transition to an essay format. In the reflective and rhetorical modes, they are still using the first person, even as the emphasis shifts to relaying information and describing learning. Put in another way, some students find it difficult to understand why all their readers don't find all the glad and gory details of their lives inherently fascinating.

This can be troublesome when the student insists on writing a lengthy and detailed autobiographical paper and chooses to include it in the Prior Learning document. Some faculty evaluators are quite put off by the "story-telling" emphasis of these presentations and do not see its relevance to the student's learning. Other faculty enjoy reading about a student's life as long as it is fairly well written, is concise, and gives substantial clues to relevant learning. In effect, as with teachers of any portfolio course, we have to be attentive to the tension between autobiography and descriptions of knowledge; between presentation of experience, however elegantly offered, and discussion of what has been learned.

In this class, students are encouraged to work on an autobiography that is no longer than ten pages in length and that they feel would be helpful to include as one part of their prior learning submission. But we also want them to write! This means encouraging them to work on more lengthy emotional pieces/memoirs on their own time and/or in preparation for their prior learning document. Such writing does help some students process emotional traumas or work with critical life moments. It also helps them see the connections between their life experiences and how they came to gain the knowledge and skills they describe in their documents. But for quite practical reasons, they sometimes need to be encouraged to lay their autobiography aside until they complete their essays.

The most difficult element to communicate in the Writing from Life course is how one can demonstrate analytical thinking in a prior learning document; that is, to go beyond merely describing to formulating and articulating insights gathered from those experiences, supported with evidence, and expressed in an evaluative conclusion. One way to encourage this kind of thinking is to ask students to pose the question "So What?" early in their essay writing attempts. Some students have no trouble writing in a voice that includes this analytical dimension, but others find it more difficult to understand the concept. Some of them never find a way to do this. Indeed, attention to "analysis" is the area found most lacking by faculty who review student prior learning documents. Readings and writing exercises that help students to work with this analytical dimension are extremely important to any successful portfolio course.

Students are expected to submit a draft of their nearly completed documents for review a quarter before the one-year completion deadline in order to get feedback, to fine-tune, and to revise. When the document is completed, two or three faculty are selected to review it, depending on its complexity. One of the three chosen faculty members must have some expertise in the subject(s) the student has written about. Because the document is shaped by personal experience, it is also important to select faculty who are knowledgeable about the student's experience, either academically or personally. This means considering race, class, gender, ethnicity, and sexual orientation in addition to area of academic expertise. Faculty read the documents, assess them individually and as a group, award credit, and write an evaluation of the student's learning.

Conclusion

Our institutional goals for the Writing from Life course have been realized when students who were shy and uncommunicative at the beginning of the quarter stand up before their peers and read their writing with confidence near the end of the quarter. Student success can also be seen when they talk about their initial discomfort in doing the collaborative assignments and then reveal in their self-evaluation how much pleasure they gained while learning from each other. Overall, they are using a course on portfolio preparation to deal with the kinds of issues and skills that are important to Evergreen's educational philosophy and to their overall intellectual growth.

At the conclusion of Writing from Life, students are asked to provide a self-evaluation not only of what they have learned about writing but about what and how they have learned about collaborative learning and the content of the course itself. These four excerpts provide some insight into this learning process:

1. A female Native American student wrote:

   I learned to be a better listener with a group of people that I was unfamiliar with, and by listening to their point of view I learned a lot more. I also learned to take a risk with others and learned to give my point of view on issues that pertain to my life and culture.

2. A white male student wrote:

   I was pleasantly shocked to find that a dozen individuals found my autobiography of interest. Likewise, I found myself hungry to read the works of the other students. The group essays forced me to think from a wider perspective and discover alternate ways of expressing ideas.

3. A female Hispanic student wrote:

   I have always been a bit hesitant about giving feedback on the work of others, but in this class the comfortable atmosphere encouraged me and made it easier for me to give feedback.

4. A white female wrote:

This is my first class in an educational system in over twenty years. The format of the class provided for self-expression and self-learning. There was freedom for all participants to engage in what we were doing, and in that context a richness and depth emerged. I learned immensely from everyone in the class. I also observed an evolution in my ability to speak in a group setting. This experience was almost more important than the writing and quite unexpected.

By the close of the course, all students who have taken Writing from Life have experienced the Five Foci or principles of Evergreen. Students are significantly more aware of their writing strengths and weaknesses by working collaboratively with each other on writing assignments and on giving writing feedback. They are able to speak before a group and present different points of view perhaps from another culture or their own culture in an unique context. They are more comfortable listening to and grappling with different opinions and cultural orientations. They can make connections between different disciplines in relation to their life experience learning. They are also able to see and utilize theory in connection to their document writing work. Most significant of all is their personal engagement in their learning. They are grounded in knowledge of who they are and have gained confidence in being able to claim their personal power. That is, they have become self-directed students who understand that they have to and can take responsibility for their learning for their entire academic career.

References

Barry, L. (1999). *The Good Times Are Killing Me*. Seattle, WA.: Sasquatch Books.

Garrison, R. (1985). *How a Writer Works*. New York: HarperCollins.

Gillespie, S., and Singleton, R. (1999). *Across Cultures: A Reader for Writers* (4th ed.). Boston: Allyn and Bacon.

THE WHOLENESS OF LIFE

A NATIVE NORTH AMERICAN APPROACH TO PORTFOLIO DEVELOPMENT AT FIRST NATIONS TECHNICAL INSTITUTE

Diane Hill

First Nations Technical Institute, a Mohawk institution on the shores of Lake Ontario, is a vocationally oriented college serving a primarily Ojibway, Cree, and Iroquoian student body. It draws on traditional Native teachings concerning competence, education, and community. Portfolio development serves a variety of purposes; it is a vehicle for documenting both prior and new learning and a record of healing from the emotional, cognitive, and social effects of oppression.

This model provides an example of a portfolio-development course that is designed to engage the cultural, economic, and political experience of a group of students who share a common history. The conversations, the exercises, and the subject matter of the course are not only about learning but also about unlearning *negative messages of self and culture. The revisiting of experiential learning thus becomes a vehicle for both personal and collective healing. As Diane Hill explains, "Exploring one's experiential learning provides a means of affirming one's own individual existence, but also of placing oneself within ever-expanding circles of involvement and interaction, from one's family, to one's extended family, clan, and community, to the environment and the world beyond."*

Acknowledgment: Special thanks to my colleague Banakonda Kennedy-Kish Bell for the use of her "wheeling-out" exercise described in this model.

Introduction

The First Nations Technical Institute (FNTI), located on the Tyendinaga Mohawk Territory near Deseronto, Ontario, is owned by the Mohawks of the Bay of Quinte and operates as an Aboriginal postsecondary educational institution. FNTI's programs offer diplomas and certificates in human services, public administration, small business management, computer science, aviation, and media studies, among other fields. The learners enrolled in FNTI's programs come primarily from various First Nation communities situated throughout the province of Ontario. These First Nation communities constitute primarily three distinct cultures: Ojibway, Cree, and Iroquoian.

From the time of its incorporation in 1985, The First Nations Technical Institute has been committed to the design, development, and delivery of learner-centered and culturally relevant educational programs for Aboriginal[1] adult learners. The human services faculty and staff[2] believe in helping Aboriginal adult learners acquire the knowledge and skills related to the concept of lifelong learning and associated learning, regardless of where it occurs. Although it is generally understood that Aboriginal learners must be proficient and competent in an occupational role, we also believe that these learners must be proficient and competent in the many roles and functions required by their unique cultural and societal affiliations. Therefore, the faculty and staff have spent much time and attention on the definition, clarification, and articulation of an Aboriginal learning model that is largely based on traditional Aboriginal teachings and that is centered on Aboriginal learners whose knowledge and skills are very much situated within the context of the culture, communities, and territories in which they live. The majority of the teaching faculty and staff are Aboriginal.

---

[1]In referring to First Nation peoples, I am following the Canadian usage, "Aboriginal," as well as "Native."

[2]The creation of FNTI's Aboriginal learning model was made possible through the efforts of both Aboriginal and non-Aboriginal people. Thanks is extended to the Loyalist College faculty, Ron Conlon and Paul Zakos, who have been assigned for many years to FNTI. James Dumont, Banakonda Kennedy-Kish Bell, Bob Antone, and Ernie Benedict are acknowledged for their contribution to the Aboriginal content of the model. Special thanks are extended to Don Groff for his work on the components related to self-evaluation and dacum charts. Jim Docherty and Janet Baker are commended for their facilitation of the occupational streams related to child welfare and general welfare legislation.

The Native Social Service Worker Program

Within FNTI, the Native Social Service Worker program offers a thirty-six-credit, two-year community college diploma, which is equivalent to one third of a university degree program. Because FNTI cannot yet offer accredited degrees and diplomas on its own, FNTI acts as the delivery agent for St. Lawrence College (previously, Loyalist College) in relation to the design and development of curriculum and the delivery of a Native-specific program of study in the social service worker field. The primary recipients of the program are adult learners who are employed in human service occupations within First Nation communities and who work as prevention workers and counselors in child welfare, general welfare assistance, substance-abuse programs, women's shelters, and the like. Non-Native people who are working with First Nation people or in First Nation communities can and do enroll in the program. However, learners are primarily mature Aboriginal adults with an average age of approximately 35 years.

Only those who have worked a minimum of three years in the social services and/or who have a minimum of five years of relevant experience in a related field can apply for admittance to FNTI. For those adult learners in the field who are not employed in social service capacities, special 300-hour work placements in the social services field are required. For example, a worker who is employed in the prison system as a guard would need to do a work placement in a social service setting where she or he can practice knowledge and skill related to a more therapeutic mode of helping. A person who is a secretary or clerical worker in a social service agency would need to do a work placement as a frontline worker under the supervision of an agency designee.

Regardless of occupation, learners in this program are trained in the subjects that constitute core competency areas related to social service work in general. Specialized knowledge and skill areas are related to three specific streams: Child Welfare, General Welfare, and Community Work.

The curriculum of the Native Social Service Worker program meets the learning outcomes set out by the Ontario Ministry of Education, Social Service Worker Occupation Standards that govern all Ontario colleges. However, as long as the program meets the general learning outcomes articulated by the province, FNTI has full creative license in interpreting what these outcomes mean in a Native cultural content. For example, at FNTI the learning outcomes associated with Community Psychology and Strategies for Community Development are often placed within an historical context that is specific to Native people. Curriculum typically includes the psychology of oppression, the development of strategies to reverse the effects of "internalized oppression" through cultural revitalization, and the restructuring of family systems according to Aboriginal norms and values.

The program is designed to accommodate the needs of working adults who cannot leave their jobs, families, and communities to undertake a conventional full-time program of study that extends from September to May. Thus, the program is delivered through a combined residency and distance-learning mode that centers on 12 one-week training sessions offered at three-month intervals over the course of three years. The average entering class is between thirty and thirty-five learners. Within that number, groups of five or six learners are developed, which then typically select a particular mentor from the faculty at hand. Faculty mentors are there to assist the learners in the clarification of subject matter, to provide individual healing/counseling, to answer questions, and to explain processes related to portfolio development. Faculty are available to assist learners both during the actual weeks of training and during the three-month interim period between training sessions.

The design of any single week of training is done by faculty members with learner input. At the beginning of the overall training program, learners are asked to fill out a self-assessment sheet that asks them to identify the areas of knowledge and skill they believe they need to perform their job. This initial list is supplemented by assessments that are filled out by the learners at the end of each week of training. Then, one month in advance, the faculty design the upcoming week of training, incorporating these learner-identified areas.

Each week of training is an integrated program of study and, combined with work done throughout the term, meets the requirements for two college courses, each of which gains learners one credit. Thus, learners gain twenty-four credits for coursework over the three years. Because the learners are already employed in the field of study, the other twelve credits can be earned through evidence provided in their individual portfolios.

The structure of each week of training usually follows this general format:

- *Day 1.* Opening ceremony; interviewing and counseling activities; traditional Aboriginal teachings
- *Days 2 and 3.* An exploration of topics associated with two college courses
- *Day 4.* Focus on the three occupational streams
- *Day 5.* Portfolio development; closing ceremony
- *Evening sessions.* Individual/group healing circles; individual help/tutoring; presentations by students

The portfolio-development component of the program is coordinated through a specific credit-bearing course and is thus, in itself, worth one college credit. However, the portfolio-development process is an integrated part of a total program of study. For example, the learning styles assessment discussed below is formally part of the course entitled Principles of Adult Learning, while the cultural and historical perspectives needed for personal and community healing are addressed in courses such as Cultural History and Interviewing and Counseling. Moreover, unlike many PLA-granting institutions that utilize portfolios, the portfolio is not finalized early in the program once credit recommendations have been made. Rather, a truly evolving portfolio is used throughout the program as a record of both prior and new learning, serving in lieu of exams and extended papers. The portfolio is submitted in its final form only at the end of the program and is, indeed, the one requirement for graduation.

Key Issues Related to Prior Learning Assessment and Aboriginal Adult Learners

In some ways, the challenges faced by our learners at FNTI are typical of those of many adults in higher education. Often the common methods of teaching do not fit either the learning styles or the interests of adult learners, thus contributing to boredom, poor attendance, shoddy academic work, and/or high dropout rates. Further compounding these problems is the educational institution's tendency to ignore what adult learners have learned through living by directing them to a common starting point in the curriculum and limiting options for meeting individual learning needs and interests.

Like many of our colleagues in adult education, we have found that a mechanism for assessing prior learning is one important solution to these problems. Implicit in the concept of prior learning assessment (PLA) are the beliefs that (a) learning can and does take place independently and outside of the formal classroom; (b) mechanisms for evaluating prior learning (e.g., PLA) should be available, and (c) adult learners should contribute to defining the competencies and learning outcomes expected in postsecondary courses and programs. FNTI is committed to the belief that recognizing, accrediting, and valuing the experiential learning of adults contribute to greater accessibility, increased adult learner retention rates, and the increased self-confidence on which educational success depends.

Aboriginal adult learners share many of the experiences and confront the same barriers associated with adult learners in general, and thus have the same need to have their experiential learning valued by the educational system. However, the unique cultural history of Aboriginal adults makes PLA both more complex and contradicted *and* more central to educational success. Specifically, the life experiences of Aboriginal adults have been tainted by the impact of generational abuse stemming from the historical oppression of their culture. These experiences have created additional obstacles to which a program like ours needs to directly respond.

In Canada and the United States, the historical impact of Western culture and the effects of cultural oppression were importantly experienced through the residential boarding school system of the late 1800s. The purpose of the residential boarding school, as explained in *The Report of the Royal Commission on Aboriginal Peoples* (1996), was to move Aboriginal peoples from their "helpless savage" state to one of "civilization" (p. 333). This "civilizing" required a concerted attack on the ontology, the basic cultural patterning, and the Aboriginal worldview. Aboriginal children had to be taught to see and understand the world as a European place within which only European values and beliefs had meaning. Thus, through this "educating" process, the wisdom of their Native cultures would seem to them only savage superstition. A wedge had to be driven not only physically between parent and child, but also culturally and spiritually (p. 341).

In Canada, because residential schools persisted until the last one closed in 1974, the grandparents, parents, and even some of the Aboriginal adult learners of today have been the recipients of this assault on their worldview. Many of them adjusted their belief systems and then passed these ideas on to succeeding generations. The changes in family belief systems created as a consequence of oppression have disrupted the psychosocial mechanisms that at one time supported the development of a healthy and positive Native self-image and self-esteem. Today, many Aboriginal people have internalized the negative imagery about their culture. Many no longer know who they are or what makes them unique.

The residential boarding school system no longer exists, but its impact lingers on in the psychological and social makeup of Aboriginal people. High rates of suicide, alcoholism, family violence, sexual abuse, unemployment, and other social ills are still a large part of contemporary Aboriginal life, as are low self-esteem and lack of self-confidence. Our learners come to portfolio development, therefore, with the need to unlearn the negative images they have often internalized concerning themselves and their culture. They have to "unlearn" the idea that Aboriginal cultures have nothing of value to contribute to learning or to the world. PLA takes on a particular powerful individual and cultural urgency in this context. It is because of this particular set of historical and cultural circumstances that Aboriginal adult learners need help in articulating and processing painful life experiences and in affirming what they know.

Purposes of Portfolio Development

At FNTI, the portfolio is a multifunctional instrument that serves five interrelated, but distinct, purposes.

1. **To assess and recognize prior learning for credit within the academic program.**

   As in other Canadian institutions, adult learners enrolling at FNTI can complete a portfolio and apply for credit for specific courses contained within their program of study. At FNTI, 75 percent of a community college diploma can be acquired in this way. Learners who have acquired the knowledge and skill areas being addressed in the courses offered within any given week of study can gain credit for those areas through PLA, though it is generally expected that a learner will be present for at least nine of the twelve training weeks.

   It is understood that a learner who is already employed in the social service worker field for a minimum of three years has prior learning acquired both from the job and from informal training seminars on such topics as crisis intervention and suicide prevention, to name but two. Given the subject matter of the program, it is important that we also take seriously the potential credit in experiential learning related to personal addiction counseling, family counseling, participation in groups such as Alcoholics Anonymous and Al-Anon, and/or participation in traditional Aboriginal healing practices as well as any knowledge gained from reading a variety of self-help books and educational texts. To apply for credit, learners complete a self-evaluation form and learning contract that describes the nature of the relevant knowledge and experience and identifies the learning outcomes that match those of the course. Further evidence in support of these claims is included in the learner's ongoing portfolio. This evidence can take the form of letters written by supervisors, peers, group leaders, and members of training institutions as well as copies of any certificates received.

2. **To recognize and articulate prior learning for vocational advancement.**

   In a related use of portfolios, adult learners interested in expanding their professional resumes often opt to complete a portfolio of learning related to the profession of their choice. Adult learners who are employed full-time can elect to complete a portfolio as a way of providing their employers with the evidence needed to substantiate their claims to competency in their field. In cases where salary raises and job security are dependent upon such "qualifications," some learners are able to argue "competency" based on experience rather than on academic credentials. This function of a portfolio is particularly useful when adult learners in outlying areas are raising families and cannot leave their families to attend conventional academic training.

3. **To set personal learning objectives and determine future educational plans.**

As social service workers, the learners in the Native Social Service Worker Program are subject to the learning outcomes set by the province of Ontario and laid out in a "dacum" or competency chart that reflects knowledge, skills, and attitudes. To a degree, and as noted earlier, our curriculum revolves around the achievement of those minimal competencies. However, it is the belief of FNTI faculty that common occupational standards are only legitimate if they are also owned and adopted by the learner as being consistent with his or her learning needs. Conflict between the need to meet learning outcomes that fit common occupational standards and the need to meet individually determined learning outcomes becomes a problem if the adult learner is not aware of what his or her individual learning needs are and therefore cannot determine the appropriate learning outcomes that will meet those needs. Over the years, we have found that the preparation of a portfolio is an important method for helping the adult learner to identify and to determine individual learning needs.

4. **To provide a mechanism for the integration of various kinds of learning.**

In some ways, the most practical function of portfolios in our program is also the most controversial: They take the place of papers and exams. That is, rather than testing the learners through a series of incremental exams and extended academic essays, we use portfolio development itself as the cumulative evidence of both prior and current learning. In it, learners give evidence of their prior learning in the areas that make up the curriculum, integrate old experience and new perspectives, and record the new learning that they gain in the three years of the program. It is for this reason that while portfolio development begins in the first weeklong session and while learners must submit sections for purposes of PLA at relevant points in the curriculum, the portfolio as a whole is completed only at the end.

5. **To affirm individual lives and the life of the Aboriginal community.**

In addition to focusing on competence as defined in a narrow academic or professional context, the majority of First Nations people also complete portfolios as a means of helping them to identify and to discover the knowledge, skills, attitudes, and insights contained within their particular journey through life. At FNTI, competence is defined broadly as the development of the whole person within the total environment, not only to survive and earn a living but also to achieve a life of quality where one can live one's life with meaning, purpose, and a profound thankfulness. In this way, the portfolio-development process provides Aboriginal adult learners with the opportunity to affirm knowledge and skills that go well beyond their formal area of academic and professional study. Exploring one's experiential learning provides a means of affirming one's own individual existence but also of placing oneself within ever-expanding circles of involvement and interaction, from one's family, to one's extended family, clan, and community, to the environment and the world beyond (Hill, 1995).

Moreover, the presentation of their prior learning experiences provides Aboriginal adult learners with the opportunity to discover and to identify the sources of conflict that many of them have had with their Native identity and with people from other cultures. It provides them with an opportunity to process and overcome the pain arising from their life experiences and to become more aware of the importance of their cultural heritage. The knowledge and skills documented through portfolio development go well beyond formal academic study; they also include knowledge and skills related to traditional Aboriginal forms of knowledge contained in cultural practices and beliefs. Indeed, many of these portfolios are handed down to both children and grandchildren as family records and heirlooms. In a large number of cases, portfolio development and prior learning assessment provide the impetus for the healing and unification of many First Nation families.

Because it functions as more than an instrument for assessing prior learning, the portfolio at FNTI's Native Social Service Worker program can contain any or all of the following:

- A narrative autobiography
- A resume
- A statement of the learner's values and beliefs regarding social service work
- A statement of one's personal philosophy and how it applies to the social service field

- An assessment of one's personal and professional strengths and weaknesses
- Specific presentations of content knowledge in the learner's field of study, including examples of theories, methods, and plans of actions
- Broad presentation of life experiences that explore one's engagement with the community and the world; these may include discussions of personal and family healing, committee and volunteer work, community involvement, work related to one's job, recreational pursuits, and hobbies
- Task analysis/learning analysis; presentation of what the learner knows and can do
- Letters of support, certificates, and other evidence of prior training, and any other supporting documentation such as awards of recognition and the like

For those sections of the portfolio that will be used to assess prior learning, there are five distinct approaches that the learner can employ. These are:

1. To describe life experiences;
2. to identify the learning(s);
3. to express the learning in the framework of his or her program of study;
4. to relate the learning to one's overall career and educational goals; and
5. to compile evidence to prove the learning and one's ability to perform.

Learner Reaction to Portfolio-Development Strategy

Orientation to the course and an introduction to portfolio development take place during the first weeklong training session of the Native Social Service Worker Program. At that first session, our learners learn what a portfolio is and what will be expected of them. We also review the various purposes of the portfolio and explain that one intent of the portfolio is to help them "pull out" the knowledge and skills already contained within them and the expertise that they have already acquired in the social service field.

Reactions in this first session to the idea of portfolio development are typically mixed. On the one hand, when they are introduced to the process of portfolio development, the majority of Aboriginal adult learners bump into painful memories and negative self-image. Many express a discomfort and, in some cases, a deep fear about recording life experiences that they feel are better left forgotten. They may be frightened at the idea of writing about themselves. For example, we discuss the history of residential schools, often a personal memory to these learners or their parents, for the purpose of giving them a perspective on negative self-images and to provide them with the opportunity to situate their fears and experiences in a broader historical context. As part of this first meeting, we put learners in pairs or small circles to talk about what worries them. Not everyone is willing to share their concerns, but just hearing about the fears of others is helpful in showing learners that they are not alone.

On the other hand, some learners react disdainfully to the portfolio as an instrument for evidencing knowledge. A "real" educational program, they reason, would require extended exams based on learning from books! For these learners, too, the discussion of the residential schools and the principles associated with adult learning is helpful because it serves as an example of how past education has been harmful and begins to challenge their assumptions about what education is all about. Over time, these learners typically come to realize that developing a portfolio is actually a more difficult task than the typical college exam because it requires engagement and participation on the part of the learner and not simply obedience. For the moment, we discuss ways in which an approach to adult learning that requires participation is more liberating and less oppressive than the kind of schooling most of them have known.

Still, for all of these difficulties and conflicted feelings, learners are intrigued by the idea of the portfolio. The suggestion that they already know something is a real inducement because it contradicts what many of them have always been told—that they are empty vessels who know nothing worthwhile. Built into our discussions during this first week is the intended use of portfolios to undo learners' negative learning about themselves and to build self-esteem.

Portfolio Development: The Course

At FNTI, portfolio development is informed by both traditional Aboriginal teachings about education and by an approach to learning styles that draws on those traditional teachings. In conjunction with a related course, Principles of Adult Learning, a focus on learning styles forms the other major topic for the first session of the Portfolio Development course.

According to traditional teachings, a human being consists of four aspects of the self—spirit, heart (emotion), mind, and body: the capacity to see, feel, know, and do. To develop the whole person, human beings must be helped to identify and to develop their innate human capacities in all four aspects of self and to do so in a way that achieves a balance, first within themselves and second in their interactions within ever-expanding circles of relationship and involvement with the outside world.

In the first training session week, our learners are introduced to the concept of lifelong learning that, we explain, usually occurs through a cycle. This cycle often begins with a spiritual, or intuitive sense—an *awareness* of one's needs in relation to one's self, family, community, nation, and/or place within the universe. Awareness of a need or problem can lead a person to *struggle* with the feelings or emotions associated with the influx of new information that contradicts the person's assumptions, beliefs, and attitudes. In this second stage of the cycle, attitudes and beliefs often change through an internal struggle with the contradictions present in one's thoughts and feelings. Resolution of the contradiction leads to a third stage of *building* new knowledge constructs, patterns of relating, and a more positive view of life. The fourth and final stage occurs when a person integrates the new knowledge and belief into a new sense of self and takes action to *preserve* the positive patterns and views of life. Thus, human beings continually move through a cycle of awareness, struggle, building, and preservation in a never-ending spiral that supports and promotes the development of a greater consciousness of themselves and the world around them.

Over time, the faculty and staff have come to understand how the four fundamental stages of learning also correlate to four distinct styles of learning. Our view of holistic education suggests that all four aspects must be present for learning to occur. At the same time, in most human beings, a certain style of learning predominates. The "awareness stage" is associated with an intuitive learning style and with the spiritual aspect of the person; the "struggle stage" is associated with a relational learning style and emotional aspect; the "building stage" is linked to a mental learning style and cognitive aspect; the "preservation stage" is connected to a physical learning style and behavioral aspect. During the first training session, learners participate in an exercise that we have developed to identify their preferred learning styles.

The differences in learning styles identified in this exercise are the basis of our strategy for helping learners to construct a portfolio. We have found that each kind of learner faces different challenges in his or her effort to identify the knowledge and meaning that resides in his or her life experience. Such challenges influence how a learner might "extract" college-equivalent learning from experience in an academic sense and how he or she tries to articulate the relationship between a given experience and the broader meaning of his or her path as a unique human being. For example, physical learners tend to present their knowledge by presenting samples of their work; a written case study, or a proposal arguing for a new policy or project, or the record of an interview. Mental learners are more likely to use the chronological charts that we provide in the student manual of what they did at various stages of life and what they learned from each experience. Emotional learners are also likely to present autobiographical accounts, but theirs will be in a narrative form rather than in charts, and they may move from one experience to another through association and patterns of meaning rather than chronologically. Spiritual or intuitive learners may also need a more holistic way of articulating learning. We offer them an example of a "mind map" that does not require a chronological structure to be understood.

Very little work on a learner's own portfolio takes place during this first week; everyone is still too overwhelmed by the process and needs the time to become comfortable with talking or writing about themselves. Instead, we present models of the kinds of portfolios typically developed by learners of the various types so as to give them examples of how they might go about it. We therefore place different types of portfolios on a table and give learners time and opportunity to reflect and to explore. After the first week, a part of each of the subsequent weeklong training sessions is devoted to portfolio-development activities. At each session, we hold individual meetings with learners. At the first training session, perhaps only one or two of thirty learners will come for individual meetings. Many are still too intimidated. Even the ones who meet individually with the faculty tend to be hesitant, and we are aware of the need to be supportive of learners taking these first tentative steps. Sometimes, a learner just wants to come and talk, to let the feelings come up about painful life experiences. Other learners will be more focused, and we can use the sessions to begin to help them organize a portfolio, for example, by mirroring back what they are thinking in a series of bullet points. Between these face-to-face sessions, support for learners working on portfolios is provided by program faculty using telephone, fax, or one-on-one tutorial sessions.

Once a year, in training sessions 4, 8, and 12, we meet with the whole group for group exercises designed to help learners articulate and gain insight into the meaning of their experiences and experiential learning. Here again, activities and exercises are organized around the strengths and demands of portfolio development for those with different learning styles. We have found that such challenges of portfolio development are quite different depending on a learner's preferred learning style; what one group finds easiest is the greatest challenge for another and vice versa. Often the same exercise works for different groups, but for very different reasons.

The "wheeling-out" exercise is an example of this (see Exhibit C5.1). It was developed by my colleague Banakonda Kennedy-Kish Bell especially

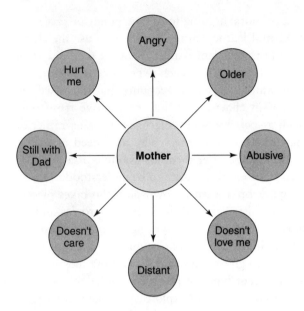

Exhibit C5.1   The "wheeling-out" exercise

for spiritual or intuitive learners. These learners typically have a sense of a larger perspective and can situate themselves in a world context. Unlike many adult learners, they have no trouble in identifying the meanings that arise from experience. Portfolio development is a challenge to them because they have trouble giving specific examples and focusing on individual experiences. Everything is connected, so they don't know where to begin.

The wheeling-out exercise is facilitated through a quiet meditation process and begins with the facilitator asking learners to visualize an image that comes to mind when asked to think about their lives. Then each learner is asked to "wheel out" from there. Using the image as a starting point, the facilitator asks the learners to place a word that comes to them in each of the four directions that surrounds the image that they have placed at the center of their page. From these initial four words, an additional word can be drawn or associated from each of these. From what is now a collection of eight words, the learner is asked to construct a sentence or paragraph that connects the words together. Often, after drawing some connecting lines, or writing out a few sentences or a short paragraph, the learner is able to correlate the words written to a particular life experience or a specific time that has informed his or her current understanding and learning (see the written example in the box, "Description of Past Life Experience at the Beginning of Educational Program").

Description of Past Life Experience at the Beginning of Educational Program

---

> My Mom hurt me. She was very abusive. She didn't care for or love me.
> She was very distant. She is older now, but she is still with Dad.

With facilitator assistance, this Aboriginal adult learner was able to explore her past life experience with her mother more fully and to unburden herself of some painful emotions. Thereafter, this is the learning description that she wrote and entered into her portfolio as a record of "new" learning:

> We had a ceremony for Mom on the 21st of December, the winter solstice,
> with all my sisters. It was a ceremony to honour Mom as a woman,
> mother, and grandmother. We did a smudge and Thanksgiving Address
> and I explained to Mom that this is the path that I have chosen. We each
> told Mom about our love for her and what we were getting together about.
> We all cried. We exchanged gifts, spent a few hours together, and shared a
> meal while talking. It was so good for us to come together as a family and
> to share this special time. It felt right.

Learning Analysis

> Through healing, I have gained some benefits. I am my Mother's daughter
> and in spite of the painful past, I can now appreciate and honour my
> Mom. In each step that I take in working towards forgiveness of my Mom,
> I move further into forgiveness of myself. I have gained the strength to
> survive all of the adversity. This is a gift that I received from my Mother.
> I know that I have a lot of work yet to do in this relationship. I can only
> hope that my Mom survives long enough for me to do the work with
> her directly.

Interestingly, the same exercise works with mental learners in spite of the fact that they have the opposite challenge. Mental learners find it easy to identify specific life experiences and to organize and present their life experiences in various forms. However, what the spiritual/intuitive learners find easiest to do is often difficult for mental learners. Thus, the wheeling-out exercise encourages these learners to develop an appreciation of the connections among things and helps them to begin to articulate what is most meaningful for them.

Other exercises are often particularly helpful to one kind of learner. Mental learners, for example, often particularly enjoy working with the competency charts developed for human service workers because they can describe certain life experiences that correlate with a specific competency area such as interviewing and counseling. Learners read the competency band descriptions and then identify the life experiences in which they acquired the knowledge, skills, and attitudes described in the band. For the purpose of self-evaluation, the learners can then go on to assess how well they can demonstrate this knowledge, perform the skills, and exhibit the appropriate attitudes. Self-evaluation of performance must be supported by appropriate documentation and letters of support from a peer or coworker, a faculty member, an agency supervisor, and/or someone who is familiar with the claims being made.

Emotional/relational learners, on the other hand, often prefer to draw meaningful life experiences from an exercise based on the Seven Stages of Life or Path of Life as described in traditional Anishinabe (Ojibway) teachings. The Seven Stages of Life are described as occurring in increments of approximately seven years beginning with the "Good Life" (age 0 to 7 years), "Fast Life" (age 8 to 15 years), the "Wandering/Wondering Life" (age 16 to 23 years), "Truth Life" (age 24 to 31 years), "Planning/Planting Life" (age 32 to 39 years), "Doing Life" (ages 40 to 47 years), and "Elder Life" (age 48 to 55 years and beyond). Learners are provided with a description of the lessons associated with each stage of development according to these teachings. In this way, learners are able to identify the life experiences that correspond to each stage of their own personal development.

Because traditional cultural knowledge is not general knowledge even to these Aboriginal learners, the majority of FNTI learners would not have received the traditional lessons associated with each life stage. Thus, through the use of this exercise, learners can divide their lives into potentially meaningful categories, which helps them better describe key learning experiences and gain knowledge and insight into their own cultural practice.

Often, learners, regardless of learning style, either participate in individual healing sessions or larger traditional Aboriginal healing circles run by the teaching faculty as evening sessions that constitute part of the curriculum. In these sessions, the learners are helped to unburden themselves of the painful memories and life experience that they carry. These sessions are particularly important as painful memories carry very intense feelings that cloud the learner's mind and prevent the learner from accurately assessing what she or he has learned. We believe that some of the most profound learning is contained within painful learning experiences. This is especially true in cases in which adult learners have led a highly disruptive or dysfunctional life as a consequence of having internalized oppressive messages about being a Native person. Through these sessions, we have found that the release of painful emotion followed by a thoughtful evaluation with the help of a facilitator has helped many of our Aboriginal adult learners to regain their self-esteem and confidence and to find pride in their Native cultural heritage. Many of the negative assumptions that adult learners make about themselves and others are reversed and transformed into more positive and healthy relating patterns. In fact, in many cases, this new awareness and understanding constitutes new learning that is then integrated into the portfolio-development process as a way of explaining and articulating what a past experience has taught them.

Integrating Two Sets of Criteria

One of the abiding tensions of portfolio development at FNTI is that there are, in effect, two sets of criteria with which learners must grapple. One set of criteria is represented by the competency or dacum charts currently being used in the human service field. These charts are concrete and professionally oriented and, as mentioned above, some of our learners find them enormously helpful in identifying and organizing what they know and can do. A sample section of a dacum chart used in the human service field is seen in the box, "Band M: Capacity for Interpersonal Communication."

But as introduced earlier, FNTI as an Aboriginal learning institution has also developed a competency chart of knowledge, skills, attitudes, and insights that relate to Aboriginal belief systems and cultural knowledge necessary for sustaining the self and the Aboriginal community. A sample section of a competency chart outlining Aboriginal learning objectives is seen in the box, "Track A8: Experiencing the Helping/Healing Ways of Aboriginal Cultures."

Learners engage with both sets of expectations as they explore their prior learning and its relationship to the curriculum of the program. While they represent two very different understandings of community service, we try to integrate them as much as possible. For example, we add a column to the dacum chart that asks learners to explore the meaning of their experiences (insights) as well as their knowledge, skills, and attitudes. While these dacum charts, performance standards, and learning objectives are available, the choice of using them always resides with the learners who will decide if they are useful in helping to define their self-determined learning needs. The important point here is the emphasis on providing the learner with a choice, even though many learners will usually choose to use the charts provided as helpful guides in assessing their life experiences.

In the Native Social Service Worker Program, we attempt to work from the adult learners' needs as defined by them and that are most appropriate to their individual work settings and community situations. We continually

---

Band M: Capacity for Interpersonal Communication (General Competency Area)

Description: This band includes the components of the communication process. It includes the skills associated with the interviewing and counseling aspects of human service work. These are the reflective skills of feedback, attending, paraphrasing, reflection of feeling, and summarizing; and the directive skills of probing, self-disclosure, interpreting, and confrontation. It also includes knowledge and understanding of the effect that physical environment has on the communication process as well as an understanding of communication dynamics.

Band M1: Ability to Confront

(A specific area of skill, knowledge, and attitude that falls under Band M. There are nine other specific areas that delineate other knowledge and skill areas related to the Band M general description.)

Description

1. Understands the purposes and uses of confrontation
2. Skill in techniques of confrontation
3. Knowledge of the guidelines for effective confrontation

Performance Stance

Level A: Function at level 4 for confrontation on the Carkhuff Counsellor Training Scale for 75 percent of the time.

Level B: Function at level 4 for confrontation on the Carkhuff Counsellor Training Scale for 60 percent of the time.

Level C: Describe the confrontation skill and its purposes, uses, and guidelines.

---

stress that adult learners must be aware of their total environment and to analyze and to determine not only what is needed to perform well in their occupation but also what is needed for them to live life within the context of their Aboriginal culture. In this sense, we see a close connection between the use of the portfolio for personal development and healing and the professional record of knowledge and skills—between what our learners understand about the pain and triumph of their own life experience and how this experience informs and determines the content of their knowledge about the communities that they serve.

Track A8: Experiencing the Helping/Healing Ways of Aboriginal Cultures

Learning Objective 1: Develop Awareness of Aboriginal Helping/Healing Styles

Knowledge	Skills	Attitude	Insights
• Concept of traditional healing and the recovery of one's true self. • Concept of the "circle." • Healing circle process that begins with oneself. • Guidelines for a healing circle process. • Levels/types of healing circles. • Different types of emotions and the ways that the body discharges feelings.	• Can list and describe the various ways of traditional healing. • Can list, describe, and share personal thoughts and feelings with others (self-disclosure). • Can identify the various levels of healing. • Can participate in one-on-one sessions. • Can share in small groups and circles.	• Respects healing processes that cross tribal and language groups. • Openness and willingness to explore traditional healing practices. • Accepts others. • Willingness to heal oneself. • Appreciation for who one is.	• That there is a need to expand one's resources for both personal healing and professional application. • That healing is universal and that one is not the only one who carries burdens. • That one can only help a person to achieve a level of healing that is equal to one's own. • That human beings are a product of their life experiences.

(continued)

Track A8: Continued

Knowledge	Skills	Attitude	Insights
	• Practices own cultural healing processes (for example, Sweat Lodge).		• That oppressive experiences will affect one's perspective and determine how a person will perceive oneself and others.

Performance Standards

1. Able to identify and to articulate one's personal awareness of issues and feelings that result from being in a helping/healing role

2. Able to struggle through one's personal healing and recovery from issues that result from the re-stimulation of painful memories associated with working in a helping and healing capacity

3. Able to describe a lifelong plan for learning how to improve one's skills in Aboriginal approaches to helping and healing

4. Able to seek further knowledge and to continue developing and strengthening one's skills in healing and helping people

The Completed Portfolio: Multiple Venues and Media

In the later stages of the program, as learners complete sections of their portfolios, FNTI faculty provide opportunities for them to present their evidence of learning in a variety of venues and media. Our program structure, which brings us together for a full week, gives us the flexibility to provide those opportunities.

In developing their portfolios, our adult learners often draw on a variety of media. Some choose to present all sections of the portfolio in written form, writing brief descriptions of each experience for the purpose of extracting knowledge, skills, attitudes, and insights for prior learning assessment. It is also possible for the adult learner to write bullet points denoting knowledge, skills, and attitudes from these experiences, and then to provide an oral explanation to a three-person program faculty committee who will ask questions and request further clarification of the points presented. In the past, adult learners have presented their learning in the form of quilts, artwork, drawings, and albums containing photographs of their work and life experiences. In these cases, portfolio development is accomplished through oral presentation and discussion while the program staff complete notes for the purpose of documenting knowledge, skills, attitudes, and insights related to the program of study and the individual's learning objectives.

Where demonstrations, videotape, and audiocassette records have been used, learners must still submit supporting documentation that can include copies of any certificates, training diplomas, awards of recognition, letters of support, and other documents under separate cover. This supporting documentation is used to support the learner's claims of exemption as well as to support his or her transcript grades that were derived from weekly processes of self-evaluation using the competency/dacum charts. In a few cases, some learners have been asked to provide additional supporting documentation where evidence is questionable or not obvious.

The choice to present the portfolio in writing, orally or through performance, is especially important for physical learners who best evidence their knowledge and skills through demonstration and activity. One learner, for example, demonstrated her human service knowledge, skills, attitudes, and insights by creating and then delivering an evening workshop for faculty and classmates related to the effects of laughter and play and its importance in social service work. Another learner videotaped his entire portfolio, including the participation of his family and friends. He provided clips of certain activities related to his social service work in his community and photographs of his birth family, complete with explanations of what he had learned from the experiences that he described. Learners may choose to present their portfolio to a three-person committee of faculty chosen by the learner or, as in the example given above, the learner chose to demonstrate her knowledge and skills in front of the entire class and teaching staff.

There are a number of reasons why we do not require that an entire portfolio be presented in a written format. English is a second language for many Aboriginal adult learners from northern Ontario, for whom Ojibway, Cree, and/or Oji-Cree are the languages of life and professional work. Even in southern Ontario, where English is a first language, high numbers of adult learners dropped out of secondary school to enter the workforce, only to return to postsecondary education with low levels of academic literacy and numeracy skills. Because we understand that an adult learner's level of literacy has nothing to do with his or her intelligence, we provide the oral option to portfolio development.

However, there is another reason why we encourage portfolios that are presented in oral and/or performance modes: to acknowledge and validate a rich oral tradition. We have found that the telling of one's story in an autobiographical section of a portfolio supports traditional Aboriginal methods of learning/teaching related to the practice of storytelling. Thus, where Aboriginal adult learners previously failed to make the connections necessary for increasing their appreciation and understanding of traditional Aboriginal "ways of knowing" and definitions of knowledge, an examination of their own life experiences helps them to comprehend the meaning of the traditional teachings associated with their particular oral tradition. For Aboriginal people, traditional knowledge and skills are part of their life experience. Portfolio development has provided a means for helping both learning facilitators and Aboriginal adult learners not only to identify but also to recognize the value and importance of traditional Aboriginal knowledge and skills.

Conclusion

While PLA has been a useful tool in our educational practice with Aboriginal adult learners, it has not been without its tensions. We have had to debate issues related to who is responsible for naming the learning and for determining the validity of knowledge and skills that do not match the current definitions of knowledge espoused by Western academic institutions. At FNTI, we have also had to work at articulating and accepting a definition of knowledge and skill that does not match the Western educational mindset. That is, we wanted to create a program of learning that is grounded in our own traditional Aboriginal teachings related to holistic learning and teaching because we work with Aboriginal adult learners whose knowledge and skills are very much situated within the context of the culture, communities, and territories in which they live. Because of these realities and of the importance of an educational process that is learner-centered, we made a conscious effort to encourage and to preserve traditional Aboriginal knowledge and skills within our particular program of study and in our use of PLA throughout the portfolio-development process.

From a traditional Aboriginal cultural perspective, portfolio-assisted prior learning assessment has been useful in helping both learning facilitators and Aboriginal adult learners understand the importance and use of life experience in educating Aboriginal people as a whole. We also know that it has been particularly effective for those who use English as a second language. In the Native Social Service Worker Program, both learning facilitators and Aboriginal adult learners have benefited from knowing how to identify, extract, and then articulate the knowledge, skills, attitudes, and insights contained within a specific set of life experiences.

In this sense, portfolio development has been an important process not only for creating awareness but also for facilitating new learning. In utilizing various portfolio-development processes, Aboriginal adult learners have come to understand how their openness and acceptance of new information has often been curtailed by some very strong opinions and views that are supported by equally strong emotions and beliefs. On the one hand, we have found that the type of self-reflective learning inherent within a portfolio-development process has been invaluable in helping Aboriginal adult learners to understand the importance of their own culture and language in a world that is moving many of them away from their unique cultural identity and worldview. On the other hand, through portfolio development, we have been able to help many Aboriginal adult learners to appreciate a reality and worldview that supports the existence of many different life forms and that includes people from many different cultures. Therefore, in facilitating a traditional Aboriginal belief in coexistence, portfolio development has helped many Aboriginal adult learners realize that they may be blocking another perspective or worldview because of the feelings and beliefs stemming from the internalization of negative experiences with people from both their own and other cultures.

In many ways, FNTI's Native Social Service Worker faculty itself has had to undergo a similar struggle. It is easy for many of our teachers to transfer a fact or piece of information, but the understanding related to its meaning and application can be subject to individual interpretation by both the learner and the teacher, which sometimes gives rise to a conflict in belief. At times, it has been difficult for the faculty who act as learning facilitators to avoid making judgments on what Aboriginal adult learners perceived and identified as being their knowledge, skill, and understanding, particularly when affective, intuitive, or experiential processes were being employed. To overcome this tendency, those learning facilitators responsible for portfolio development and prior learning assessment have had to examine their own educational philosophies in order to identify the cultural assumptions that conflicted with those presented by our adult learners. Although the FNTI program faculty consists primarily of Aboriginal people, many of us have been educated within Western institutions and have had our own traditional Aboriginal cultural beliefs co-opted in favor of the Western concepts of what constitutes valid knowledge. Many of us have been well socialized by the

Western educational system and have been conditioned to operate on cultural assumptions that are based in Western ideological thought rather than in our traditional Aboriginal thought and practice.

Over the years, the teaching team has become very cognizant of the personal, situational, and cultural issues that affect the learning and teaching of Aboriginal adult learners. Great efforts have been made to meet the educational needs of Aboriginal adult learners and to help them overcome the barriers that they perceive are blocking their learning and educational success. Thus, knowledge and understanding of the learning process have enabled Aboriginal adult learners to take control of their learning in such a way that the differences in learning styles can now be seen and understood. Also, the portfolio-development processes employed in the program have provided them with the opportunity to develop themselves as whole people who have the capacity to learn in four primary ways. The Aboriginal approach to understanding one's total environment for the purpose of achieving balance in each and every circle of one's many relationships requires adult learners to become aware of the spiritual, mental, emotional, and physical realities of the world surrounding them. Because of this approach, the portfolio-development processes employed in the Native Social Service Worker program have provided them with the opportunity to transform the perceptions that they hold of themselves, others, and the environment around them.

Finally, as an Aboriginal educational institution, we have found that portfolio-assisted prior learning assessment has helped our learners to overcome the effects of their historical oppression. First, the documentation or presentation of their prior learning experiences through a portfolio-development process of their choice provides Aboriginal adult learners with the opportunity to discover and to identify the sources of conflict that many of them have with their Native identity and with people from other cultures. Second, the portfolio-development process provides Aboriginal adult learners with the opportunity to document life experiences that contain knowledge and skills related to their traditional Aboriginal cultural practices and beliefs. Third, it has become clear over time that the knowledge and skills associated with their traditional Aboriginal cultural heritage and life experience can now be expressed and validated in a way that has never been done before. In fact, portfolio development, when placed within an Aboriginal cultural context, has provided not only a mechanism for validating knowledge and skills but also a means of empowering Aboriginal people with confidence and self-esteem as human beings and as Native people who possess a valuable cultural heritage.

References

Hill, D. (1995). *Aboriginal Access to Post-Secondary Education: Prior Learning Assessment and Its Use within Aboriginal Programs of Learning*. Deseronto, ON; Canada: First Nations Technical Institute.

Minister of Supply and Services Canada. (1996). *Report of the Royal Commission on Aboriginal Peoples* (Vol. 1, pp. 333–389). Ottawa: Canada Communication Group-Publishing.

CRACKING THE CODE

THE ASSESSMENT
OF PRIOR EXPERIENTIAL LEARNING
AT LONDON METROPOLITAN UNIVERSITY

Helen Peters, Helen Pokorny, and Linda Johnson

London Metropolitan University, one of the "new" British universities that strives to promote greater access to higher education, serves a broad population of Londoners, including many immigrants, refugees, and groups of working adults. Like many portfolio-development courses, LMU's Making Your Experience Count encourages students to explore the relationship between their experiential learning and formal academic courses, outcomes, and ways of knowing. Unlike many courses, however, Making Your Experience Count helps students make connections between their personal history and the broader history of societies in transition.

    LMU also brings groups of adults from a given profession together in portfolio-development courses designed specifically for them. In an environment in which assessment of prior learning is not widely accepted, the authors note, the mutual support and the explicit congruence between professional experience and the course of study made for a more successful portfolio-development process. While the professional homogeneity constrains the possibilities for APEL somewhat, Peters, Pokorny, and Johnson argue, "it is nevertheless evident that in many ways the APEL process is more straightforward

Acknowledgments: The authors would like to acknowledge the important contribution to this model made by Azar Sheibani, project manager, Refugee Advice and Guidance Unit; Jo Skinner, academic leader in community nursing; and Gill Venn, academic leader for continuing professional development in education, and to thank them for sharing with us their expertise and their approaches to APEL. Any errors remain those of the authors.

*and easier to grasp than for students who do not go through the process as a
professionally homogeneous group."*

Introduction

Dramatic changes took place in higher education in the UK in the last decade
of the twentieth century, changes aimed at opening universities to a broader
spectrum of society and producing a much greater proportion of graduates in
the population. In 1992, polytechnics and colleges of higher education were
upgraded to university status. (These are known as the "new" universities.)
Further changes came in 1998 with the proposed establishment of 500,000
new openings for students in further and higher education by the Department
for Employment and Education. Still other changes, stemming from the highly
influential *Dearing Review of Higher Education,* included the introduction of
tuition fees and the abolition of student grants. The *Dearing* report had set out
to reconsider the future of the academic track: In its wake, "notions of work-
based learning, experiential learning, accreditation of prior learning and the
assessment of learning outcomes" started to develop as an expression of dis-
trust of the established educational system (Williams and Raggatt, 2000, p. 81).

One result of these changes was to encourage more mature students to
take up opportunities for study and to gain academic and professional credentials. It was during this period that the concept of "lifelong learning"
began to gain currency in the UK and, with it, the notion that higher education institutions should be collaborating more closely with the world of work
in offering opportunities to adults who missed out on education earlier in
their lives. Former polytechnics such as the University of North London, now
part of London Metropolitan University (LMU) had not typically attracted
large numbers of 18–22-year-old students and responded positively to these
changes, seeking to increase their appeal to adults returning to education
through both the nature of the programs of study offered and their methods
of delivery. The changes that have had perhaps the most impact have been
the modularization[1] of the curriculum, greater student choice and flexibility,
and, for adult students, the principle of credit accumulation, credit transfer,
and credit for learning from experience.

---

[1]British higher education has traditionally been offered in yearlong "blocks," with
little student choice and few options for part-time or alternative study. In the 1980s
modular schemes and semesterization, which already existed in some HE institutions,
primarily polytechnics, were expanded and can now be found in all but the most
traditional establishments.

As a "new" university serving a predominantly local population, LMU seeks to open up lifelong learning opportunities to the diverse communities of London; to provide an educational experience that adds value to all students' capabilities, skills, and qualifications; to serve populations of students exposed to discrimination in the past; and "to be a sector leader in the promotion of an inclusive and equal opportunity society" (Strategic Review, 1993). Our student body is reflective of the North London community, with a range of ethnic groups substantially represented. There are slightly more female students than male, and nearly half the students are over 25 on entry. Over a third of all students study part-time. So-called mature students do not necessarily need formal qualifications for entry but may be accepted on the strength of interviews provided they meet language and math requirements for the courses for which they apply. LMU is on record as having the most accessible entry qualifications in the country, demonstrating an open and welcoming admissions policy.

An interest in the accreditation of prior experiential learning (APEL)[2] began to develop at LMU in the mid-1990s, both from a pedagogical standpoint and as a useful means of attracting mature learners and helping them progress. To a large extent, this was due to the interest and commitment of certain individual members of staff rather than as a result of policy decisions on the part of management or of demand from students. As elsewhere in the UK, the enthusiasm of academics for APEL has been hampered by a number of financial and policy constraints.[3] The University had a university-wide APEL Policy and quality assurance systems in place for APEL that integrated into the mainstream systems, but the levels of practice varied enormously across the university. As we discuss later in this chapter, APEL was most successfully introduced where it was linked to subjects with a clearly professional focus and where there was congruence between this professional experience and the student's course of study. However, we recognized that there were students outside these fields who had significant learning we wanted to accredit. The question was how to reach these students and how to introduce an individualized process into a steady-state structure aimed at providing mass higher education.

---

[2]The preferred nomenclature in Britain is APEL, for the accreditation of prior experiential learning, or APL, for the accreditation of prior learning.

[3]For example, government-induced expansions in higher education have not been accompanied by any corresponding increase in spending, and lecturers are experiencing higher staff/student ratios and heavier workloads. Moreover, performance measures have been introduced that encourage a focus on statistical outcomes and financial performance rather than educational processes.

LMU therefore decided to develop a credit-bearing module, Making Your Experience Count, that all students wishing to undertake the APEL process could choose as part of their studies. The hope was that such a module could support students from a diverse range of backgrounds across the institution. The module explores the theoretical and practical connections between experience and learning and asks how these connections can be made within an academic environment. In common with other such modules, it has three main outcomes: (a) to help students to adapt to higher education, (b) to promote personal development, and (c) to prepare students to undertake an APEL process. Because the module is at an introductory level and must be taken as one of a student's first eight modules, we are able to introduce these concepts during a time at which students can maximize the opportunities for credit. This means, however, that many of the students taking the module have not acquired confidence in academic literacy.

This chapter will describe the APEL module, Making Your Experience Count, and how it has operated as an elective module chosen by and designed to serve a range of different students. It will also describe how APEL forms part of a degree in Community Nursing, a Certificate of Professional Development for Refugees, and a Registered Teachers Programme. We will explore the implications for APEL of the quite different issues raised by these contexts.

Making Your Experience Count

Making Your Experience Count begins with an introduction to APEL, an exploration of the principles behind it, and the mechanics of how it works at LMU. It then goes on to examine the learning process and how learning from experience differs from learning in a "formal" context. Early in the course, we introduce students to a variety of concepts having to do with experiential learning. In a discussion of learning styles, for example, we review Kolb's (1984) learning cycle and use Honey and Mumford (1992) to help students examine their personal learning styles. In addition, we use the notion of "transferable skills" to help students identify their areas of learning, understand the different ways of describing and categorizing skills and abilities, and demonstrate the breadth and depth of learning from experience. Students are introduced gradually to these concepts by means of a range of participatory activities aimed at raising awareness of how learning takes place, how to recognize and describe it, and how to recollect and analyze their previous experience. Activities include drawing a lifeline and focusing on particular aspects of it, devising a personal banner of key life events and pinning it up for the rest of the group to see, and carrying out a small group exercise followed by analysis of roles within the group. After the establishment of ground rules covering confidentiality and mutual respect in terms of views, opinions, experience, and willingness to share, students are encouraged to examine and discuss their experience from a whole range of situations, both personal and professional, and to look at these in terms of learning gained. Readings are assigned each week and are discussed at the beginning of each session. These include articles and selections from texts such as Boud and Walker, "Barriers to Reflection on Experience" (1993); Boud, Keogh, and Walker, *Reflection: Turning Experience into Learning* (1985); Kolb, *Experiential Learning* (1984); J. Mezirow, *Fostering Critical Reflection in Adulthood: A Guide to Transformative and Emancipatory Learning* (1990); and Schon, *Educating the Reflective Practitioner* (1987).

Among the most important concepts introduced early in the course is that of learning outcomes. In our modularized system, twenty-four modules (each roughly equivalent to a 5-credit course in the United States) are necessary to earn an undergraduate degree. The learning expected in each is specified to students in the form of a list of statements of what they will know and be able to do after completing that module. These statements are known as learning outcomes.

Although learning outcomes frameworks are not without problems, their use as a means of equating experiential with formal academic learning has become well established in the UK.[4] At LMU, learning outcomes are crucial to the APEL system, since claims for credit need to be formulated in terms of these. As in many other UK universities, credit can be claimed for up to sixteen modules (two-thirds of a degree) on the basis of prior learning. Two options are available. First, students may apply for subject-specific credit toward the named subject of the degree (what many U.S. institutions refer to as a student's "major"). In this case, they may either claim credit by demonstrating how their learning from experience matches the learning outcomes of an existing module, or they can articulate a series of learning outcomes that match their experiential learning and that relate to the subject matter of their degree. Alternatively, students can apply for generic credit for up to six "free choice" modules outside their subject area, again either by matching their learning to existing modules or by devising their own set of learning outcomes relevant to their experience. It is difficult to get the level of specificity right, and, as we discuss later in the chapter, approval of the learning outcomes by subject specialists can often reinforce a traditional view of what

---

[4]For a critique of learning outcomes, see Usher (1989).

counts as academic learning. However, this flexibility plays an important role in facilitating a wider recognition of learning that has taken place outside the university context.

For their first assignment, students produce a written reflective resume and a series of learning outcomes that are submitted both in writing and as an oral presentation to the rest of the group. The purpose of the resume is to aid the reflective process and provide an opportunity for students to practice autobiographical writing, a process that even established authors who write in the field of experiential learning find difficult (Boud, Cohen, & Walker, 1994). The learning outcomes described by the student provide the basis for developing an APEL claim and establishing the level and volume of credit that the student could potentially be awarded through submission of a portfolio.

The development of the ability to relate experience to specified learning outcomes and to create learning outcomes to match experience is probably the key element of the module and the most important factor for success in the APEL process. It is a difficult process to work through alone, and the support of the group is important. As one student put it: "I find when working things out that, paradoxically, I seem to think I can do many things, and yet nothing at all—that is to say I am very successful when people already believe I am, but am unable to persuade anyone who does not already believe in me."

Students undertake a number of activities related to interpreting and creating learning outcomes and assessing the level at which they consider these to have been achieved. This involves both a conceptual and a linguistic process, whereby experience is broken down into elements, which then need to be described in terms that will gain recognition from academic staff in a relevant school or department of the University. This "breaking down" process is approached from two directions, firstly by starting from the perspective of the students' experience. Students are asked to consider an incident of their choice from which they feel they learned. They are then asked to consider what they learned, how they learned it, and what this tells them about themselves. Secondly, approaching the analysis from another direction, students are given lists of skills, abilities, and attributes and asked to identify which ones apply to them, and then to explain how they gained them. At a later stage, they are introduced to a number of taxonomies for categorizing knowledge and cognitive ability—specifically those of Bloom (1964), McLure and Norris (1991), and Eraut (1990)—and are asked to break down examples of learning from their own experience in relation to one of these taxonomies. In this way, Making Your Experience Count combines personal exploration with the acquisition of an academic vocabulary for the description of the learning gained from this experience. Although students are encouraged to present their experience in different ways—through charts, diagrams, video, and, in some cases, artifacts—the process of completing the first assignment nevertheless constitutes a schooling in academic discourse and is presented as such, with exercises in looking at examples and discussing terminology.

The second major assignment, an essay, gives the students the opportunity to examine the literature and debates surrounding the accreditation of prior experiential learning and requires a formal essay style with correct academic referencing. It thus allows students both to develop their academic writing skills and to demonstrate their awareness of APEL issues. This assignment is framed by a series of readings on APEL and by a discussion of issues of equity, quality, and equality of opportunity. Readings at this stage of the module include Coben and Hull, "Professional Training or Academic Education" (1994); McKelvey and Peters, *APL: Equal Opportunities for All?* (1993); Merrifield, McIntyre, and Osaigbovo, "Changing but Not Changed: Mapping APEL in English Higher Education" (2000); Lueddeke, "The Accreditation of Prior Experiential Learning in Higher Education: A Discourse on Rationales and Assumptions" (1997); and Wylde, "Coming to Know: A Personal Experience" (1996).

In addition to giving students the tools to develop their own view of APEL, framing the discussion of APEL in social terms is important for another reason. Our experience has emphasized for us the fact that there is no such thing as "the adult learner." Rather, the experience of each individual has been shaped, constrained, and enriched by social histories and socially determined subjectivities that are shared in socially and personally significant ways. In our experience, students voluntarily raise factors that they feel have had a significant impact in their lives, including race, gender, disability, health issues, bereavement, parenthood, mental and physical abuse, and prison; and they have felt able to examine these experiences in the group context and gain valuable insights from this process.

One group, for example, included two disabled students, one who had suffered from cerebral palsy all his life and another who had been through a long process of gradually losing his sight, regaining some of it, and losing it again. Both of these students recognized the learning they had gained, in their very different situations, from experiencing their disability and from experiencing being a disabled person in society. For them, gaining independence, travel, and study are very different learning experiences from those of able-bodied people, and the APEL process needs to provide the means to recognize these experiences by giving the student the tools to analyze and describe the learning that each had gained. Thus, students are encouraged to make links between a life history and relevant social, historical, or cultural frameworks and perspectives. A woman who witnessed domestic violence as a child and now works in an organization for the protection of battered women has transcended her childhood experience and turned it toward a job, an awareness, and expertise in an important social field. A refugee who undertakes advocacy work for others as well as lobbying and campaigning on immigration and asylum issues has developed the broader knowledge of world issues that enables him to place his own experience in a political context.

There is no automatic presumption in the module that students will complete a portfolio and make a claim for APEL credit. Rather, the module is seen as *preparation* for portfolio development. The structure of a portfolio is covered in the module, and the assignments given in the module aim to prepare students for this task. This is particularly true of the first assignment, the reflective resume, which will probably form the basis for their claims for credit. Similarly, the most important part of the portfolio is the students' written reflective account of their learning, an account that requires students to combine autobiographical and formal writing, both of which have been practiced in the module. Finally, completion of the assignments encourages students to value their experience, builds their confidence, and in some cases can lead them to view their studies in a different light and make changes. As one student said: "This module helped me to evaluate much more of my experience as valid in academic terms than I expected. It also helped to clarify my thoughts vis-à-vis other modules."

As Boud, Cohen, and Walker (1994, p. 15) state, "one of the most powerful [influences on learning from experience] is that of confidence and self esteem." The confidence-building that takes place during the module has been observed to be useful preparation for students when they must deal with assessment tutors who may be less well informed about the APEL process, or who may not be particularly sympathetic to their aims.

All students completing the two assignments satisfactorily gain fifteen credits as they would for any other module. Students then decide whether they wish to produce a portfolio for the purpose of claiming credit. Those who choose to do so decide whether they wish to claim specific or general credit and draw up lists of learning outcomes that are then discussed with the relevant lecturer in the faculty in which credit will be claimed. The student then proceeds with the portfolio. In this way, the candidate has a clear idea of what is required in the finished product and is reasonably assured of his or her efforts being worthwhile in terms of gaining credit. This enables students to make their own decisions about proceeding with APEL in full knowledge of what will be expected of them. After successfully completing the module, students have access to tutorial support for as long as they need in order to complete their claims. This includes advice and help with formulating the claim and help in connecting with the subject specialist who will be assessing it. Some students choose not to proceed further with the APEL process, preferring to see the module in terms of personal development. This may be in some cases a reflection of our inability within the module to do more than introduce these concepts or, as we explore in the next section, a reflection of APEL's inherent tensions and complexities.

Cracking the Code

For those who go on to claim credit, the module is a preparation or training for the process of presenting knowledge/learning from outside the academic sphere to academics and convincing them to accept it as of equivalent value. Students are supported throughout this process, a triangular relationship developing between the assessor, the student, and the APEL tutor. Generally the student will be put in contact with the assessor by the APEL tutor, and the assessor will advise students on whether they have the necessary evidence for a successful claim. The student will then write up the evidence, consult the APEL tutor, present it to the assessor, and may be asked to make changes or additions. This process can be more or less challenging depending on the staff and students concerned, the subject area, and the nature of the experience. For example, it could be a relatively simple task to provide evidence for an assessor that one has covered the elements of a basic IT module through work experience, but much harder to demonstrate that one's work in a voluntary organization has given one a grasp of human resource management, or that years of experience as a teacher in the developing world have instilled concepts relevant to a program in Education Studies in a UK university. Theory is often a sticking point. An academic may acknowledge that a student has valid learning from experience, but ask for evidence of theoretical knowledge. This can be difficult to provide, especially for candidates for APEL who are new to higher education and have had little time to become initiated into the ways of thinking and reasoning that are considered to be an integral part of academic study.

Students perceive Making Your Experience Count in a number of ways: as an opportunity to bring themselves as individuals into the academic context in a way that may not be possible elsewhere in their studies, as a chance to make sense of what has gone before, and as an opportunity to examine their own perception of themselves and their place in the world in a group context with other students. When students are asked, in the first session of the semester, to describe an experience from which they feel they have learned, they almost never mention any kind of formal education as the learning context.

Personal experiences, such as giving birth to a child, the death of a close friend or relative, or serious health problems are experiences that single out but at the same time unite individuals with others in society, often leading to participation in specific groups with communal aims. Other significant experiences are those that by their very nature change or redefine the place of an individual in society, such as exile, unemployment, or bankruptcy. The APEL module is a small window where issues such as these can be explored and examined in general and specific terms as part of students' learning at university.

APEL can also make promises that cannot be fulfilled and therefore needs to be handled with extreme care. As Brah and Hoy (1989, pp.70–77) argue, "The value of any experience will depend not so much on the experience of the subject, important though this is, but on the struggles around the way that experience is interpreted and defined and by whom." In our experience, three issues specifically impinge on the APEL process and the relationship between students' learning and academic recognition: professional expertise versus academic language, informal versus formal theory, and relative willingness of academics and institutions to value what students know.

One important part of the APEL process is being able to describe and discuss learning in a language that is considered appropriate to the academic environment. Students who are extremely capable in their sphere of activity, or indeed across a number of spheres, will often not be proficient in the discussion of this activity in an academic context, and the relevance and importance of their knowledge and ability may not be recognized by academics for this reason. Jordan (cited in Lave and Wenger, 1991) uses the example of a group of Mexican midwives to make this point. Jordan argues that verbal instruction given to midwives in Mexico on state-sponsored training had the effect of teaching them how to talk in biomedical terms, whilst having little or no effect on performance. In other words, even those who are extremely skilled and competent in their profession may need to acquire another, different skill in order to describe what they are able to do, this latter skill being in many ways unrelated to the actual performance of their work. In the same way, workers or practitioners who aspire to gain academic qualifications, however experienced they may be in the field, need to learn how to talk (and write) like academics, or in fact need to learn to be academics. This is the "code" that the students need to crack.

Usher (in Bright, 1989) makes another, related distinction between the "practitioner" or informal theory that a person might develop through work and the formal theory that is taught in educational institutions. "Informal theory is created through practice and is the result of the interaction between practitioners' experience and the cognitive models they use to structure their interpretation. In this view, practitioner theory has the status of a discourse in its own right" (Butterworth and Bloor, 1994). In our experience, however, even when academics are willing to take account of this practitioner theory, it is usually tempered by references to "the formal theory" for the purposes of accreditation. Thus, unless the relationship between practitioner theory and formal theory is made absolutely clear to the student, there can be very negative consequences. As Trowler (1996, p. 25) states:

> Where academic staff are equivocal about the relative status of academic and personal understanding . . . the implications for students can be serious. . . . The danger for many mature students who receive mixed messages is that they perceive the APEL processes as minimizing the worth of the learning they have derived from personal experience because it is inadequately related to the literature or does not "match" the program.

Making Your Experience Count provides an opportunity to raise these issues, to provide a process of formal induction into the discourse of higher education, and to enable participants to make connections between their experience and the curriculum. The delicate task in the APEL process is, first, to help students to clarify how and what they have learned from such experiences and, second, to facilitate its expression in terms that will gain them credit without exposing them to failure or disappointment in situations where they have been encouraged to lay themselves open. One struggling APEL candidate wrote: "My confidence is pretty fragile at the moment. I get the impression that my work is not of a high enough standard if as XXX says my approach to theory is lacking. I am not sure if I can improve it enough to warrant continuing with the degree."

This student eventually went on to gain forty-five APEL credits at advanced level and is succeeding in her degree studies, but not all have had the perseverance to do so. Even students who are relatively successful in making claims for accreditable learning find the power relationships embedded in the process disturbing. One student who was successful in her claim, though unhappy with the grade awarded, put those power relationships in terms of gender, in which the more personal and emotional qualities of experiential learning were not honored by the patriarchal culture of the traditional academy. APEL, she argued, was seen as "a difficult area, emotional, feminine and marginal."

Community Nursing and the Registered Teachers Programme

There is no doubt that, for many of our students, APEL is a difficult process to go through alone. It places high demands on both academics and students, particularly in situations such as Making Your Experience Count, where each student is fighting his or her own individual battle, albeit with the support of the group and tutors. This situation also lends itself to possible bias on the part of assessors making decisions about accreditation outside the context of an established framework and guidelines and where they are making individual decisions concerning the relationship between experience-based and university-based discourse and theory.

The situation is quite different in two programs at LMU in which APEL is undertaken with homogeneous cohorts of students. In our experience, many of the issues discussed above are less fraught where groups of students have broadly similar experiences that are seen to be relevant to their course of study, where there is congruence between students' professional backgrounds and the university course of study, and where there is both a close link between formal theory and practice and a willingness among academic staff to work with balancing formal and informal learning. A Learning from Experience Trust report (Merrifield et al., 2000) on APEL in higher education in England confirms that this reflects the national picture. Where institutions have university-wide APEL policies, which a surprisingly high proportion do, practices are likely to be unevenly spread across the institution and are to be found in areas with a ready market and a strong connection between academics and practitioners. The relative success of APEL in these areas may also be explained by its taking place in contexts where a framework has been established within a given subject area, with staff trained in the process, and with norms and criteria established. From the students' point of view, success is attributable firstly to the fact that they are a group with a collective aim, and therefore more powerful, but also because the way forward has been opened for them by others in similar situations.

One such area is Community Nursing, where the principle of APEL has been incorporated into national qualification systems. In the nursing profession in the UK, the development of many professional programs and the need for practitioners to continue their professional development fueled demand for APEL. The English National Board (ENB) introduced a requirement that all nursing programs incorporate a process for accrediting experience, and the United Kingdom Central Council for Nursing, Midwifery and Health Visiting now requires that every nurse and health visitor maintain an up-to-date profile of his or her experience. Thus, in the context of nursing, APEL is a now-routine practice and is viewed by the ENB as integral to their members' professional development opportunities. In 1996, for example, they funded a two-year national study into APEL practices led by LMU Health School staff with the purpose of sharing practice and highlighting issues.

At LMU, three entry routes to the Community Nursing Programme are available, based on academic level. The entry point for potential students is determined by their individual profile. All candidates are required to fill in a profile form with their application that addresses all previous learning, whether from formal courses or work experience. Three half-day workshops are offered at fortnightly intervals.

At the first workshop, students are introduced to the course "profiling pack," which contains the learning outcomes, syllabus, and assessment details of all modules on the program. Through a process of individual and group discussions, the students match their prior experience with the learning outcomes of the modules. First they check "Can I meet the learning outcomes of this module?" Staff encourage students to consider claiming credit for those modules for which they have 50 percent or more of the learning outcomes. This is by way of recognizing that students often have more relevant learning or certification than they may realize at this point, and to make the processes less frightening. In assessing the final evidence, the criteria is that of equivalence and not necessarily an exact match. Secondly, students ask: "Can I demonstrate that I have achieved these outcomes through certificated and/or noncertificated learning?" The requirement to evidence learning and to link this to the formal University APEL quality assurance processes are explained to students. If they do not have the learning outcomes of a module or are unable to evidence them through APEL, the module will be taken as a part of their taught program. If students feel they can demonstrate equivalence through experience, they discuss the nature of the appropriate APEL assessment with the tutor. The need to contextualize informal theory with formal theory and academic referencing is made clear to the students.

In order to support students in making APEL claims, the processes of academic writing are introduced in the first session, and students are provided with essay exercises to complete before the group meets again. Library induction and research exercises are introduced in the second session. The process of making an APEL claim is facilitated by the fact that the profiling pack contains comprehensive module details and students are clear as to what is expected of them. The details will include the module context, aims, learning outcomes, content, and reading list, as well as assessments for students taking the taught module, for prior study equivalence, and for APEL. The APEL assessments often refer to the provision of a Learning through Work Report— guidelines for which are provided for students. For example, the Developmental Psychology module APEL assessment requires students to "complete a Learning through Work report which analyzes key factors in human development in relation to a range of client groups or one particular group in detail." This report is described and assessed as a piece of academic writing and must be at least 2500–3000 words; demonstrate reflection, analysis, and discussion of the work situation; and identify what has been learnt and relate it to specific learning outcomes on modules. At the start of the process, a plan of content for the report is agreed upon with a member of the health school staff to ensure students focus upon the right areas and make the best use of their time. In other modules, the students are given essay titles, which relate to their area of work with an accompanying reading list. For example, in the module "Health Promotion," APEL students are given a choice of three essay titles including: "Health professionals frequently help clients and patients to make health choices, discuss this in relation to ethical issues."

At the third workshop, students will be given individual feedback on the profiling evidence submitted and details of the taught program to be undertaken. The outcome of the process is the choice of an individualized program of study for the candidate, with entry and choice of modules at a level appropriate to the candidate's previous experience and qualifications. Students can choose to study part- or full-time and are free to take a break from study or move to a different institution if they wish. As a result of this process, 80–100 nurses are gaining credit annually toward programs of study, compared to numbers of up to ten in other faculties.

Three important principles are established by the APEL component of the nursing programs. Firstly, it has been nationally acknowledged that the learning from experience that nurses achieve through their work can be considered equivalent to the outcomes of degree-level studies in a university. Secondly, it is recognized that for credit to be awarded, learning from experience does *not* have to match taught modules exactly. Thirdly, the balance of formal and informal learning required in assessment is made clear to the students beforehand.

Another context where APEL is the norm has been established at LMU in the shape of a Registered Teachers Programme (RTP) for those working in schools without a degree and who want to gain Qualified Teacher Status whilst continuing to work. As in the case of nursing, this program has the approval of a national body, the Teacher Training Agency. The program consists of a taught element, which builds on 240 prior learning credit points. Whilst the potential students have extensive experience of working in schools, few have had opportunities for traditional study within HE. A pre-program element of APEL is therefore offered throughout the year prior to their starting the taught element, in order to assist them in the preparation of claims for credit. The experience of all candidates will again be common in many respects, as all will be working in schools in the UK.

As with the nurses, this makes the preparation of evidence for APEL a very different process from Making Your Experience Count. Students have a common language, are surrounded by a common culture, and hold professional values and expectations in common that identify their role in society and clarify their purpose for and route through higher education. The task of the tutor is to help draw out each individual's particular strengths and gains within a common framework.

To be sure, the difficulties of APEL are not eliminated by this commonality. The issue of theoretical background still arises, and students need to familiarize themselves with the discourse of study in education as opposed to that of teaching, which may not come easily to those accustomed to focusing on the task at hand. A key focus of this program is the demonstration of critical reflection on established professional practice and understanding of the literature and theory related to practice. While recognizing that this is not an easy task, it is nevertheless evident that in many ways the APEL process is more straightforward and easier to grasp than for students who do not go through the process as a professionally homogeneous group. On the other hand, the possibilities for APEL are more constrained. Whereas there is scope for them to contribute to the knowledge and understanding of their field within its existing parameters, they do not have the option open to other students of pushing back the boundaries of accepted knowledge in the way that students claiming credit for free modules can, since the experience they claim credit for must fall within the professional area of expertise (nursing or teaching). Students claiming credit for free modules can claim for virtually anything as long as they can present a case for it being equivalent to academic study. In our experience, students have claimed for areas such as writing poetry, learning to live independently as a disabled person, producing books with children, teaching traditional dance, and understanding alternative therapies.

The Certificate in Professional Development for Refugees and Asylum Seekers

Clearly, the learning experience and degree of difficulty posed by APEL will be different for different groups of students and will vary considerably depending on the circumstances of those concerned. As the example of the teachers and community nurses suggests, APEL is made easier in some ways the more homogenous the group undertaking the process. On the other hand, it is all the harder for individuals within the group who find that they and their experience do not "fit in." This constitutes the dilemma for APEL: If it becomes routine, the process becomes easier for many of those experiencing it, but at the same time this narrows down what knowledge is acceptable to that gained in a particular set of circumstances. It then loses an element of its main advantage, that of opening up the curriculum by acknowledging new forms of knowledge gained outside the world of education.

These issues are raised most compellingly at LMU by an APEL program offered as part of the Refugee Assessment and Guidance Unit, with the aim of enabling refugees and asylum seekers with qualifications and/or experience to claim credit and gain access to higher education or employment in the UK. Here the issues of language and the relationship between prior expertise and current expectations are further heightened, as is the promise of "belonging" implicitly offered by APEL.

For most participants in this program coming from developing countries or from Eastern Europe, the concept of APEL is one that they have not considered before and that can arouse dismissive or negative feelings. Those who have gained qualifications or completed part of a qualification under very difficult conditions may feel that the idea of awarding credit for experience *diminishes* the value of their studies. Those who have full qualifications but no documentation to prove it or who find that their qualification is not recognized as equivalent to a British one may also feel bitter and disillusioned. This, added to the negative feelings that all have experienced from the very fact of being refugees, means that the task of welding a group and achieving positive outcomes from the portfolio-building experience is a delicate one for all concerned. However, the gains from sharing experience with those in a similar position to themselves in the group, coupled with intensive expert individual tutorial support, contribute to making this program often a crucial turning point in participants' lives.

The content of the APEL program for refugees and asylum seekers includes information on the education system in the UK, on careers and employment, and on equal opportunities legislation, in addition to sessions on portfolio development. In this way, the program becomes a means for the students of reorientating themselves; gaining new perspectives on past experience, whether negative or positive; and making positive plans for future action. Racism and other forms of discrimination are issues that have to be confronted, since many of the students will have experienced this or may experience it in the future. Boud et al. (1985) emphasize the importance of attending to feelings in the process of turning experience into learning, and this is particularly important in the case of refugees. The program can be part of a process of overcoming apathy or depression, rebuilding confidence, and setting realistic goals. For example, many of the students have never had to compete for a job, write a CV, or go through an interview, and they often voice embarrassment at having to tell others about their own abilities, knowledge, and qualities. They may also find it strange to attach any importance to voluntary activities such as sports or music or to unpaid work experience such as involvement in family businesses or the informal sector.

Gaining access to and familiarity with the language of learning outcomes is an important part of the program and one that students usually find particularly useful, as they often feel language is the main barrier to the acceptance of their true worth in the UK. This is an issue that needs to be addressed realistically as part of the whole situation of any individual refugee or asylum seeker. A lack of knowledge of the English language may well be a block to progress toward their aims, but many other factors also come into play. Seeing language learning as a solution may actually be a strategy for avoiding confronting other issues that pertain to the future prospects of an individual. APEL is one way of helping people assess their strengths and weaknesses realistically in a situation where hard facts need to be faced. A person who was a high court judge in Peru, a diplomat for Somalia, or a popular leader in Kurdistan will have to do some hard and clear thinking about future prospects in the UK in terms of career path and appropriate direction.

The program begins with exercises that explore a student's present situation. For example, are they working or studying? Have they finished their studies in their country, or do they need to do more? Do they need to improve their English? What other activities are they involved in at present? Are they seeking accommodation or helping family members? These questions lead to others about where they would like to be in one year's time: Do they see themselves involved in training, studying, or working? What new skills do they expect to gain? What changes would they like to see in their lives? Students then consider how APEL could help to get them there. For example, do they know their strengths and weaknesses? Do they know how their skills and abilities could best be used in this country? These issues underpin the rationale for the portfolio-building exercises students undertake and help to focus their resume on relevant skills and understanding derived from their experience. Kolb's (1984) learning cycle is used as the basis of an exercise, which aims to help them draw out and describe their learning. Students consider, for example, a specific task or role they have undertaken— what they enjoyed about it, their dislikes, and what they learned about themselves, about their attitudes to work, and about their attitudes to other people. They can then link this learning to exercises in which skills, qualities, and abilities are articulated. This gives students a vocabulary for some of the skills and knowledge they may want to describe in their portfolio.

On the portfolio-development program for refugees and asylum seekers, a large number of students complete the portfolio and oral presentation required for accreditation. Accreditation in this case does not fall within the degree system, but successful students gain a Certificate in Professional Development, which is a qualification the University offers as the outcome of a variety of programs aimed at students from professional backgrounds. There is also a high success rate in terms of students gaining advanced standing on degree programs or access to master's level programs at LMU or at other universities. Others gain access to work experience and sometimes jobs. Feedback is almost invariably very positive, students valuing the input, the learning and teaching processes, and especially the involvement with the group, which often leads to ongoing mutual support. One student's comment was, "This is the first time in the UK that I feel I am one of you, I belong."

However, it has been our experience that it is often harder for older adults to achieve their aims and reconcile themselves to what they have lost, particularly in the case of those who enjoyed very high status previously. Student approaches seem to fall roughly into three modes: those who are immediately drawn to the concepts of APEL and embrace the process with enthusiasm and generally produce highly reflective portfolios, those who view it with a certain skepticism but nevertheless see it as a useful strategy in their progression, and those who find it hard to accept the ideas and to commit themselves to the process. Far more men than women attend the programs, perhaps because more qualified and experienced refugees are men or because in the family, the priority has been made the reorientation of the man's career before the woman's. However, women often seem to have a more immediate understanding of the process and a greater willingness to engage with their past experience and share it with others. This could be because the questioning of traditional values that APEL can encourage and the implicit challenge to patriarchal domination of education and the professions is less threatening to them.

Conclusion

We feel at LMU that the future for APEL lies in breaking down the boundaries between learning from experience and learning through academic study by gaining official acceptance of the potential value of the former. Just as importantly, however, we would like to see acknowledgment of the value of the process of reflection, evaluation and description of learning from experience for those returning to study, and the necessity of making space for this process in the HE curriculum. Mezirow (1990, p. 368) has mentioned the importance of time to allow adults "a temporary respite from the pressures of action and convention to experiment with reflection on all aspects of their lives," and the crucial importance of this for effective educational intervention to take place. In our new massified, modularized university system, this time for reflection is often precisely what is missing. We would like to see battles for recognition of the value of learning gained outside the university being fought at a national and institutional level and students given structured time to undertake a process of synthesis between their previous experience and their integration into the sphere of academic study.

Making Your Experience Count and the Certificate of Professional Development for Refugees only offer this opportunity to a tiny minority of students. Programs such as those in Community Nursing and Teaching open up this possibility to far greater numbers, and if this approach can be further developed, it will constitute genuine progress in opening up the academy. We feel that the way forward lies in developing routes through higher education that incorporate space and systems for recognition of the fact that many students have made valuable gains from their experience between leaving school and returning to study. As Stephen McNair (1997) says: "Because adult learners are members of society, not 'apprentices' preparing for entry to it, they have a different status, they have the right to challenge what is offered in the light of their experience in the world and of their rights as citizens." The revolutionary potential of APEL lies in the challenge it poses to the deficit view within higher education of any experience gained outside. Programs such as those described above offer the space for students to mount challenges and to support them in so doing.

References

Bloom, B. S. (1964). *Taxonomy of Educational Objectives: The Classification of Educational Goals.* London: Longman.

Boud, D., Keogh, R., and Walker, D. (1985). *Reflection: Turning Experience into Learning.* London: Kogan Page.

Boud, D., Cohen, R., and Walker, D. (eds) (1993). *Using Experience for Learning.* Buckingham, UK: SRHE/Open University Press.

Brah, A., and Hoy, J. (1989). "Experiential Learning: A New Orthodoxy?" In *Making Sense of Experiential Learning: Diversity in Theory and Practice,* edited by S. Weil and I. McGill, pp. 70–77. Buckingham, UK: SRHE/Open University Press.

Bright, B. (1989). *Theory and Practice in the Study of Adult Education.* London: Routledge.

Butterworth C., and Bloor, M. (1994). "The Professional Development Model of APEL—Some Problems of Assessment and Validity." In *Reflecting on Changing Practices, Contexts and Identities,* edited by B. Armstrong, B. Bright, and M. Zukas, pp. xx. Proceedings of the 24th Annual Standing Conference on University Teaching and Research in the Education of Adults (SCUTREA), UK.

Coben, D., and Hull, C. (1994). "Professional Training or Academic Education—A Common Problem." *Journal of Interprofessional Care* 8(1), pp. 45–55.

Eraut, M. (1990). "Identifying Knowledge Which Underpins Performance." In *Knowledge and Competence,* edited by H. Black and A. Wolf, pp. xx. Sheffield, UK: Sheffield Employment Department.

Honey, P., and Mumford, A. (1992). *Using Your Learning Styles.* Maidenhead, UK: Peter Honey.

Kolb, D. (1984). *Experiential Learning.* Englewood Cliffs, NJ: Prentice Hall.

Lave, J., and Wenger, E. (1991). *Situated Learning: Legitimate Peripheral Participation.* Cambridge, UK: Cambridge University Press.

Lueddeke, G. (1997). "The Accreditation of Prior Experiential Learning in Higher Education: A Discourse on Rationales and Assumptions." *Higher Education Quarterly,* 51(3), pp. 210–224.

McKelvey, C., and Peters, H. (1993). *APL: Equal Opportunities for All?* London: Routledge.

McLure, M., and Norris, N. (1991). Knowledge, Issues and Implications for the Standards Program at Professional Levels of Competence." Internal report to Employment Department.

McNair, S. (1997). "Is There a Crisis? Does It Matter?" In *The End of Knowledge in Higher Education,* edited by R. Barett and A. Griffin, pp. 27–39. London: Cassell.

Merrifield, J., McIntyre, D., and Osaigbovo, R. (2000). *Changing but Not Changed: Mapping APEL in English Higher Education.* London, Learning from Experience Trust.

Mezirow, J. (1990). *Fostering Critical Reflection in Adulthood: A Guide to Transformative and Emancipatory Learning.* San Francisco: Jossey-Bass.

Schon D. A. (1987). *Educating the Reflective Practitioner.* San Francisco: Jossey-Bass.

Trowler, P. (1996). "Angels in Marble? Accrediting Prior Experiential Learning in Higher Education." *Studies in Higher Education* 21(1), pp. 17–30.

Usher R. (1989). "Qualifications, Paradigms and Experiential Learning in Higher Education." In *Access and Institutional Change,* edited by O. Fulton, pp. 63–80. Buckingham, UK: SRHE.

Williams, S. and Raggatt, P. (2000). *Government Markets and Vocational Qualifications. An Anatomy of Policy.* London: Routledge-Falmer.

Wylde, J. (1989). "Coming to Know: A Personal Experience." In *Making Sense of Experimental Learning,* edited by S. W. Weil and I. McGill. Buckingham: SRHE/Open University Press.

BUILDING ON THE PAST, MOVING TOWARD THE FUTURE

PRIOR LEARNING ASSESSMENT IN A CHANGING INSTITUTION AT METROPOLITAN STATE UNIVERSITY

Susan T. Rydell

Like many of the nontraditional colleges and universities founded in the 1970s, Metropolitan State University saw the assessment of prior learning as fundamental to its mission of providing an appropriate education to adult learners. It developed both a high-quality prior learning assessment (PLA) process and a curriculum that could respond to the typical strengths and challenges of adults returning to formal learning. Through "Perspectives: Educational Philosophy and Planning" and the institution's theory seminars, Metropolitan State offered ways both to accredit students' practical expertise while addressing their sometime-lack of formal theory.

As Metropolitan State has evolved into a more traditional university serving younger students, it has been forced to rethink the relationship of PLA to the university's mission and to recreate assessment practices that would remain relevant to new student populations and institutional goals. At a time in which many nontraditional institutions are being challenged to become more "traditional," the story of Metropolitan State's evolution is especially important. "The challenge," as explored here by Susan Rydell "would be to allow PLA to 'fit' the expanded mission . . . of Metropolitan State."

Metropolitan State University, originally known as Minnesota Metropolitan State College, was authorized by the Minnesota Legislature in 1971 to serve adult students in the Minneapolis–St. Paul metropolitan area. In its original design, it resembled many of the nontraditional colleges founded in that era: It was an upper-division, competence-based university without a campus whose small core of full-time faculty facilitated student learning and access to community-based resources. Its focus was on student learning outcomes, whether the learning was achieved through a course or was the result of prior experiential learning.

The hallmark of Metropolitan State, and originally its only program, was the individualized baccalaureate degree. In this program, whose first fifty students were admitted in February 1972, students designed individual degree completion programs within the context of a required course, now called Perspectives: Educational Philosophy and Planning. Perspectives provided all students the opportunity to consider the question of what it means to be an educated person, to do a personal self-assessment of their previous formal and nonformal learning, to identify areas that could be considered for assessment of prior learning, and to design an individualized degree plan in light of their educational goals.

Initially, the individualized degree plan was viewed as an umbrella, with individually developed study units negotiated with community faculty as part of the overall degree plan. By the end of 1972, however, some courses ("group learning opportunities") had been introduced, and student degree plans quickly evolved to a combination of courses, prior learning assessments, internships, and independent studies that would allow a student to meet his or her learning goals. Independent studies evolved in two directions: student-designed studies similar to the individually negotiated learning contracts mentioned above, and faculty-designed studies announced in the class schedule along with courses each semester. Currently, about 14 percent of all Metropolitan State registrations are independent study registrations, with the vast majority of those being faculty designed.

From its inception, both prior learning assessment and new learning at Metropolitan State were competence-based, with a focus on student learning outcomes. We define a competence as what you know and what you can do with regard to a particular subject at a specified level. With respect to prior learning, competences can be equivalent to courses or they can reflect unique student learning, but they must include both theoretical and practical knowledge.

One outgrowth of this approach to prior learning assessment was the "theory seminar." The faculty had observed that although many students pursuing assessment of prior learning had gained extensive practical expertise, they often did not have the theoretical components expected of college-level learning. The example given was of a student with a business background who understood and was skilled at management techniques, but did not have an in-depth understanding of the theories of motivation and human behavior that provide an academic framework for those techniques. The options facing such a student were either to take an entire semester-long course in management or else to omit the area completely from a baccalaureate degree program. To address this, the new learning format for theory seminars was developed.

The learning format for theory seminars gives students the option to gain full academic credit in a learning/assessment setting requiring fewer classroom hours than a regular semester course. The theory seminar process is initiated when the student takes a faculty-prepared, self-administered diagnostic evaluation in the subject area in which he or she has some experiential learning. Students who have extensive theoretical and practical experiential learning in a subject directly pursue assessment of prior learning options, while those with limited knowledge of a subject are asked to consider taking a regular semester-long course or independent study. Students are encouraged to consider the theory seminar as an option when both their practical expertise and their limited theoretical knowledge are affirmed by the diagnostic exercise. An integrated assessment of student prior and new learning is part of the theory seminar, and students successfully completing the seminar receive full academic credit in the subject area, generally four semester credits.

Metropolitan State: A Changing Institution

Since the chapter on Metropolitan State was published in the first edition of this book, fundamental shifts that have occurred in our organizational structures, academic program developments, and student clientele. This, in turn, has produced major changes in our prior learning assessment program, including a new role for the Perspectives course. The first major changes in Metropolitan State's mission were implemented in the early 1980s when, in response to local educational needs, we initiated a baccalaureate degree in nursing and a graduate program in management. In the late 1980s, a more extensive change took place. Metropolitan State was directed by its governing board and the Minnesota State Legislature to become a comprehensive urban university with expanded numbers of majors, lower-division offerings, and master's-level programming. If it were to respond to that imperative, our educational model had to change. As the institution evolved into a comprehensive urban university, the physical plant was developed; formal academic departments were established; freshmen students were admitted; and majors, minors, and graduate programs were created.

At the present time, Metropolitan State owns a campus in St. Paul and has leased facilities in downtown Minneapolis, the Midway area, and several other locations in the Twin Cities metropolitan area. The ninety-nine full-time resident faculty and 487 part-time community faculty are organized into four colleges and two schools, with twenty-five academic departments. In addition to the Individualized Bachelor of Arts Program, Metropolitan State now has sixty-six majors, twenty-eight minors, and eight graduate programs. In keeping with this set of changes, the full-time faculty role has shifted from "facilitating" student learning to developing discipline-based curriculum and teaching in a discipline.

Prior Learning Assessment and Institutional Change

In 1995, the university faculty eliminated the requirement that all students take Perspectives. Students and faculty generally shared the view that spending time on such a course was superfluous when most students followed prescribed degree programs outlined in the university's catalog. One result was that prior learning assessment declined dramatically. Between 1985 and 1999, student numbers at Metropolitan State increased from 4,068 to 7,428 and, measured in full-time-equivalents, grew by over 250 percent. Yet by the fall of 2000, registrations for assessments of prior experiential learning had fallen to 0.8 percent of all registrations, and registrations for theory seminars had fallen to 0.5 percent of all registrations. Even students taking Perspectives tended to select courses from the catalog to meet the learning goals described in their individualized degree plans.

The profound changes within the university in a relatively short period of time were not made without a great strain on the university's human and financial resources, which further marginalized the assessment of prior learning. With the creation of formal academic departments, for example, oversight of faculty evaluators was assigned to departments already overburdened with other significant responsibilities and with little time to train and supervise a core of prior learning evaluators. The faculty within the newly created First College, which now houses the Individualized B.A. degree and coordinates the university's assessment program, began to consider how prior learning assessment could be redesigned. The challenge would be to allow PLA to "fit" the expanded mission and more traditional institutional structure of Metropolitan State and serve a student body that was now more racially and ethnically diverse and that had more full-time and lower-division students.

Faculty agreement was reached that the following principles would continue to be used as a guide to the assessment of prior learning at Metropolitan State:

- Individual student prior learning would continue to be *directly* assessed by experts in the field in which the learning is claimed.

- A student portfolio would continue to be considered only one *indirect* indicator of areas of potential learning. The faculty subject matter expert would determine the particular assessment techniques to be used and would meet with the student to evaluate directly the extent and level of learning.

- Assessment of prior learning would continue to be competence-based, with competence defined as what you know and what you can do, with regard to a particular subject at a specified level.

- With respect to prior learning, competences would be recognized whether they were directly equivalent to university courses or reflective of unique confluences of student learning.

- Faculty training in assessment of prior experiential learning, centrally coordinated, would be an ongoing process, and faculty evaluators in a variety of subject areas could not be listed in the Metropolitan State class schedule without having attended a recent training session.

- Theory seminars would be retained as part of the prior learning assessment continuum at Metropolitan State.

Outreach to the Student Body

One of the main challenges facing the faculty and administrators of First College was the need to disseminate information about prior learning assessment. With Perspectives no longer a required course, the challenge was to create other university-wide options for giving students information and initial support. The following workshops and courses have been developed to expand student access to prior learning assessment:

- *Transitions to College,* a free, noncredit, two-hour workshop that was originally designed for employees at the Ford Motor Company, helps students determine if college is for them. It explores the benefits of going to college, what college options exist, and how to make good choices. Brief self-assessment exercises assist students in identifying some of their personal learning strengths and learning styles. Though this workshop has now been opened to current students and is announced in the student newspaper, to date, very few students have registered for it. Future efforts to market the workshop will be coordinated through new student recruitment and admissions.

- *Creative Learning Strategies,* a free, noncredit, three-hour workshop that was introduced when the Perspectives course was dropped as a requirement, is open to all currently enrolled students and is offered once each semester. In the workshop, students identify one or two specific subject areas they would like to include in their degree programs and discuss whether the areas could be pursued through new learning, assessment of prior learning, or theory seminars. University procedures related to independent study, assessment of prior learning, and theory seminars are reviewed in the workshop. Approximately 20–25 students now register for the workshop each semester.

- A required *New Student Orientation* has been phased in over the past four years. Prior learning assessment as an option for students is mentioned briefly in the two-hour program. The focus of the orientation, however, is on undergraduate degree programs offered and student services.

- A new one-credit course, *Getting Credit for What You Know,* was offered for the first time at the end of the summer of 2000. First College faculty members and university admissions counselors anticipate that this course will be of interest to students throughout the university. The course, which meets four times during a semester, is designed for entering students who wish to examine the various options for gaining credits for learning outside the formal college or university classroom. Options that are explored include using military experience toward a degree, taking standardized tests (e.g., CLEP), earning credit from approved courses offered by businesses and human service agencies (e.g., ACE-approved courses), pursuing assessment of prior experiential learning, and Metropolitan State theory seminars. In this class, students do a self-assessment of their skills and abilities, write a statement of their educational goals, and identify ways to earn credit from nonclassroom learning that are consistent with their goals. Within the class, students also assemble the necessary evidence to pursue these alternative options of earning credit. Following course completion, students may register for assessment of prior learning or theory seminars in each competence subject area identified. *Getting Credit for What You Know* has been an instant success, and sections of the course fill very quickly.

The Reconceptualization of Perspectives: Educational Philosophy and Planning

One important component of our effort to foster prior learning assessment in spite of major institutional change has been the reconceptualization of the original Perspectives course. As in earlier versions of the course, students do an in-depth self-assessment and identify possible areas for assessment of prior learning, examine the concept of what it means to be an educated person, and reflect on their prior learning and future learning goals within this context. At the same time, the reconceptualization of the course has included an extensive revision of the materials, an updated training program for resident and community faculty teaching the course, a new stress on journal writing, and an attempt, still in process, to integrate learning outcomes into the course content.

Although individual faculty members select their own supplementary readings and design their own syllabi of readings and written assignments, all instructors must use three resources created for the course: a reader with a collection of essays, a course workbook with text and exercises that also includes information about policies and procedures, and a *First College Reflective Journal* (Meyers, Anderson, Burton, Fox, & Holmberg, 1999) in which students record their reactions to and reflections on a number of topics. The basic course reader, *The Educated Person: A Collection of Contemporary Essays* (Jones & Meyers, 1998), was originally developed for this course in 1983. The current reader includes essays by a culturally and ideologically diverse group of authors on a variety of themes: "The Ideal of an Educated Person," "A Liberal Education," "Diverse Perspectives," and "Disciplinary Perspectives." The question "What is an educated person?" is the overarching theme.

The *First College Reflective Journal* (Myers, 1999) provides an opening for students' personal reflections on their education. In the introduction to the *Reflective Journal*, the question "Why write a journal?" is posed:

> The Danish philosopher Soren Kierkegaard said that though we obviously live our life forward, we can only understand it by looking backward. Writing in a journal gives us the opportunity to pause in our often too-busy lives, to gather our thoughts, and to write them down, reflecting on what has happened and on our responses to those occurrences. Then, periodically, we reread what we have written to see what our thoughts and feelings were at that time and how they may have changed. By reflecting on, or thinking about, our life experiences, we can often learn from them. (p. 1)

In addition to weekly open-ended entries for students to complete, the *Reflective Journal* has topical journal assignments for each of the fifteen weeks of Perspectives. Thus, before considering assessment of prior learning as part of a baccalaureate degree program, students now complete topical *Reflective Journal* entries in the following:

Topic 1. The educated person—attitudes and skills: Students are asked to record some of their thoughts about what it means to be an educated person, where they got their ideas on what it means to be educated, and what attitudes and skills characterize an educated person.

Topic 2. Educated person—specific content areas: Students are asked what kinds of specific knowledge they believe educated people have in addition to attitudes and skills. Examples include a knowledge of the historical record and skills in how to effectively communicate.

Topic 3. Educated people in your life: Students are asked to think about one person in their life who exemplifies some aspects of being educated and to write down their thoughts explaining why they feel he or she is an educated person.

Topic 4. Responding to a reading: Students choose any reading the instructor has assigned at this point in the course and write a response to the author. They are asked to tell the author what they liked or disliked, and agreed or disagreed with, and to share their ideas with the writer.

Topic 5. Critical thinking: Students are asked their thoughts on critical thinking. Questions include: "What are some of the character traits of a critical thinker? How do you assess your own critical thinking abilities? Is there a difference between critical and creative thinking?"

Topic 6. Challenges or roadblocks to getting an education: Students are asked what they see standing in the way of completing a B.A. degree and what personal or external resources they can draw on to overcome those roadblocks.

Topic 7. Pivotal life experience: Students are asked to think back on one important experience in their lives that was really pivotal, that changed their way of thinking about things, and to write about that experience.

Topic 8. Midsemester evaluation: Students are asked to write something about how the course is going for them, what they need less and more of, what they are confused or anxious about, and what the single thing is that the instructor could do to help.

Topic 9. Multiculturalism: Students are asked to write about their thoughts and feelings on the issue of multiculturalism, with some reference to class readings and discussions with fellow classmates.

Topic 10. Prior Learning: Students are asked: "In looking over your own life/work experience, is there any prior learning that you might want to get credit for?" Thus, the students' exploration of their own prior learning is embedded in a broader discussion of what it means to be an educated person, challenges to getting an education and earning a baccalaureate, and the development of critical thinking and communication skills. Many students conclude that there is no inherent relation between being an educated person and earning a degree, but the reality is that they want to earn the degree—and they can achieve some of their ideal of the educated person while doing so.

The *Reflective Journal* continues with weekly open-ended and topical entries through the end of the Perspectives course. The last half of the *Reflective Journal* is entitled "Looking toward the Capstone." This last section is to be completed by students throughout their educational journeys while at Metropolitan State and is used as a source of reflection and discussion in the First College senior year capstone course, a requirement for all First College students.[1]

Beginning around the tenth week, the preparation for prior learning assessment becomes a central theme of the course, and the course instructor refers students to related assignments in the *Workbook* (Perspectives, 1999). As noted earlier, Metropolitan State faculty have determined that a portfolio is only an indirect indicator of potential prior learning. Students therefore learn about the entire spectrum of different ways of learning and evidencing learning and are given concepts related to competence-based education.

In reflecting on different ways to learn, students read about and discuss alternatives to formal classroom learning, which Metropolitan State calls "creative learning strategies." Creative learning strategies include (a) prior learning, (b) theory seminars, (c) internships, (d) faculty-designed independent studies, and (e) student-designed independent studies. The related *Workbook* assignment is "Building Creative Learning Strategies into Your Degree Plan":

> The purpose of this exercise is to get you to consider how you might use creative learning strategies as part of your individualized degree plan. We are not asking you to make a formal commitment . . . but only to consider some of these different strategies. To do this exercise, look over the subject areas of your educational goals. Many of these goals will be achieved

---

[1]Stephen Bookfield, who evaluated our redesigned course, suggested that this emphasis on journal writing is a successful part of the new course. In his review of the materials used in all First College courses, Brookfield (2000) observed:

> The *Reflective Journal* was about the right size and therefore not too intimidating. I've seen some examples of journals which are more like large 3-ring binders, and which freeze the student's writing impulse. Yours seems more like a private diary, something one could jot down fleeting thoughts in. I also liked the examples you gave at the outset of "typical" diary entries. It's this kind of autobiographical data I'm arguing be inserted more strongly in other course materials.

through formal classroom learning, but some of your goals might better be addressed through creative learning strategies. There are five strategies listed below. We want you to consider including at least three of these learning strategies in your degree plan. So, choose any three strategies below and list in the blank space a subject area you would like to study. (*Perspectives*, 1999, p. 67)

Once students have identified subject areas, they move on to the next section of the *Workbook,* "Understanding Competence-based Education." Students read about the definition of competence as "what you know and can do with regard to a particular subject at a specified level." After considering the key words—"theory," "practice," and "specified level"—they work on writing competence statements for the subject areas identified in the previous assignment. The final exercise in the series is to fill in a competence description page for each subject, including how the competence was or will be achieved, suggested measurement techniques, and the name and qualifications of faculty evaluators selected from the list of evaluators included in each semester's class schedule. These competence description sheets are included as part of the student's individualized degree plan.

The Perspectives course instructor never approves competences for university credit; rather, the instructor indicates that a competence appears appropriate to pursue at a later time in close dialogue with a content expert on the faculty. Metropolitan State differs in this regard from other institutions that use portfolios as a mechanism for prior learning assessment. First, rather than relying on the Perspectives instructor to help students present evidence of learning, faculty who are content experts in the field and who will evaluate the learning play a prominent role. Students bring the competence descriptions described earlier to the initial meeting with the faculty member who will eventually do the assessment and then assemble and/or prepare the specific materials requested by the content-expert faculty member.

Second, while written portfolios play an important role in PLA at Metropolitan State, they are not considered a necessary part of all assessments. When Metropolitan State was founded and began to seriously consider assessment of prior learning, faculty noted how some other institutions were beginning to have students develop portfolios as part of the assessment of prior learning process. They then noted that what they had considered originally as only part of a process became an end in itself. At Metropolitan State, the faculty who assess the students have a great say in determining which measurement techniques are most appropriate: oral interviews, written tests, performance tests, situational observations, simulation exercises and case studies, and/or product evaluations in addition to written portfolios.

Building on the Past, Moving toward the Future

In many ways, our efforts to preserve and foster the assessment of prior learning in the face of overall institutional change is still a work in progress. Two specific issues, theory seminars and learning outcomes, need to be addressed in that regard.

Theory Seminars

As noted earlier in this chapter, the importance of the role of theory seminars was reaffirmed during the reexamination of the assessment of prior learning program. As academic departments had been formed and some discipline areas increased the number of courses and major requirements, departmental budgeting favored offering high-enrollment courses rather than low-enrollment theory seminars, and, as a result, fewer theory seminars were actually scheduled for students to take. Yet, although theory seminar registrations had decreased over the years, requests from students for the diagnostic materials indicated that student interest remained strong.

Recent external funding from the Minnesota State Colleges and Universities and renewed administrative commitment have rejuvenated faculty interest in developing these learning options for students. Moreover, now that the university has shifted from a quarter to a semester system, theory seminars that can be completed in less than a full fifteen-week semester are viewed as learning options that fit many adult learners' busy schedules. Theory seminars currently being developed reflect some of the newer topics in the curriculum and areas in which students have prior experiential learning: Disability and Career Development, Database Management Systems, Social Casework Methods, Public Relations, Institutional Corrections, Family Communications, Adolescent Chemical Dependency, Quality Management, Human Services and Diversity, Social Gerontology, Special Education, and Urban Teacher Education. Close to fifty theory seminars are now available on the Web. Students can print out the diagnostic tests, get the self-scoring key, and look at the requirements on the syllabus.

Learning Outcomes: A Theme for Further Development

The concept of learning outcomes was central to the Individualized B.A that formed Metropolitan State's original educational model. As part of the reconceptualization of Perspectives, faculty returned to the concept and explored how learning outcomes could be a part of the redesigned Perspectives course. The following learning outcomes have been identified by First

College faculty as those they would like all graduates of the Individualized BA to have:

- *Self-Directed Learning.* Students have learned:
  - To learn and think critically;
  - to assume responsibility for and authority over their education; and
  - to self-assess their particular vocational strengths.
- *Lifelong Learning.* Students have learned:
  - To be aware of the ongoing need for lifelong learning and of resources available to them;
  - to self-assess "gaps" in their learning through the process of reflection;
  - to plan in relation to their perceived gaps in learning, including intentional as well as serendipitous learning; and
  - to identify their own "love of learning," that is, to identify and apply their particular gifts (skills/knowledge/attitudes), perhaps through community involvement and/or avocation.
- *Reflective/Self-Transcending Learning.* Students have learned:
  - To appreciate a variety of perspectives on vocation, education, and life;
  - to achieve some distance from their immediate ego needs;
  - to cultivate a healthy sense of humility, an awareness that there is so much more to learn; and
  - to contribute to the "common good" and our collective responsibility by
    - developing a sense of how their own skills/knowledge/talents can contribute to the larger local, state, and national community; and
    - sensing their ethical and spiritual place in the even greater human community.

It is not yet correct to say that these learning outcomes are uniformly built into all of the aspects of a First College degree. First, only the two required courses, Perspectives and the Capstone course, address these outcomes explicitly, and students incorporate courses into their degree programs from other Metropolitan colleges, where the learning outcomes do not obtain. Second, while in their degree programs, it becomes more problematic to say that the entire university judges all learning against these outcomes.

While Perspectives, for example, clearly addresses issues of lifelong learning and educational planning, independent expert evaluations of actual Perspectives assignments have found the connection between articulated learning outcomes and specific student products unclear. In other words, when educators other than the Perspectives course instructors looked at both the expected learning outcomes, example, "be aware of the ongoing need for lifelong learning," it was difficult to determine what assignments would assist students in achieving this learning outcome and what completed assignments could be used to determine that the learning outcome had been achieved. Some independent course evaluators indicated that many "learning outcomes" were not learning outcomes at all, but rather statements of educational philosophy. Thus, faculty are currently reconsidering both how the outcomes are articulated as well as how students can achieve and demonstrate those outcomes through the given assignments. This will be a topic for future development by First College faculty.

Ongoing Evaluation and Development

At Metropolitan State, we continue to evaluate and develop both the Perspectives course and opportunities for all students to pursue prior learning assessment. In one such development, the Summer 2000 semester was the first time Perspectives was available as an Internet Study course with two optional class meetings. Twenty students took the course and carried on course discussions, including discussions of prior learning, on the electronic bulletin board. At the end of the course, one student e-mailed her instructor: "I learned things so subtle through your guidance I never even imagined them before." The First College recently received a second grant from the Minnesota State Colleges and Universities to put the Individualized B.A. on the Web.

In another arena of ongoing work, we have focused on student evaluation and feedback. Currently, formal university course evaluation forms do not solicit student feedback regarding revisions in course materials, course delivery modes, and specific assignments in courses. A major First College goal is to solicit appropriate student feedback to assure the continued success of its academic program with its holistic approach to education, linking prior and new learning within the context of what it means to be an educated person.

First College is now in the position of looking to the future, while maintaining the best features of an earlier program: individualized, student-centered adult learning. As the entire institution has moved in recent years to develop formal majors in numerous discipline areas, First College has provided a home for students who wish to harness university-wide faculty expertise to achieve their own learning goals and earn a baccalaureate degree. First College has also been the champion for providing opportunities for prior learning assessment across the entire university for our adult students. In addition to developing prior learning assessment options for students, the First College has led the faculty development program to train new faculty in prior learning assessment as the founding faculty, who developed the original assessment program, have retired. We look forward to assessing the effectiveness of providing alternative ways for students to earn credit for learning outside of the formal classroom within our changing institutional context.

References

Brookfield, S. (2000, April 18). "First College Student Learning Outcomes Assessment Program." Personal communication.

Jones, T. B., and Meyers, C., eds. (1998). *The Educated Person: A Collection of Contemporary Essays.* St. Paul, MN: Metropolitan State University.

Meyers, C., Anderson, M., Burton, J., Fox, B., and Holmberg, C. (1999). *First College Reflective Journal.* St. Paul, MN: Metropolitan State University.

Perspectives: Educational Philosophy and Planning Workbook. (1999). St. Paul, MN: Metropolitan State University First College.

ALL OF WHO WE ARE

FOUNDATIONS OF LEARNING AT THE SCHOOL FOR NEW LEARNING, DEPAUL UNIVERSITY

Marixsa Alicea, Deborah Holton, and Derise Tolliver

Like Alverno, the School for New Learning of DePaul University (SNL) uses a competence-based model of assessment and learning to help students integrate their own experiential learning with the traditions of the liberal arts and sciences. In SNL's portfolio-development course, Foundations of Adult Learning, students use the competence framework to identify their learning, design their programs of study, and relate the competency framework to their educational interests and needs. As in many programs, adults are helped to articulate their individual needs and goals in the Foundations course. But because SNL's curricular framework includes competencies such as collaborative learning, cross-cultural issues, globalization, social justice, and service learning, students are encouraged to explore their societal roles and identities.

One of the important aspects of this model is the ways in which individual faculty use their unique identities, perspectives, and values as a basis for teaching the Foundations course. Writing and teaching explicitly as women of color, the authors of this chapter focus the course on the relationship between individual experience and social context. The authors draw on their own ethnic, disciplinary, and artistic backgrounds in order to engage students in critical analysis of social institutions and the ways in which individual lives are affected by gender, race, and class. This model is therefore a more personal account than many others. "Rather than live and work out of a Western compartmentalization

---

Note: Please note that the names of the authors in this essay are listed alphabetically. Each of us contributed equally to its writing.

of self," the authors say, "we bring to the classroom many aspects of who we are and encourage students to do likewise."

Introduction

The School for New Learning (SNL) is one of eight colleges of DePaul University. Established in 1973, it offers several competence-based programs including a Bachelor of Arts degree, a joint Bachelor of Arts and Computer Science degree, a Master of Arts in Integrated Professional Studies, and a Master of Arts in Applied Technology. Because the bulk of our work and experience lies within the Bachelor of Arts degree, we will focus our attention on this program and, in particular, on our experiences in teaching Foundations of Adult Learning, SNL's closest equivalent to a portfolio-development course. This model integrates our own experiences as learners, as women of color, and as members of historically disenfranchised groups and seeks to explore how these experiences shape the ways in which we teach the Foundations course. In doing so, we hope to showcase the work that we are doing with our students, but also to offer our own perspectives concerning issues in adult higher education and how they differ from mainstream adult education theories and practices.

In the first section of this model, we present the general approach to Foundations of Adult Learning shared by the faculty of SNL. Later, we speak in our own individual voices because we believe that our approaches to the course importantly reflect our own experiential learning. Like our students, as learners we are the products of distinctive personal and social histories.

Foundations of Adult Learning

SNL is built upon a competency-based framework that offers students flexibility and opportunities for choice in achieving their Bachelor of Arts degree. To earn their degree, students must demonstrate fifty competencies, twenty-one of which are prewritten and required of all students. The remaining twenty-nine competencies are either written by the student with the assistance of an academic committee or are chosen from a menu of prewritten competency statements. Students must fulfill two required competencies and six elective competencies in each of the three liberal learning categories (see Exhibit C8.1).

Students work with an academic committee to design their programs and relate the competency framework to their own educational interests and needs. Each committee is composed of the student, an academic advisor, a

Exhibit C8.1   SNL Undergraduate Program

Lifelong Learning Area (12 competencies)	Liberal Learning Area (26 competencies)			Focus Area (12 competencies)
	Arts & Ideas	The Human Community	The Scientific World	
L-1 Learning Assessment Seminar: Can assess one's strengths and set personal, professional, and educational goals.	Competence in Interpreting the Arts (A-1-_)	Competence in Communities and Societies (H-1-_)	Competence in Experiencing Science (S-1-_)	**F-1 Focused Planning:** Can design a plan for development in one's Focus Area based on an analysis of elements that comprise that area.
L-2 Foundations of Adult Learning: Can use one's ideas and those of others to draw meaning from experience.	Competence in Creative Expression (A-2-_)	Competence in Institutions and Organizations (H-2-_)	Competence in Patterns and Processes (S-2-_)	F-X Focus Area Elective (written by student/faculty)
L-3 Foundations of Adult Learning: Can design learning strategies to attain personal and professional goals.	Competence in Reflection and Meaning (A-3-_)	Competence in Individual Development (H-3-_)	Competence in Science, Technology, and Society (S-3-_)	F-X Focus Area Elective (written by student/faculty)
L-4 College Writing: Can write clearly and fluently.	Any competence in Arts and Ideas (A-_-_)	Any competence in The Human Community (H-_-_)	Any competence in The Scientific World (S-_-_)	F-X Focus Area Elective (written by student/faculty)
L-5 Critical Thinking: Can analyze issues and reconcile problems through critical and appreciative thinking.	Any competence in Arts and Ideas (A-_-_)	Any competence in The Human Community (H-_-_)	Any competence in The Scientific World (S-_-_)	F-X Focus Area Elective (written by student/faculty)
L-6 Quantitative Reasoning: Can use mathematical symbols, concepts, and methods to describe and solve problems.	Any competence in Arts and Ideas (A-_-_)	Any competence in The Human Community (H-_-_)	Any competence in The Scientific World (S-_-_)	F-X Focus Area Elective (written by student/faculty)

L	A	H	S	F
L-7 Collaborative Learning: Can learn collaboratively and examine the skills, knowledge, and values that contribute to such learning.	**A-4 Ethics in the Contemporary World:** Can analyze a problem using two different ethical systems. (required competence)	**H-4 Power and Justice:** Can analyze power relations among racial, social, cultural, or economic groups in the United States. (required competence)	**S-4 Interconnections in the Natural World:** Can describe and explain connections among diverse aspects of nature, (required competence)	**F-X Focus Area Elective** (written by student/faculty)
L-8 Research Seminar: Can pose questions and use methods of formal inquiry to answer questions and solve problems.	**A-5 Creativity:** Can define and analyze a creative process. (required competence)	**H-5 Globalization:** Can analyze issues and problems from a global perspective, (required competence)	**S-5 Information Technology:** Can use current information technology for integrated solutions to problems. (required competence)	**F-X Focus Area Elective** (written by student/faculty)
L-9 Research Seminar (written by student/faculty)	**E-1 Advanced Elective** (written by student/faculty)	**E-2 Advanced Elective** (written by student/faculty)		**F-X Focus Area Elective** (written by student/faculty)
L-10 Externship: Can reflect on the learning process and methods used in an experiential project.				**F-X Focus Area Elective** (written by student/faculty)
L-11 Externship (written by student/faculty)				**F-11 Advanced Project:** Can design and produce a significant artifact or document that gives evidence of advanced competence.
L-12 Summit Seminar: Can articulate the personal and social value of lifelong learning.				**F-12 Advanced Project** (written by student)

professional advisor, and, if the student wishes, a peer advisor. The academic advisor is usually the instructor with whom the student completed the Foundations course. The academic advisor, in turn, helps the student to identify a professional advisor, someone in the student's field of interest who will provide guidance and support with respect to professional and educational goal setting and planning and who will assess the student's work in the focus area.

Working with their academic committees, students design an individual "focus area" around a specific area of concentration and write nine of the twelve competencies that are required in that area. Students can fulfill competencies through SNL courses, transfer courses, independent learning options, or prior experiential learning. SNL differs from programs that offer credit for experiential learning on a course-equivalent basis. Instead, students are awarded credit if they can demonstrate competence in a particular area. This aspect of our program and the fact that students have the option of writing their own competence statements means that there are almost endless possibilities as to the types of experiences students can draw upon in order to earn college credit.

Many of our adult learners come to SNL with a wealth of experience. Our job as academic advisors is to help students identify how they can demonstrate some of the SNL competencies by drawing on these experiences. We begin this process with students in the Foundations of Adult Learning course. With the help of their Foundations instructors, students design their curriculum, identify professional goals, and design a plan for attaining their goals. The Foundations course also examines principal concepts of adult learning and their practical applications. It emphasizes learning through collaboration and at the same time supports knowledge of self and of the self as a learner. We are concerned with developing the potential of the whole person, not just one who is a good employee or who has gained a necessary credential. In the words of Olivia Castellano, through the Foundations course we want "to bring about changes in the way [students] view themselves, their abilities, their right to get educated and their relation to . . . the world" (Castellano, 1995, p. 309).

One of the primary outcomes of Foundations is the development of a Learning Plan in which students identify how they intend to demonstrate each of the fifty competencies in the SNL framework. This document is largely a grid or matrix where students not only list the various competencies they intend to fulfill but also indicate what SNL courses they plan to take or what evidence of prior learning they plan to submit for each of the competencies. As part of the learning plan, we also ask students to briefly describe their educational goals, their professional goals, and the title and rationale for their focus

area. In the process of developing their Learning Plan, students begin to identify relevant prior learning from experience and come to understand the
nature and process of learning from experience. At SNL, we see the Learning
Plan (and its development) as a tool for helping students become familiar with
the SNL competence-based approach; we encourage them to see how it supports the traditions of liberal arts education and the skills of liberal learning.

In addition to the Learning Plan, another key assignment is the Professional Goal and Action Plan, in which students define their professional goals
and develop a plan for attaining them. In completing this assignment, regardless of whether they are experts or new to a field, we ask students to research
their field of interest and to address questions such as "What are the changes
your professional area of interest is undergoing?" and "What skills, knowledge, and abilities are necessary to be effective in your field?" As part of
researching their career area of interest, we not only ask students to read
books and articles and to investigate useful Web sites, but also encourage
them to conduct interviews with people who are in the field or in positions in
which they would like to see themselves within five or ten years. We also ask
students to investigate professional associations and to visit our Career Center
at the University.

Many members of the faculty ask students to entertain questions about
their personal goals and aspirations. Through the use of readings, typically
essays and poems, we also ask students to explore questions concerning the
meaning of work and the relationship between work and leisure and their
personal lives. Several of us who teach Foundations find Levoy's (1997)
book *Callings* useful for encouraging students to define goals and plans that
stem not only from a sense of what society and their current life situation
dictate they should be and do but also from a deeper sense of their own
longings and desires.

As part of the process of developing these two assignments, instructors
often have students meet in small groups with individuals who share similar
educational and professional goals. Students submit multiple drafts of both
the Learning Plan and the Professional Goal and Action Plan in preparation
for their first committee meeting where the two documents are reviewed by
both the professional and academic advisors. For some students who are in
the process of changing careers, have not yet established their career, or are
uncertain about the career path they want to pursue, the Professional Goal
and Action Plan assignment can be particularly challenging. For many of the
students who fall in this group, it is impossible to research and decide on
their career of choice within the ten-week format of the course. For these students, we have devised an alternative assignment in which they articulate

where they are in the process of thinking about their professional goals and their plans for continuing to explore various career options.

To students who are reasonably clear about their professional area of interest or who have been in their field for many years and know much about what is happening in their industry, this assignment can seem tedious and unnecessary. When they first hear about the assignment, some students question whether there is any value in researching an area about which they feel very knowledgeable. We often encourage these students to use the assignment as a way to "check out" or confirm the knowledge they already possess about their field. For students who are well established in their career, sometimes researching and learning about graduate programs for which they might want to apply or learning about how they can mentor others in their profession represents new learning for them.

Because much of the content of Foundations centers on students' experiences and professional and educational goals, instructors must be sensitive to students' diverse situations. Each student enters Foundation at a unique point in his or her history. Some people have been in college before; others have not. Some students have moved high on the career ladder; others are newly reentering the job market. Some people appear very assured in what they want; others seem more tentative. Some people are well into middle or late adulthood; others are still under 30 years of age. Given this diversity, we urge students to come to Foundations with a sense of adventure that will allow them to look at their experiences as though they are on a new journey. We urge them to come with a sense of openness and to be imaginative in creating new learning possibilities. We ask that they come with a sense of trust that they will find the structure and support they need to learn how to be their own agents of learning.

One of the challenges of Foundations is to help students relate their experiences and experiential learning to the SNL competence framework. As instructors, we use a dual approach. Often, we begin by talking about students' experiences and examining the competencies embedded in them. That is, we brainstorm and elicit examples of experiences and examine these carefully, sometimes creating mindmaps showing the many facets and areas of their experiences and what they might have learned from them. We then draw connections between students' experiences and the competence framework. At other times, we start with the SNL competencies themselves and begin to ask students questions about which of their experiences pertain to particular competencies. Our hope is that by applying their experiences to the SNL competence framework and the liberal arts, students will assess their learning in a broader context. That is, we hope that as students review their life experiences and discuss them with others, they will gain an extra measure of learning simply through the process of analyzing what they know.

One strategy is to offer students vignettes of previous students' experiences and how they used them as a basis for demonstrating competencies in the framework. Below are some sample vignettes.

> J. Walsh grew up speaking the Polish language in his home. For the last three years, he has worked for a hospital as an administrative assistant where he is often asked to translate for the Polish-speaking patients.

> M. DeAngelis is an amateur sculptor. He has always been fascinated with working with clay and took some noncredit courses at his local community college. He has also been sculpting for several years and recently sold two pieces at a community art show. Mr. DeAngelis views sculpture as an avocation. His goal is to work his way up in the data processing field.

> S. Lopez has been volunteering at a local environmental agency. Recently, she tried her hand at running several workshops for high school students concerning environmental issues in the surrounding area and about efforts to clean up the local river. She is also an avid reader on these issues and has assisted in raising money for local education campaigns.

Identifying links between these kinds of experiences and academic competencies is a major goal of the Foundations course.

As many of us in the PLA field have noted, it is difficult to get students to move beyond describing their experiences, to begin to explore what they have learned, and to draw meaning from experience. At SNL, we use the competency framework as a tool for helping students with this kind of exploration. In addressing a particular competence, we ask students to read each statement carefully—to notice the verbs in the statement and to consider the category in which the competence appears. We also ask students to consider their overall educational goals when reading a competence and to interpret the competence statement in relation to their own experiences as well as to their professional and educational needs. We encourage students to relate their experiences to their work, family, community, and leisure pursuits. For example, for the competence statement that reads, "Can employ the skills of negotiation, mediation, or interpersonal communication in the resolution of a problem," we ask students to think about ways in which they have employed these skills with members of their family, with people with whom they work, and with members of their community. We then ask students to think about the similarities and differences between negotiation and mediation skills and interpersonal communication. From this discussion, we then develop a list of what we believe are the basic principles of effective negotiation, mediation, and interpersonal communication. An instructor might then end this discussion by relating students' ideas with the ideas of experts who have written about effective interpersonal skills.

Besides the specific criteria we have developed at SNL for each of the competencies, we also have developed general criteria for the assessment of both liberal learning and independent learning projects in the focus area based on students' experiences. In Foundations, we make students aware of these criteria. These criteria are divided into three areas: content, analysis, and presentation. In the content area, criteria include (a) the student connects his or her experience/knowledge and subject matter to the competence and addresses key criteria of the competence, (b) the student describes and reflects on his or her own experiences/knowledge, and (c) the student relates others' views to his or her own learning experience and/or demonstrates the ability to view experiences from multiple perspectives. In the areas of analysis and presentation, our criteria include (a) assertions are supported by evidence; (b) focus and conclusions are clear; (c) the presentation format is well-organized, coherent, skillfully executed, and appropriate to both the topic and audience; and (d) grammar, syntax, spelling, and citation form are appropriate.

Of course, much of the work with helping students draw meaning from their experiences revolves around exploring questions about learning. How does learning occur? What are some models of learning that might be effective in exploring what they have learned from their experiences? What are their learning style preferences?

There are several movies we use at SNL to stimulate students' thinking about learning itself. The movies *Shirley Valentine, Educating Rita,* and *Lorenzo's Oil* all provide wonderful stimuli for engaging students in discussions about learning—and the relationship between learning and their goals and dreams. As part of their Foundations assignments, students also complete the Kolb Learning Styles Inventory and learn about Kolb's model of experiential learning (1983). Many members of the faculty assign readings concerning experiential and self-directed learning from *An Orientation to College* (Steltenpohl, Shipton, & Villines, 1996), which we like because the readings are short, but provide key and useful information.

The work of Foundations does not end at the end of the course or quarter. One of the unique features of the SNL program is that the tasks begun in Foundations continue in each student's academic committee. Committees are required to meet at least twice during a student's tenure in the program, although additional meetings often take place.

Critical Perspectives on Foundations of Adult Learning

While the previous ideas and descriptions represent general approaches to the Foundations course that are shared among the faculty, each of us at SNL has his or her own approach to the course and to our work as academic advisors. For example, while some of us may focus more time in the course on exploring learning styles and theories of learning, others focus more attention on helping students learn from experience. Others dedicate more time to helping students identify professional goals and design a plan to attain them. In addition, as with any course one teaches, our own personal histories, academic training, social commitments, and experiences as learners influence how we approach the course. Our academic backgrounds in the humanities, arts, or social sciences account for some of the divergence in our approaches, as does our understanding of where we stand intellectually and professionally as adult educators. Our sense of social, artistic, and spiritual connectedness accounts for some as well. Viewed broadly, we teach and learn out of our own experiences of self and our own memories of and commitments to personal development, community identity, and connectedness to others.

The connections between Foundations and our own experience of self are deeply meaningful to the three of us who have authored this model. Each of us has taught at SNL for a number of years. In many ways, SNL's philosophy and approach to education and teaching are consistent with our own. For each of us, the college's ability to integrate students' experiences into the learning process is exciting. The use of experiential learning theories in the design of the curriculum seems to provide a more welcoming environment for students of color, women, and others who have been traditionally underserved by higher education. Competencies such as those that focus on collaborative learning, social justice, cross-cultural issues, globalization, and service learning are consistent with many of our values concerning education and our thoughts about the qualities of a competent and educated individual.

Yet despite these areas of overlap between our philosophies and those of SNL, there are some areas where we believe our perspectives and strategies differ from those of other colleagues. For example, while alternative paradigms informed SNL's history and early curricula, aspects of the program still operate out of the individualistic and technicist paradigms that have traditionally dominated American adult education. As our colleague Mechthild Hart (1992) explains,

> the adult education enterprise defines "competent" primarily in terms, which reflect a narrowly instrumental as well as starkly individualistic approach.

> Since the overall social, political, and cultural context is entirely taken for granted, to be competent therefore . . . means merely to function within this pre-given context. . . . This notion of competence is undergirded by the ideology of economic growth and competitiveness, an ideology that never appears to be worthy of questioning. (p. 9)

As in other adult education programs, strong ties to business complicate our efforts to engage students in critical analysis of social institutions and the ways in which individual lives are affected by institutional and structural determinants of gender, race, and class discrimination.

The approaches taken by the three of us in Foundations are, in part, an attempt to balance these individualistic and often instrumental biases. We do this in a number of ways. First, insights taken from the arts and humanities help us to present a more holistic notion of competence. We approach our work in Foundations with a belief that, as Diane Hill of First Nations Technical Institute explains in Model 5 of this volume, learning is a holistic process that utilizes the spiritual, intellectual, emotional, and physical aspects of self. Our inclusion of issues concerning spirituality, cooperation, personal growth, community development, authority, art, and creativity is also grounded in the idea that our task in the Foundations course is to assist in the holistic development of the learner. Second, we approach our work with advisees and in our Foundation class not only from an individualistic model of lifelong learning but also from a philosophy of life that stresses interdependence and collective responsibility. Third, we explore with students the ways in which human experience is shaped by gender, class, and race.

As we describe in the next section, this work requires that we take risks and that we bring all of who we are into the classroom. Once concerned about speaking Spanish to Latino students before and after class for fear it might offend other students who did not know the language, Marixsa now chooses to speak Spanish when appropriate in an effort to establish a sense of connection with Spanish-speaking students. Deborah takes risks as she engages students in creative experiences, and Derise does so by incorporating rituals and ceremonies into her classroom teaching. Rather than live and work out of a Western compartmentalization of self, we bring to the classroom many aspects of who we are and encourage students to do likewise.

Next, we reflect on who we are as human beings, and how who we are influences how we teach the course. We also discuss the relationship of what we do in the course to the goals of the course and to the ways in which we encourage students to explore and articulate their own prior learning and to connect it to the competence framework.

Our Personal Stories and Our Teaching of Foundations

Foundations is not only about providing students with a framework, resources, and tools with which to explore their educational and professional goals and to evidence prior learning. It is also about inviting students to explore themselves as learners and to explore the question, "Education for what?" Our mission as educators of adult learners is to help students become more fully developed individuals who will live optimally (Akbar, 1985) within larger communities of which they are members. We attempt to encourage both individual development and collaborative development, learning to value the interconnections between the self with others, between the self with environment, and between the self with the self. This approach to Foundations is one that is grounded in each of our lived experiences as women of color. Our growing up experiences and lessons we learned about "giving back what you know" informs our understanding of the public uses of knowledge and thus forms a context in which to understand the relationship between experiential learning, professional and educational goals, life goals, and community. The value we place on the integration of student's experiences in Foundations is also informed by our participation in African American, Latino, and women's studies programs—all of which were grounded in and developed expansive, life-affirming, and inspiring experiential learning theories that would help inform the creation of a more socially just world.

For example, Marixsa's experiences as a member of a traditionally marginalized and colonized community initially propelled her into academia. Leaders of the Puerto Rican community where she lived, her teachers of color, and her parents all possessed a strong conviction and instilled in her the belief that education could be a profound strategy of resistance—a "radical space of possibility" (hooks, 1994, p. 12). The belief that education can be an important catalyst not only for individual growth but also for community empowerment defines her professional identity and scholarly work. Although trained in sociology, she sees herself as an activist educator/scholar who believes that a broad spectrum of people should "claim knowledge as a field in which we all labor and that scholarly work can be an important catalyst for improving conditions among oppressed groups" (hooks, 1994, p. 14).

As a junior high school student, she attended one of the first state-funded bilingual programs in the country. In the segregated environment of her bilingual classroom, she had largely Latina teachers, who, like bell hooks' African American teachers in the segregated schools of the South, brought an ethic of care to their work. The bilingual teachers and the counselors that she and her classmates encountered were more than teachers and counselors; they were cultural workers and healers "struggling against society to undo the damage of years of abuse" (Castellano, 1995, p. 308). They sought to help students cure the "clear cut [and deep/profound] scars" of "internalized self-hatred and fear of [our] own creative passion that racism, sexism and colonialism had already carved into their young bodies and minds." Even at the young age of 8, 9, and 10, before she and her peers entered the bilingual program, Marixsa and her classmates were "fragmented souls" (Castellano, 1995, p. 309). They had grown too shy to speak up in class and had no passion for learning because they had heard a loud and clear message that they were not capable of learning. Little of what they were taught had any relevance to their lives or inspired them to want to learn. Like many others, Marixsa and her school-mates came into their classroom with a "deep sense of personal shame about everything—[their] poor skills" and for being brown (Castellano, 1995, p. 312). Their shame left them silent and with no desire to want to speak for fear of being noticed, called upon, and further shamed.

It took a "conjurer, a magus" for Marixsa's teachers and counselors to deal with their students' fragmented souls and to bring her and her peers back to life (Castellano, 1995, p. 309). Besides sharing with them their knowledge and enthusiasm of Puerto Rican history and culture, these bilingual teachers helped Marixsa and her peers *name,* acknowledge, and go beyond the psychic pain of the constant discrimination that they experienced within the community at large and even from teachers and students within their own school.

Marixsa's bilingual teachers nurtured her and her peers' intellectual growth, and, as hooks writes, taught them "that [one's] devotion to learning, to a life of the mind, was a counter-hegemonic act, a fundamental way to resist" gender, race, and class oppression (hooks, 1994, p. 2). Her teachers taught with conviction and with a sense of purpose and mission. In retrospect, it was in these bilingual classrooms that she learned that education was not only about acquiring specific skills and existing information and knowledge, but also that students/learners should be viewed as "subjects acting in and on the world, not as passive recipients of information" (hooks, 1994, p. 2).

Deborah, having attended a historically Black college, also connects the work she does in Foundations to the legacies of those institutions, namely, a clear mission on the part of its students and graduates to help others and to expand and share knowledge. "Give back what you have learned" is the message she recalls being taught. Derise too describes how her family expected and promoted academic excellence throughout her childhood, often extolling the value and importance of "getting a good education." As did many in the African American community, they looked to education as a means for liberation from oppressive social and economic living conditions.

For both, academic accomplishments were "owned" not only by them but also by the larger community, the relatives, the friends, the neighbors, and the elders. They learned early that identity and the self are rooted in the larger cultural group. For Marixsa, Deborah, and Derise, education was centered within a community context and was an early means to learn about themselves and those around them.

Thus, at the same time that we try to "center" our students, helping them understand who they are as learners, how they can learn from their experiences, and how they can define goals and create plans for attaining them, we also try to "decenter" them by encouraging them to think about the communities of which they are part and to which they see themselves as accountable. One exercise that we have used, designed by our colleague Patricia Monaghan, asks students to consider the various communities of which they are part and to then articulate what others in these communities would expect of them as college graduates. We ask them to consider what possible impact their education might have within the neighborhoods and city in which they live and other groups of which they feel a part. Another writing assignment, designed by our colleague Morris Fiddler, asks students to address the following questions: What does it mean to be educated? To what extent do you consider yourself educated? This assignment offers us another opportunity to explore with students the public uses of knowledge. As part of writing this essay, we ask students to consider who they are as learners within the larger context of the communities of which they are a part.

Our own lived experiences also inform our belief that Foundations must address how race, class, and gender, and not only students' status as adults, shape who they are as students. This, in turn, informs how we walk students through the process of developing prior learning projects, honoring their own learning and developing goals and plans for attaining them. Each of us, recalling how our own cultural and community experiences were often erased in our educational experiences, seeks to find ways for all students to feel honored in the classroom.

Derise, for example, enjoyed and was fascinated by school in her early years. She was a good student who worked hard and did well. She was taught by her family that she could thrive, prosper, and achieve, and be herself while doing it. This could be done in the context of fairness, justice, sharing, and helping others to thrive and prosper. She was taught that she came from a people who had a rich cultural heritage to be proud of, even if, economically, many were poor. In retrospect, she realizes that her parents were planting the seeds of an African-centered perspective, although they would not have described themselves as having that worldview at that time. She also had some wonderful teachers who encouraged her to explore the range of her abilities and to investigate the great legacies of her cultural heritage.

However, this kind of early nurturance and confidence in her was in contrast to far too many negative, often demeaning educational experiences later in childhood, experiences that devalued the humanity and questioned the abilities of people who looked like her. After three years in an all-Black elementary school, her family moved and she transferred to a predominantly white school system, where she remained until she graduated from high school. Some teachers emphasized the "desire" for her to be, as one teacher said, a "good Negro girl." This translated into being silent, culturally alienated, nonassertive, and lifeless. Some expected less of Black students, even in the face of their accomplishments and achievements. When an all-Black school system was ordered to merge with the predominantly white one she attended, Derise recalls, many of the white parents protested, alleging that the integration of "those students" would result in a decrease in academic standards. What she discovered was that far more Black students received national commendation for scholarship prior to their integration into an assumedly better educational system. "Those students" essentially had been placed into a hostile environment that neither appreciated nor was prepared to nurture their strengths, accommodate their ways of knowing, or believe in their academic capabilities. The predominantly white women's college she later attended provided many wonderful educational opportunities, but she was falsely accused of plagiarism when she turned in a paper that was "better than most journal articles," according to her professor, and again when she uncovered an obscure reference that helped her solve a chemical equation in organic chemistry.

Many of her undergraduate and graduate school experiences convinced Derise that to be optimally educated, she would have to unlearn inaccuracies that had been taught, and then relearn truths. Much of her relearning has been outside the traditional educational system because of its exclusion or marginalization of people, ideas, issues, and worldviews that are integral to her being. As Derise pursued studies of traditional African philosophies and spirituality, she began to apply some of the concepts to her professional practices. Their teaching of the importance of maintaining balance and harmony in life and seeing things holistically has informed her personal and professional life. The Akan (a group of people in Ghana, West Africa) beliefs that everything and everyone in nature is programmed for success, that nothing is good or bad in and of itself but is there to serve its purpose, and that, if we but listen, we have the answers we need have guided her work in the classroom.

Although she had access to invaluable resources and scholars at Northwestern University, Marixsa also recalls that her educational experiences in college were not entirely positive. Having grown up in an inner-city neighbor-hood and coming from a working-class immigrant experience, attending Northwestern was a huge culture shock for her. It meant crossing racial, eth-nic, and class boundaries as she found herself in classrooms with students whose prior educational opportunities far surpassed hers. While there were aspects of her traditional liberal arts education that she enjoyed and that con-tributed to her intellectual development, she also found that her lived experi-ences and the ideas to which she had previously been exposed were rarely represented in the courses she took. With a strong conviction that she had to be an active participant in her own education and intellectual development, she used whatever resources she could to create alternative learning opportu-nities. Using independent learning courses, for example, she identified topics she wanted to pursue and identified teachers willing to work with her to more clearly define her questions and to help her identify resources, learning tools, and strategies.

Deborah grew up in an environment that placed great emphasis on edu-cation and on cultivating a refined appreciation for the arts and humanities. She attended a private integrated, yet predominantly white, high school, with small classrooms and attention to individual development. Although she did well in her studies, she could not fathom why she was treated differently when her white peers received enthusiastic counseling for college. Attendance at historically black colleges at both the undergraduate and graduate level, as well as the swirl of the civil rights movement in the North, helped her identify what was missing and understand that there were aspects of herself that she did not know. In college, she sought to learn more experientially about her-itage and culture and what parts of herself could flourish with this knowl-edge. She remembers, for example, that when growing up she virtually never heard gospel music and had to go to college to discover the power and majesty of that musical form that is a part of her heritage. Similarly, she could not speak in the African American vernacular; she had to learn it when she got there. College was a time of planting and watering and pruning, of unlearning and relearning, of developing confidence and developing voice.

Because of these kinds of personal and collectives experiences, we find it important to explore with students the ways in which human experience is shaped by gender, class, and race. This means that we balance the explo-ration of individual goals with a broader discussion of social justice and make explicit the relationship between identifying learning experiences and coming to value them. Students often dismiss some of their experiences because they have preconceived ideas about the type of experiences they believe are even worthy of being discussed in the classroom, let alone granted academic credit. Students often believe that the only experiences worthy of consideration are traditionally mainstream, middle-class, white, and male. We have all faced the female student who has been raising children for twenty years, but manages to think that she has had *no* experiences worthy of college credit. On the opposite end, we often have students in Foundations who are very accomplished in their careers and who are rarely questioned or asked to "prove" what they know. Typically coming from more privileged social categories, they find it almost insulting to be asked to demonstrate or document their expertise. Often, the challenge with these students is to assist them in stepping back from the details of their experiences to articulate the general principles, concepts, and ideas that are "behind" what they do. Our invitation for further self-discovery encourages students to expand their thinking about prior learning and to supplement what they already know with new knowledge.

Brainstorming ideas in both large groups and individual advising sessions and deliberately exploring those experiences that are different and fall outside of students' expectations about what is "appropriate" in an academic setting are effective ways for Foundations to help students consider and value diverse experiences. Coming to know students well and approaching our advising with a sense of personal involvement are also effective tools for helping students come to value their experiences. Marixsa recalls how it was only through lengthy advising sessions with a female student that she was able to convince her student that there was probably much that she had learned from volunteering for twenty years in a mental health institution. From the student's perspective, her volunteer work was just something she did to keep her busy while her young children were in school. Marixsa's student believed what many women believe, that there is no "true" skill or knowledge involved in the traditionally female "caring work" in which she was engaged. It was only after several advising sessions, class discussions, readings about experiential learning, and short readings by feminist scholars that Marixsa's student became aware that she had learned much about mental health issues, mental health institutions, and effective strategies for working with individuals with severe mental health problems. In the end, her student was able to demonstrate her knowledge and earn credit.

We also explore with students the ways in which human experience and development is shaped by gender, class, and race by assigning readings that cross disciplines, race, gender, ethnicity, and power. We try to draw on the experiences of others as they have written about their own experience, within the context of their own experience, rather than elevate the interpretations of others outside those experiences. For example, we assign excerpts of *The Autobiography of Malcolm X*. We find this reading invaluable not only for engaging students in discussions about how race and class shape human experience but also for generating dialogue among students about education as transformative and in examining public uses of knowledge. Alice Walker's *In Search of Our Mothers' Gardens* is another reading we use to encourage students to think about individuals who possess a great deal of knowledge or skills that we are not likely to recognize or value because it falls outside mainstream traditional notions of what is valuable knowledge. We also show videos such as *Maya Lin,* which examines this artist's work on the Vietnam Memorial. Maya Lin's story provides students with a wonderful example of someone who had to draw on many areas of the liberal arts to complete the design of the Memorial, but also as she fought against racist groups and individuals who sought to disqualify her design because she was Asian American.

As another example of how we try to integrate different cultural traditions, Derise begins each class with proverbs, succinct yet profound statements of values about and expectations of the learning process. Examples include "When the student is ready, the teacher will appear" and "She or he who learns, teaches." These two ancient African proverbs inform the learner of Derise's belief that their work together is purposeful, that learning and teaching are a mutual and reciprocal process, and that she has an investment in collaborative and shared learning. These proverbs (and others throughout the term) are presented, and the learner both determines his or her personal meaning and hears others' interpretations. Proverbs often speak to learners on an affective and spiritual as well as intellectual level, thus appealing to a variety of learning preferences. The use of proverbs, which are widely utilized as instructional tools in many non-Western cultures, speaks to Derise's belief in the legitimacy of different ways of knowing and learning.

Again, drawing on diverse traditions, practices, and ways of knowing, Derise also utilizes other "spiritual technologies" in Foundations, such as centering/meditation and visualization, affirmations, group symbols, and rituals, to help orient and remind learners of their purpose and goals. These activities are designed to stimulate awareness, awaken imagination, foster creativity, and prepare learners for optimal learning. Derise invites students to participate in centering and meditation activities as a way to help them focus on aspects of their experiences that need to be articulated as evidence of learning. In addition, by using visualization exercises, Derise hopes students can become more aware of elements of their experiences and learning that they perhaps had forgotten. Her aim with the use of these "technologies" is to also help learners remember their *passions* and to apply these to the development of their academic program.

Both Derise and Marixsa use decorations, celebrations, and food as a way to welcome students into the learning environment, but also as a way to welcome the affective as well as cognitive aspects of learning. For example, Derise begins her course with a celebration, complete with food, party favors, and decorations. This often-surprising first activity reminds students that learning can be and should be fun. It helps to create a particular kind of space—physically, emotionally, spiritually—to facilitate the work ahead. Derise encourages the learners to celebrate and honor themselves and their lives and to acknowledge their successes, both past and present. She asks students to name the things they have done as a way to obtain an initial list of experiences around which students might be able to develop prior learning projects. This activity also invites the playful parts of students' personalities to be present and also communicates that Derise values and honors who they are and what they've done.

Marixsa also decorates her classroom with fabrics and plays music at the beginning of class as a way to welcome students into the learning environment. In addition, at the end of Foundations, she hosts a "graduation" ceremony celebrating students' completion of the course. In place of a "diploma," Marixsa gives students a small gift that she has selected especially for them and that represents something about them. It might be a gift that speaks to an insight a student had during the term, which gives her the opportunity to review important ideas presented in the course. Some of the gifts she chooses are meant to motivate students to take courses in areas that they "feel they are not good in" or that they claim they hate. For example, she has given students who insist that they are not creative and are not looking forward to taking a course in the arts a set of watercolor paints. By personalizing the experience and by introducing humor, she shows students that she has been paying attention, that she has heard their joys as well as concerns about learning. Students leave the course feeling like she has come to "know" them.

Deborah uses techniques and strategies informed by arts and humanities disciplines to assist her in her work with students. Over the years, she has tried to help students expand their capacity for creativity by asking students to bring their creative projects or engage in some creative activity for competence development. Deborah gets students talking about their creative work as well as fears with each other and helps them brainstorm ideas about how they can expand their perceptions about the arts. By focusing on their visual, kinetic, and aural modes of expression, among others, students begin to identify and value previously unconsidered aspects of their lives that may lead to demonstration of competence. In addition, Deborah exposes students to visual tools for organizing ideas that provide nonlinear approaches to thinking and writing. For example, she uses mind-mapping and models its use in various classroom activities. For those students who are uncomfortable with outlines, this exposure to alternative methods acknowledges their past frustration and provides an important tool to help them develop greater comfort with the writing process, an essential in demonstrating competence. Students quickly see the applications of this accelerated learning technique and go on to use it in work and other settings successfully.

Deborah also uses her theater background to help students break out of their more traditional—and sometimes unpleasant—college experiences. In exercises designed to reinforce student learning, she encourages students to present to the class their assignments in game-show formats, role playing, and debates. Through these exercises, students not only reinforce their learning but also work on their collaborative learning skills. Often these exercises lead students to take courses that help them develop public speaking and improvisation skills embedded in their lifelong learning.

For all of us, the arts and humanities can give students access to information about themselves and the world that they would not otherwise have. In short, these techniques and ways of knowing can become effective tools for drawing meaning from experience as students develop evidence of prior learning and identify and articulate their goals.

For example, drawing on a Native American tradition where masks were created as a way to influence the future, we ask students to create a mask that communicates something about their professional, educational, and personal goals. Students can create a collage, a painting, or some other visual artifact as their mask. As they create their masks, we also ask students to be aware of the attitudes and feelings they bring to the project. Students then share these masks in small groups, not only discussing their goals but also the "energy" they bring to the project. The act of physically having to create something, we believe, makes them aware of how much information their bodies hold. Being aware of and sharing these attitudes can help students understand the belief systems surrounding their professional, educational, and personal goals. Often, in addition to including images in their masks that speak to their goals, we also find that students include images about significant events in their lives. This provides an opportunity to engage students in discussions about these events and whether they represent significant learning experiences for them.

Conclusion

We understand and believe, as bell hooks (1994) describes, that education can be liberatory and that

> to educate as the practice of freedom is a way of teaching that anyone can learn. That the learning process comes easiest to those of us who teach who also believe that there is an aspect of our vocation that is sacred; who believe that our work is not merely to share information but to share in the intellectual and spiritual growth of our students. To teach in a manner that respects and cares for the souls of our students is essential if we are to provide the necessary conditions where learning can most deeply and intimately begin. (p. 13)

It is an "ethic of care" and respect that we believe best captures what we bring to our work as teachers and advisors. It is our deep sense of care for the intellectual growth of our students that pushes us to find ways continuously and intentionally to work with diverse students and the wealth of experience and knowledge they bring to Foundations.

Collectively we believe that the various perspectives and strategies we bring to Foundations are grounded in African-centric, Latino-centric, and feminist perspectives that see the process of reflection and learning not as detached disembodied processes. Our aim through the various practices we utilize is to help students "re-integrate cerebral ways of knowing with what Adrienne Rich has called 'thinking through the body' " (Michelson, 1996, p. 450). We want our students to believe, as Michelson states, that "emotional, sensual and physical being informs our knowledge of both self and others; empathy, anger, desire, interestedness are moments of connectedness to self and world that provide important evidence about the world. . . . The emotional and the sensate mediate our social and moral selfhood" (p. 450). Rather than valuing detached observations, we want our students to "value knowledge claims that are rooted in personal testimony and constructed through dialogue with others." We want to "transgress" the boundaries of "acceptable" classroom and teaching strategies by creating spaces that invite neglected or forgotten aspects and elements of students' learning experiences to emerge (hooks, 1994).

Given the deeply rooted middle-class, white, masculinist values and norms in our society, which are in many ways reflected in SNL's general philosophy of adult learning, we also aim to renarrate SNL's story and practices, thereby reshaping them and broadening them. We address these issues from a politically radical perspective by making students aware of the racial, social, and gender hierarchies in our society and how their experiences are shaped by gender, class, and race. Given these hierarchies, we want to challenge students' perceptions about what experiences are considered valuable enough to be heard. We also want to expand students' understanding of the kinds of knowing that can bring life to what people know or can learn.

Through the Foundations course and by using diverse and holistic teaching and learning strategies, we aim to cultivate a kind of educational and social agency among our students that will guide future learning both outside and inside the classroom. By helping them reflect on and become more aware of their attitudes toward learning, themselves as learners, and what it means to be educated, we hope students will gain more confidence in developing learning goals and executing learning activities that will contribute both to their personal growth and to community development.

References

Akbar, N. (1985). *Community of Self.* Tallahassee, FL: Mind Productions.

Castellano, O. (1995). "Canto, Locuray Poesia." In *Race, Class, and Gender: An Anthology* (2nd ed.), edited by Margaret L. Anderson and Patricia Hill Collins, p. 000. Belmont, CA: Wadsworth Publishers.

Hart, M. U. (1992). *Working and Educating for Life: Feminist and International Perspectives on Adult Education.* New York: Routledge.

hooks, b. (1994). *Teaching to Transgress: Education as the Practice of Freedom.* New York: Routledge.

Kolb, D. (1983). *Experiential Learning: Experience as the Source of Learning and Development.* Upper Saddle River, NJ: Pearson-Prentice Hall.

Levoy, G. M. (1997). *Callings: Finding and Following an Authentic Life.* New York: Harmony Books.

Michelson, E. (1996). "Usual Suspects: Experience, Reflection and the (En)gendering of Knowledge." *International Journal of Lifelong Education* 15(6), 438–454.

Steltenpohl, E., Shipton J., and Villines, S. (1996). *An Orientation to College: A Reader on Becoming an Educated Person.* Belmont, CA: Wadsworth Publishers.

DELINEATIONS ON THE WEB

COMPUTER-MEDIATED PORTFOLIO DEVELOPMENT AT THE UNIVERSITY OF MARYLAND UNIVERSITY COLLEGE

Theresa A. Hoffmann

The EXCEL Through Experiential Learning Program of the University of Maryland University College (UMUC) has grown from a small program to a major institutional activity that serves thousands of adult learners, including U.S. military personnel, internationally. The transformation of portfolio development from a print-based to a Web-based study has given access to greater numbers of learners but at the same time challenged the faculty and staff to replicate the supportiveness and immediacy of face-to-face interaction.

At a time in which many institutions are considering a Web-based process of portfolio development, UMUC's systematic and carefully articulated EXCEL curriculum is an important model. Equally importantly, UMUC has led the way in addressing the challenges of Web-based portfolio development and generating creative and learner-centered solutions. Theresa Hoffmann describes how the UMUC staff asked and answered a multitude of questions: "How do we design a Web course for portfolio development? How do we use the Web to provide the kinds of support students and faculty had gained from the course guides and videos that formed our previous materials? How do we provide the counseling and coaching support that was critical for student success?"

The process of developing and refining a prior learning program is like discovering the many nooks and passageways of an old cave; some take you deeper and deeper and lead to new openings and others, to the end of the path. It is an adventure that takes us on the same rigorous path anyone in search of learning must take.

—EXCEL Course Guide, 2000.[1]

Introduction

By definition, any experiential learning program for adults begs many questions concerning the meaning of learning. How is learning identified and quantified? How do we retain the uniqueness of the individual's knowledge yet have it fit within a finite system? What is the meaning of a college degree for adults?

This model will focus on EXCEL Through Experiential Learning, the portfolio-development program of the University of Maryland University College (UMUC). It will explore not only the nuts and bolts of the course but also how it was developed and why we chose the configuration it finally took. Specifically, this essay will explore its newest delivery design, a Web-based course designed to meet the needs of a greatly expanded student body. The first section contains a brief overview of our program. Next is a descriptive narrative of the developmental process by which we arrived at the logistical and theoretical framework for our course, and, finally, the Web course itself is described and illustrated.

Overview

Prior Learning at the University of Maryland University College (UMUC) is similar to that of other adult-centered institutions in that we offer a portfolio-development program housed in a part of the university designed to serve adults. Like other programs, UMUC provides a broad range of undergraduate and graduate degree programs serving students who have work-based experience in many fields and differing levels of academic achievement. Like many of our sister institutions, we develop partnerships with employers and offer classes on-site in addition to our campus-based undergraduate certificate programs. To ensure that our students benefit from both scholarly and "real-world" expertise, we draw our faculty from both academic ranks and from the public and private sector.

[1]The EXCEL course at UMUC is a collective effort. I am grateful to my colleagues Charles Aldrich, Jerry Bellenker, Barry Butts, Catherine Campbell, Ed Guss, Anne Kirchgessner, Jeanette Kreiser, Stanley Lacienski, Kevin Michel, Peter Porosky, and John Van Brunt for their creativity in working with our students and their help in writing this model. I am especially grateful to our students and former students who over the years have taught us about experiential learning and student needs.

UMUC requires 120 credits to graduate, ninety of which can be transferred from other accredited institutions and sixty of which can come from non-collegiate-sponsored learning, with a maximum of ninety nonresident credits in all. Non-collegiate-sponsored learning can be demonstrated through the military occupational specialties (MOS) and other courses that have been evaluated for generic credit by the American Council on Education; examinations such as DANTES, ACT/PEP, and CLEP; and/or documented through portfolio. Although EXCEL students apply for credit in specific academic areas, often the content of a portfolio does not precisely match the syllabus of existing courses. Evaluators are therefore able to develop "course" titles that accurately name a student's knowledge, thus enabling students to earn credit for a wider range of college-level learning.

Portfolios at UMUC are organized around a series of what we call "delineations" in a given area of expertise. Each delineation consists of a list of competencies; a list of targeted course equivalents that, while not necessarily exact, provide guidance and focus; and an academic narrative. For example, a student writing a delineation in General Management might choose to target courses such as Leadership and Management in an Age of Diversity, Total Quality Management, and Managerial Communications Skills. Competencies in this same area might include statements such as "I can create reorganization plans for a large organization" or "I am able to operate a small business." In the academic narrative, the student describes the knowledge he or she has gained from related life experiences within the academic discipline. The narrative must be a detailed piece; we therefore require a minimum of fifteen pages.

In important ways, our portfolio-development course resembles that of other institutions that serve adults. The role of EXCEL301: Learning Analysis and Planning (three credits) is to support and encourage students to complete and develop their portfolios. EXCEL has a maximum class size of twenty students and runs a full semester, typically giving students fifteen weeks to complete the portfolio documenting their lifelong learning. After the course, the Prior Learning office sends portfolios to appropriate faculty experts for evaluation of credit. Like comparable institutions, we follow CAEL guidelines. A portfolio consists of the following sections: goals, chronological table of life events, autobiography, competencies and targeted courses, narratives, and documentation.

At the same time, UMUC is different from other adult-friendly institutions in that we have served a large military and civilian population both stateside and overseas since the 1940s. Thus, we faced the particular challenges of prior learning assessment at a distance earlier than many other institutions. Our new Web version of portfolio development is the result of a long process that took us from an obscure, institutionally marginalized program to one that makes PLA an institutional priority—literally worldwide. The process of its development, and the challenges it was designed to address, has more often than not driven the content of the course.

EXCEL (Portfolio Development Program): A Developmental Process

In 1991, EXCEL was a small, classroom-based program with approximately 100 students a year and 300 delineations. At the time, our main concerns were program maintenance, the institutional environment, and faculty and employer involvement. Our greatest challenge seemed to be letting students know we existed, since students had to look hard in the course catalog to learn about the program.

Yet even then, we were asking ourselves how we defined the concept of "articulated learning." To many students and even many faculty, learning seemed to mean "what I did and where I did it." There also seemed to be what I call a "MOS" mentality in some students who, like those who had received ACE credits for competency-based learning in the military, thought the portfolio credit was earned the same way. Faculty evaluators had to decipher what courses the learning overlapped, if any, and at what level, or whether they had to create a course title to reflect what the student knew. Students often found evaluators' comments vague and sparse, and they felt a gap between the credits they imagined receiving and the reality. Identifying course credits and assigning levels of knowledge were sources of serious frustration for both students and faculty.

Thus, even as a small program in the early 1990s, we were struggling with important issues of both quality and service to students. Prior learning staff read all evaluators' reports and met with course faculty each semester as a group. We talked with faculty who were often unsure about how to help students conceptualize their experience. We wrestled with the original policy of awarding credit based on content alone, not on the quality of students' writing. When that policy was changed, we confronted the apparent relationship between retention and writing skills.

Thus, we were already engaged in trying to improve EXCEL when new institutional priorities led to greatly increased student numbers, specifically in providing access to U.S. military personnel around the world. We needed to address the issues of motivation and retention, work with students to improve their writing, provide supportive process guidelines and feedback, help students define the difference between applied learning and theoretical understanding, and provide training, technical support, and materials for faculty. At the same time, we also needed to address the problems of large student numbers, which, for example, had forced us to computerize our administrative processes, lists of assessors, and student database. The main issue, of course, was how to deliver portfolio development within a massified system to a worldwide network of students who differed widely in learning styles, technological savvy, writing and organizational skills, academic confidence, time management skills, and access to materials and support services. Many students served in businesses and military services that imposed unusual hours and unpredictable travel schedules. Some had been out of the work and academic environment for many years and needed detailed guidance to navigate the university system. Still others required academic support and tutorial assistance to promote their success in the program.

The solution was the Web.

Evolution of the Web-Based EXCEL Course

Although the Web medium was enticing and convenient, designing a Web-based portfolio-development course brought a whole new set of issues into play. First of all, how do we design a Web course for portfolio development? How do we use the Web to provide the kinds of support students and faculty had gained from the course guides and videos that formed our previous materials? How do we provide the counseling and coaching support that was critical for student success? So many EXCEL students, we knew, would continue to take EXCEL as their first course after returning to college after many years. They would need help in sorting out their goals, assessing which experiences were most likely to yield credits, and making the shift from narrating experience to documenting learning.

EXCEL: The Web Course[2]

The Internet Web course, developed in 1998, currently has the highest enrollments of the two course formats that UMUC now offers to students: a classroom-based course and the new Web-based version. Most students elect the Web-based delivery method for EXCEL because of its convenience, worldwide access, and asynchronous time frame. The Web site for the course is organized into the following major topic areas: faculty introduction and biography, syllabus and assignments, course content and modules, conferences,

---

[2]The EXCEL Web course (UMUC, 1998), *EXCEL Course Guide* (UMUC, 1999, 2000), and all related materials are protected by copyright. All rights reserved.

study groups, chat room, class rosters, and e-mail addresses. Web-based materials include a course syllabus with time lines for each section of the portfolio, written and visual instructional materials, training on using the Web if needed, course assignments, and samples from student portfolios. The Web is also used for creating dialogue among students and between students, instructors, and the Prior Learning office. A "Read Me First" module links to time management and organization tips, student and faculty audio and video testimonials, writing guides and tutorial assistance, EXCEL philosophy, course description, and grading policies.

There are seven instructional modules in the Web course, corresponding to the parts of the portfolio. As indicated below, the course also contains an "Assembling the Portfolio" module.

Module 1: Goals

Module 2: Chronological Table

Module 3: Autobiography

Module 4: Competencies and Targeted Courses

Module 5: Writing the Narrative

Module 6: Documentation

Module 7: Assembling the Portfolio

Within each module, students are given directions through the combination of a mythological theme and a "nuts and bolts" approach. Each module is divided into a theoretical framework, approach, student and faculty tips, assignments, targeted student portfolio samples, and exercises to help in the completion of the particular task. One faculty role is to remind students to use parts of these modules as needed throughout the course. We try to use the technology in ways that speak to a multiplicity of forms and learning styles, especially for the student who participates more often and more deeply. Pictures, videos, diagrams, maps, and samples are infused throughout the course to provide visual clarification. Some students have a strong computer background, and many offer technical support to those who need more help.

From the beginning, EXCEL faculty use a variety of approaches to engage students in the process. Many establish initial contact with students through e-mail in order to establish logistics. Typically, faculty begin by reviewing the course syllabus, which refers students to readings in the course guide, and Web course modules and the *EXCEL Course Guide*. The goal in this initial stage is to inform students about grading methods, give them guidance in producing each part of the portfolio, provide help with exercises and delineation strategies, and offer examples of students' work.

Class conferences are organized by portfolio topic or by special topics. The purpose of the conference is to provide tips for success and an opportunity for questions and answers. Throughout these conferences, the instructor advises students on managing the project and on possible pitfalls, opens and moderates discussions, responds to questions, and makes appropriate referrals. For example, in the Goals conference, Module 1, an instructor may inform students about ways to view their goals, give examples of goals, and suggest ways to phrase their statements and link them to their educational aspirations. Often this process encourages other students' reactions and suggestions.

Some instructors also divide students into study groups on the Web, with a small number of students assigned to each group. Each study group receives assignments such as completing the exercises in the course guide or on the Web. For example, one exercise asks students to develop a time line of significant life events and describe what was learned from them. Students can compare their stories and provide feedback on each other's work by e-mail or in the chat room. Study groups have proven successful as students progress in their portfolio development.

Students access support from faculty, staff, and other students using a variety of media. Each day, our EXCEL faculty and the assessment staff receive phone calls, e-mail messages and attachments, and letters requesting clarification or feedback on various portions of the portfolio or aspects of the process. Many students who are ultimately referred to advisors want information about how courses will fit into their curriculum; others want feedback about whether they are on track in identifying learning or clarification about which courses fit into which delineations. Most requests are for assistance in organizing and developing their academic narratives.

Although the phone and individual e-mails are used, the Web itself is the major venue for individual communication, small-group conferences, and class discussion. People have been very creative in finding ways to connect on the Web despite its electronic and deceptively impersonal character. Many of our Web students are very sophisticated and knowledgeable about communicating via the Web and often act as models for other students and faculty. For example, some will submit their entire portfolio online for faculty and peer review. Class lists and e-mail addresses are provided for fellow students to communicate with each other and develop cohorts that review each other's work throughout the process. Pictures and biographies are submitted online to make introductions more realistic and friendly. Conference groups are set up to work on exercises, discuss questions, or share information. Students' work is submitted on paper by mail, by fax, or electronically.

Despite the EXCEL student manual (UMUC, 2001) and the standard formats we have devised, EXCEL faculty find many ways to *individualize* their classes. Although we have created the "voice" of a generic instructor on the Web, and although the course guide offers a variety of instructional information, our predesigned course materials have been developed as resources for faculty and students, not as rigid requirements. Individual faculty members create their own syllabi and guide students through the process of portfolio development by referencing useful course materials and referring students as appropriate to the Web information, exercises, or text. The Web format allows faculty to design personalized guidelines and mini-lectures that elicit student responses online. All material is archived for easy student referral.

According to Yalom (1995), the beneficial results of group dynamics hinge on eleven therapeutic factors: installation of hope, universality, imparting of information, altruism, corrective recapitulation of the primary family group, development of socializing techniques, interpersonal learning, imitative behavior, group cohesiveness, catharsis, and existential factors. Despite the Web format, our EXCEL course gives students access to the beneficial factors Yalom describes. The Web and course guide provide students with information and a feeling of hope; the "I can do it" feeling is enhanced by providing examples and models for writing the portfolio. Increased accessibility of faculty and students online from any location and time encourages a sense of universality, altruism, interpersonal learning, and community. EXCEL students can emulate and learn from others through conference groups and exercises, online questions and answers, the course guide, and videos. Students are encouraged to contact each other, form groups, share work, and provide feedback. Ultimately, existential factors come into play when students realize that no one else can write their life story and articulate its lessons.

The Course Modules: Writing the Portfolio

Module 1: Goals

The mythological theme in Module 1 is "Daedalus and Icarus." The story is described and students are told that "the goal of human flight was realized only after 2,500 years of starts and stops, small successes and major failures. . . . Goals are not always clear at first, and they must be defined and refined before we can accomplish or even recognize and state them. . . . The purpose of this module is to help you define and refine your personal, educational, and professional goals."

The approach section in Module 1 asks students to use the goal-setting exercises and format: "short- and long-term personal, educational, and career goals." The assignment section asks students to review the guide, look at examples of goals and evaluators' comments, and formulate their own goals. Students are referred to five topics to help them formulate their goals and identify roadblocks to achieving them: "Guidelines for Goal Setting," "Setting Goals for EXCEL," "An Example of a Plan of Action for EXCEL," "Life Goals Checklist," and "Goal-Setting Exercises."

Module 2: Chronological Table

This section focuses on Chronos, the god of time. We tell students that this section is "a capsule overview of your most significant life events (personal, professional/vocational, educational, volunteer/community)," and that the module will help prepare them to write an autobiography and statements of learning, identify potential sources of knowledge, and supplement the documentation. Students are advised that "life does not happen in a linear fashion . . . the lessons can be harsh at times, but if we know how to learn from them, they can be opportunities for growth and change." There are two exercises in this section: One helps students identify significant life events by drawing a time line stating what was learned from each significant event and why it was important; the other provides a chart of life stages to identify a person's earliest memory and how it might have impacted the student as a learner, patterns found throughout life, successes, mistakes (opportunities to learn), and what they taught. Students refer to a variety of student examples and student/faculty videos and comments.

Module 3: Autobiography

This section uses the story of Echo and Narcissus for the self-reflection aspect of the autobiography. Students are instructed in this module that the story of Narcissus expresses humanity's basic fear of self-reflection and that one can look at oneself in a benign and safe fashion: "Many people feel uncomfortable looking at themselves because they are afraid of what they might see. We encourage you to look at both positive and negative life events and grow fond of yourself despite what has happened." In the rationale section, students are given the reasons for the inclusion of the autobiography: to put learning into broader context and give it credibility, to get accustomed to writing in the first person, and to help the instructor identify potential college-level knowledge.

Because the autobiography is such a critical piece of a student's decision-making process, we provide optional resources: an abbreviated, self-scoring, online Myers-Briggs Inventory (1995; adapted from Keirsey Temperament Sorter); a link to an online Interactive Autobiography guide; and an exercise on "Building Your Autobiography" based on developing recurring themes and significant learnings.

Module 4: Competencies and Targeted Courses

This module uses the metaphor of the goddess of the moon and hunt, Diana, because she never misses her target. At this point, students are reminded about the importance of having their evaluation of transfer credit completed. Faculty typically create an exercise to have students look at the courses they need for graduation and identify which transfer credits have been accepted by UMUC. This is the point where students write their competencies and identify target course equivalents based on their goals and significant learning. As students identify a body of knowledge they feel comfortable writing about, we ask them to look for recurring themes and patterns throughout the process of developing their expertise. Outlining connected and related events maps them for the student, which helps the student to develop the narrative that will be written in the next module. Examples of themes and patterns might be cross-generational parenting methods; variances in management responses to employee needs; connecting one's childhood interests, values, and skills to career, educational, and personal choices; constructive and dysfunctional responses to stress; and the interplay of internal and external political structures on the development of policy.

Module 5: Writing the Narrative

This section uses the Greek Muses as a sign of inspiration. Students are directed to seek their source of inspiration to explain the targeted competencies. Resources for this section include examples of narratives; student tips and faculty videos in different disciplines describing what they are looking for; sections in the course guide that break down courses into delineations in Business Management, Computers, and Behavioral Sciences; and a model student's whole delineation. The exercise "Developing Your Narrative" focuses students on questions to use as a standard throughout the narrative(s).

Module 5 also returns to some of the basic dilemmas of any PLA course, one that we had wrestled with: our concept of learning. Our concept of learning had been evolving from what seemed to be a mystical, elusive force of nature expressed as implied knowledge to something more explicit, measurable, and recognizable to faculty and students. Instead of the faculty discovering the learning, we wanted the students to be explicitly aware of what they had learned. The greatest challenge of the EXCEL course is teaching students how to identify learning experiences and then extract knowledge, principles, and theories from them.

In EXCEL, students do not receive credit for experience but for articulated *learning*. This concept has been one of the most difficult to teach. For example, one student who had worked for over twenty-five years in law enforcement felt that he deserved credit for his experiences because he could not have achieved a high rank without knowing the concepts. In EXCEL, however, this student and all students must spell out what he or she knows.

UMUC awards credit for both applied learning and theoretical understanding. We give credit for learning that is articulated on many levels. Although UMUC accepts competency-based credit such as that awarded through ACE, competencies are only the first step; thus, in writing their academic narratives, we ask students to look beyond their competencies. Similarly, we ask them to look beyond any targeted courses they have identified; students are told not to describe their learning with exact reference to courses, but rather to use them as guidelines for writing about an academic area. The delineation is defined here as a combination of "competencies, targeted courses and academic narrative." An exercise on decision making helps students identify important life decisions and think about what made them successful or unsuccessful to look at knowledge areas, while other exercises help them discuss their knowledge in terms of academic area, targeted courses, methods and techniques, and specific competencies.

According to Sheckley and Keeton (1997), "Research on tacit knowledge suggests that experience helps adults to know that something's going to happen (tacit knowledge) even though they do not 'know' why it's going to happen (explicit knowledge)." We realized early in the development of EXCEL that students were learning intuitively and that somehow we needed to facilitate the process of making the unconscious learning conscious. Because we recognized the complexity of identifying and describing "explicit knowledge," we wanted to create helpful instructional materials. In response to this issue and to the problems we faced in earlier versions of the course, the Web course includes a model to help students get beyond the surface levels and go deeper to uncover and discuss their learning and knowledge. The model has the student ask six questions about an experience:

What did you accomplish?

Where did you do it?

How did you do it? What were your methods?

What was/were the rationale(s) or guiding principles?

What worked, what did not, and why?

How would you generalize it to other settings?

Students are also asked to give specific examples to demonstrate the learning principle from their own experience.

The most significant role of the instructor in every EXCEL course format is to help the student identify and articulate college-level learning, to review drafts and give feedback, and thus to help the student complete the portfolio. EXCEL instructor Anne Kirchgessner understands the importance of carefully reviewing drafts of the students' narratives and providing feedback. She regularly gives students comments that help them to expand their discussions and be precise about what they have learned. For example, in helping a student to think about management contracting principles, she might ask:

> What are the best practices, and how have you learned them through your experiences? Take what you have learned from experience, analyze it, and discuss the guidelines you recommend for best practice. Add vignettes or examples to show your specific involvement and how you gained the learning you are claiming. Think about training seminars and how they helped you do what you are doing. Describe what you learned in these seminars concretely. What are the standards for best practice in this area (field)? Describe the theory and outline the steps to take or the process to accomplish your task. How would you develop a Web page or marketing plan? What are the pros and cons of the processes outlined? Describe concretely and specifically what you have learned. When you say you understand something, define it and give examples.

Other faculty members use their own styles and strategies to guide students in the process. Peter Porosky (2000) tells students to imagine they are writing a textbook in which their experience is being used as an example. Kevin Michel uses a Socratic approach to draw out explicit learning by engaging students in dialogue. He asks them to think about their usual work or professional practice and consider "In what situations would it not work? If it went wrong, what would it be like? What is the worst-case scenario? What would happen if you broke the rule? Would it create better results? If you started over, what would you do differently?"

However, some students need more visual cues to conceptualize how to "extract learning from experience." Our new EXCEL course guide provides a "diamond" model incorporating the six questions above, but expands the process to help the student move from experience to learning in a more detailed fashion. This diamond is part of our careful attempt to provide support to students of differing learning and personality styles with specific hands-on techniques to direct students around Kolb's (1984) learning wheel.

The diamond model divides the process of extracting learning into five phases: (a) "scratching the surface" (course preparation, including evaluating transfer credit, evaluating finances, collecting documentation, and purchasing materials), (b) identifying "learning facets" (developing goals, writing the autobiography, comparing evaluation of transfer credit to autobiography, and identifying significant learning events), (c) "cutting deeper" (defining—accomplishments, implications, methods, what worked, what didn't, and supportive documentation), (d) "hitting the core" (synthesizing information into rationale, philosophies, best practices, and guiding principles), and (e) "polishing and setting the stone" (generalizing the knowledge).

Using Kolb's (1984) learning wheel and Myers-Briggs personality styles (1990) as a base, the assumption was made that students will have different approaches to writing their learning narratives and that EXCEL students will feel more comfortable beginning the writing process in one of the four quadrants: practical/sensing, reaction/feeling, philosophical/intuitive, or analytical/thinking. A set of sample questions was developed for each. For example, a people-oriented person might start writing by asking such questions as "How did you react to the event? How were others affected? Who inspired you to do this? What were the rough spots? Who helped?" The second quadrant would ask about patterns noticed over time and about your beliefs or hunches; the third, about the characteristics of the event and the methods used; and the fourth, about outcomes and how the learning was applied.

Module 6: Documentation

In this module, Libra represents balance of mind, body, spirit, and emotions. This section helps students understand how the documentation supports the narrative and how to provide evidence for evaluators that backs up the knowledge and skills claimed. Students are asked to link their documentation to the text within the narrative and provide a table of contents, and they are given a checklist of possible items to use. Other resources are the course guide, video, and Web videos.

Students can provide various types of documentation to support their academic narratives. Documentation can include photographs, letters from employers, computer programs, newspaper articles and other written materials, videotapes of performances, audiotapes of speaking events, graphic designs, business letters, and training certificates.

Module 7: Assembling the Portfolio

In this module, students' efforts are compared to the twelve labors of Hercules, which were known for being virtually impossible. We tell students, "You have written all of the individual components of your portfolio, and now it is time to put it together." Our intent here is to provide humor and present the assembling of the portfolio as a task that is easier than the trials of Hercules. Instructions are provided for assembling a complete portfolio with the essential components, structure, format, and logistics. The sequence is provided in the Portfolio Checklist, and the Portfolio Submittal form must be submitted with a portfolio for each delineation.

Student Support and the Web-Based EXCEL

As adult educators know, many adult students need a specialized environment that both provides convenience and sensitivity. Our greatest challenge has been to provide sufficient support for students over great distances and through a computer screen. One important step in the development of the Web-based EXCEL course was to try to understand the causes of Web course attrition and to put appropriate interventions into place. We contacted students who withdrew, received an incomplete, or were given an "F." We discovered that students left the course for a variety of reasons, which include not having the time required to do the work in the course, difficulty understanding or managing the task, technical difficulties, job pressures, personal or family illness or death, and divorce. We attacked the retention issue on a number of fronts. We studied the incomplete rates and found that the longer students were given beyond 2–3 months after the end of the course, the *fewer* completed. Interestingly, students now have a shorter incomplete time and we have found that more students are completing.

From the beginning, one important aspect of our design was to ensure personal contact with a mentor in order to balance the potential experience of anonymity and alienation. We provide students with a mentor on the EXCEL staff who contacts them initially and provides support throughout the process. Students are told they can contact the mentor if they encounter any course or technical problems. If faculty identify students who plan to withdraw, the mentor calls to work with the student and help sort out issues. Although most adult students who choose the Web format are very successful, there is a portion of the population that requires more "hand-holding" throughout the process. Close personal connection with students has been most successful in reversing decisions to withdraw.

A third intervention concerns the initial exposure to the course and students' own decisions to register. Through a study of over 450 students, we learned that the EXCEL orientation could be of crucial importance to the process of self-selection, and we therefore focused attention on providing that orientation on a large scale. The orientation includes student testimonials on video, faculty comments, and samples of portfolios. In effect, it encourages students to begin reviewing the instructional materials prior to taking the EXCEL course itself. Equally importantly, initial stages of the course include materials on time-management skills. We saw from experience that many students who did not finish were unable to plan and organize their time. Finally, we have been careful to provide concrete, "hands-on" examples at all stages of the process to show students what successful portfolios looked like, and why.

Challenges

While our students are very successful on the whole, earning an average of nineteen credits, we are devoting our efforts to make the process as tangible as possible so they can maximize their efforts to receive the credits they deserve. UMUC Prior Learning has used many models throughout the years as we continuously refine our program. We are breaking new ground in the area of Web education and are pleased with the great degree of student success. A critical factor in this type of program is faculty training. To ensure quality and consistency, our EXCEL course instructors and over 230 faculty evaluators receive ongoing training and development.

Developing and managing a Web portfolio course presents us with academic, technical, and administrative challenges to ensure a smooth process for students, faculty, and the Prior Learning administration. With a program of this kind, it is essential to have the technical support that UMUC provides with the Webtycho system upon which to build and maintain the course structure. However, even with a sophisticated system, there are technical repairs and inactive links to update that can contribute to some downtime. The asynchronous nature of a Web course creates an increase in e-mail and course discussions that augment the faculty and administrative workload and necessitate developing information and time-management strategies.

It is crucial to student retention that instructional materials are provided that reflect new ways to present models that facilitate extracting learning from experiences and that encompass various learning modalities. By encouraging student and faculty feedback, we can create new responses to ensure consistency, to ensure the highest possible quality, and that can also increase retention rates. (For example, students expressed the need to access whole portfolio samples on the Web, since it was difficult for them to visualize all the parts together.)

Our future efforts will include continuing to track student retention and success rates on the Web to gauge the impact of new practices and instructional materials. It will be essential to continue to simplify the administrative responses for students and faculty. One example is to provide students with a Web portfolio template that provides an interactive structure. By converting binder-bound portfolios to Web-generated documents, efficiencies can be realized for all.

For the moment, and always, we are fortunate to have the support and expertise of UMUC faculty and administration providing the necessary resources we need to pursue the "state of the art."

References

Kolb, D. A. (1984). *Experiential Learning: Experience as the Source of Learning Development*. Englewood Cliffs, NJ: Prentice Hall.

Myers, P., and Briggs I. (1995). *Gifts Differing: Understanding Personality Type*. Palo Alto, CA: Consulting Psychologists Press.

Porosky, P. (2000, March). Correspondence to Theresa A. Hoffmann.

Sheckley, B., and Keeton M. T. (1997). *Improving Employee Development: Perspectives from Research and Practice*. Chicago: CAEL.

UMUC. (1999). *EXCEL Course Guide: Great Possibilities* (6th ed.) Prior Learning in cooperation with Office of Instructional Development, Undergraduate Programs. College Park: University of Maryland University College.

UMUC. (2000). *The EXCEL Course Guide*. Prior Learning in cooperation with Office of Publications, Undergraduate Programs. College Park: University of Maryland University College.

UMUC. (1998). *EXCEL 301: Learning Analysis and Planning* (Web version). (1998). Prior Learning, Undergraduate Programs in cooperation with Office of Instructional Development, College Park: University of Maryland University College.

Yalom, I. (1995). *The Theory and Practice of Group Psychotherapy*. New York: Basic Books.

CORPORATIZING
KNOWLEDGE

WORK-BASED LEARNING AT THE UNIVERSITY
OF TECHNOLOGY, SYDNEY

Nicky Solomon and Julie Gustavs

The Work-Based Learning (WBL) initiatives are part of the University of Technology–Sydney's emphasis on practice-based teaching and the close relationship of the university and the workplace as sites of learning. The curriculum, which can be individualized to meet the needs of particular students and industries, is developed in a three-way partnership consisting of the student, the workplace, and the university. Portfolio development in the WBL program takes place in the context of that three-way partnership as students are planning their degree. In a series of four workshops, students are helped to develop a conceptual understanding of their learning path, plan the degree, and provide evidence of prior learning.

The WBL portfolio-development process is interesting from a number of perspectives. First, it is a notable example of portfolio development and assessment at the postgraduate level. Second, it makes explicit the relationship between work and schooling in the lives of adults, the often unspoken and implicit negotiations that occur between universities and employers, and the power relationships contained therein. Third, it emphasizes that, for working adults, the workplace itself is the major site of learning. "Learners," say Nicky Solomon and Julie Gustavs, "have many opportunities to use their work as a site of learning and as a learning resource. Professional placements, cooperative education arrangements, and practica are available, and many learners are involved in action-learning projects and individual learning contracts in the workplace itself."

The Work-Based Learning (WBL) programs at the University of Technology, Sydney (UTS), are a set of postgraduate[1] programs in which the source of the curriculum is learners' work, work experience, and workplaces rather than academically defined bodies of knowledge. In this model, we will explore the various teaching and learning practices involved in the development of individual learning portfolios at WBL. We will begin with a description of the institutional context of these WBL programs, then provide a detailed discussion of the four daylong workshops through which learners are given educational support to facilitate the development of their programs and portfolios. Finally, we will explore some of the issues that arise from the three-way partnership among learners, employers, and universities.

UTS is one of five technological universities in Australia. UTS was constituted as a university in 1988 as an amalgamation of two colleges of advanced education and an institute of technology. UTS is one of Australia's "new" universities, and its degree offerings and the identity of its academics have been shaped by a different history and a different positioning than that of the older universities in Australia. Specifically, the newness of UTS means that it has not been characterized by conventional disciplinary structures. While these exist at a macrostructural level, the university's image lies in its reputation for practice-based teaching. It describes itself as "a new and progressive university, non-elitist and egalitarian, with a distinctive focus on professional practice" (Blake, 2000). This focus has a number of manifestations. First, UTS has strong partnerships, alignments, and networks with industries and organizations in both the public and private sectors. Second, the student population is predominantly employed and studying part-time.

A third manifestation of our work-based focus is in the way work and professional practices are integrated into almost all programs at UTS. Learners have many opportunities to use their work as a site of learning and as a learning resource. Professional placements, cooperative education arrangements, and practica are available, and many learners are involved in action-learning projects and individual learning contracts in the workplace itself. Further, there is a recognition that learners bring to the learning situation a considerable amount of knowledge and experience that can "count" toward a degree. Therefore prior learning opportunities are recognized and processes have been established for students to claim credit for workplace-based learning. In the main, these claims for recognition are made against existing learning outcomes articulated in subject and course documentation.

---

[1]The term "postgraduate," which is used in most English-speaking countries, is the equivalent of "graduate" in American English.

The WBL initiative offered at UTS sits within this practice-based framework as an extension of existing connections with organizations and the world of work. It takes the notion of partnerships and the focus on work one step further by recognizing not only the importance of situated learning in the professional development of graduate students but also the way in which learning takes place during everyday work. In WBL programs, work *is* the curriculum. This curriculum is individualized and is negotiated within a three-way partnership among the university, the learner, and the workplace.

WBL programs are currently offered at postgraduate level (Master's, Graduate Diploma, and Graduate Certificate) in the Faculties of Education, Business, and Information Technology at UTS. Exhibit C10.1 represents the WBL model we have developed and implemented at UTS.

While space does not allow for a full discussion of the global context of this innovation, it is worthwhile considering why this kind of partnership—an educational partnership that was once inconceivable—now has such a marketable legitimacy (see Boud & Solomon, 2001; Symes & McIntyre, 2000). At a macrolevel, its legitimacy emerges within the broad social, technological, and educational changes that we are all experiencing in our professional as well as everyday lives. These changes entail and indeed rely upon changes in the microprocesses of work, that is, the way in which individuals do their work and relate with one another while accessing and producing knowledge. The emphasis on ongoing skills development and on the workplace as a site of knowledge production is reflected in the contemporary management literature with concepts such as the "learning organization" (Senge, 1990) and the "knowledge worker" (Gee, Hull, & Lankshear 1996; Reich, 1991) as well as in the expanding training industry.

This understanding of the changing nature of work helps to locate the new roles, patterns, and expectations being constructed for each of three partners in educational innovation—that is, the learner, the employer, and the university. And it helps explain why each of them finds a close educational alignment to be an attractive opportunity. A work-based learning program is attractive for learners who are seeking initial or further credentials in order to enhance their employment choices. Many WBL participants have a great deal of scope in their work positions and have many years of on-the-job experience. The WBL degree provides them with the opportunity to gain formal recognition for their learning. WBL also suits learners who want more "relevant" learning and increased choice in delivery modes so that their education can fit into their busy professional and domestic lives.

For employers, the appeal of the partnership is linked to an increasing understanding of the importance of supporting learning practices at work in

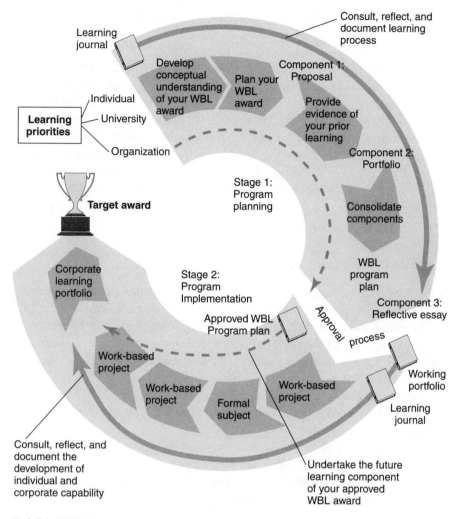

Exhibit C10.1

order to enhance organizational capability at a time of ongoing change and uncertainty. It is an opportunity for organizations to professionalize their workforce in order to be more competitive and to retain their "best" employees. For universities, in turn, WBL is one of many educational responses to political, economic, and social change. Collaboration with employers reaps rewards for universities in terms of their image and success in student recruitment in a fiercely competitive local and international marketplace. Moreover, the focus on work and the individualization of learning programs links to government policy directions in lifelong learning and demonstrates how educational practices have shifted from a stress on teaching to a stress on learning.

While the rhetoric of collaboration, flexibility, and learner choice is appealing, numerous conceptual and practical challenges surface during the implementation of a WBL program. This is inevitable given the fact that the program has to negotiate the particularities of each of the organizational structures and the similar yet different ways the partners talk about and understand learning. These changes have resource implications (such as reduced government funding), but they also problematize conventional understandings of what counts as legitimate "academic" knowledge. Following our description of current practices, we will explore how UTS has responded to these challenges.

Portfolio Development and the WBL Curriculum

WBL comprises two stages: program planning and program implementation. Portfolio development takes place during the program planning stage.

Program planning, the first stage of the WBL degree, is twenty-eight weeks in length. Each learner negotiates a WBL program plan in consultation with his or her line manager and an academic advisor with the relevant content expertise. The program plan comprises three assessment components: a proposal, a portfolio, and a reflective essay. At the end of the twenty-eight-week period, these components are submitted to UTS for approval as an integrated WBL program plan.

The proposal is the "blueprint" for the participant's program plan. It is organized around a number of areas of learning that correlate to the "subjects" in a conventional university degree but that take into account the skills, knowledge, and understandings the learner has and what his or her future learning needs are. Some of these areas of learning correspond to the learner's claim for what we call "recognition of current capability" (RCC) as demonstrated in the portfolio, while others focus on "future learning," which is organized around conventional university subjects and/or work-based projects.

Work on the portfolio begins once the learner has completed a proposal. The portfolio provides a learner with the opportunity to present a case for the formal recognition and assignment of credit points for learning that demonstrates current capabilities. A claim of up to two-thirds of a degree can be made through the portfolio. The portfolio is also a mechanism that facilitates learners' understanding of the relationship between their work and learning. Therefore, the portfolio-development process focuses not only on planning but also on the development of capabilities that go beyond the design of the program and include, for example, the ability to respond actively to the combined learning requirements of the workplace and the university. These require an engagement with academic literacies and practices involved in the negotiation and writing of a WBL program plan that meets degree requirements. In other words, learners need to "translate" their existing knowledge and experience into a form that "counts" in the university.

Finally, prior to submitting their program plan for approval, the learners write a reflective essay that focuses on the learning gained from engaging in stage one of their degree. Upon approval of their WBL program plan, learners undertake the Future Learning component of the proposal developed during the first stage of their degree. Both the formal subjects and work-based projects are linked to specific areas of learning and learning outcomes as outlined in their proposal.

Work-Based Learning Support Strategies

WBL learners have a range of support strategies to assist them in drafting their portfolios and developing and implementing their program plans. First, prior to their commencement of the program, it is important that learners are assisted in managing their expectations. We therefore co-present briefing workshops for potential WBL participants with the WBL coordinator in our partner organizations. On expressing interest, participants and their line managers meet on an individual basis with the WBL coordinator in the organization who discusses a range of issues including the benefits of the WBL program to the individual and the organization and some of the main challenges involved in postgraduate study, including time management and the academic expectations. Strategies are discussed that help both managers and learners prepare for this commitment. These may include discussing study leave offered by the organization and ensuring that the participant has enough scope in his or her work. In some cases, the engagement in a WBL degree is incorporated into the participant's performance agreement at work. The participant and manager also complete a joint application form in which they outline their understanding of the WBL program and reasons for the application. The WBL team at UTS and the WBL management team at the partner organization review applications prior to the participant's acceptance into the program. Any questions that emerge from this review are followed up in further discussions with the applicant and the line manager prior to acceptance in the program.

During the program planning stage, we focus on helping learners gain the conceptual underpinnings for the proposal and portfolio text; on producing the required proposal, portfolio, and reflective essay; and on understanding the interrelationships among the three. Many WBL learners have not undertaken formal study for many years, and this presents a range of challenges. Concerted efforts are made to encourage WBL learners to build their learning support networks from the very outset of their involvement in the WBL program by drawing on the university, their organization, and personal contacts.

The main venues for student support in stage one of the program are the four daylong, face-to-face workshops. Workshops are held for individual client groups, and each group comprises 15–20 WBL learners. The four workshops are intentionally staggered throughout the twenty-eight-week period of stage one to allow learners time to work on drafts of their work. The WBL team at UTS designs and presents the workshop activities. The WBL coordinator from the organization attends all workshops and supports learners during group activities. The workshops are organized around the four processes in program planning.

Workshop 1. Develop a conceptual understanding of your WBL degree

This workshop occurs in the first week of the WBL program. Its main purpose is to provide learners with conceptual understandings of their WBL degree.

Workshop 2. Plan your WBL degree

The second workshop occurs in week five of the program. Its main purpose is to provide learners with the opportunity to consolidate their evolving understandings of the WBL degree and to focus on the development of the proposal component of their degree.

Workshop 3. Provide evidence of prior learning

In week fifteen of the WBL program, learners attend the third workshop. The main purpose is to further consolidate their understandings of their degree and to focus on the development of the portfolio.

Workshop 4. Consolidate the components of your WBL program plan

In week twenty-two of the WBL program, learners attend a final workshop. The main purpose of this final workshop is to refine the work they have done on their WBL degree and to focus on the development of the reflective essay.

Between the four workshops, participants work through readings and a series of writing tasks that scaffold the development of each of the components of the WBL program plan.[2] Learners are also encouraged to consult with their academic advisor and their line manager, whose respective roles are to ensure that the learner's developing WBL program plan both aligns with university standards and reflects organizational learning priorities.

Finally, learners are engaged in online group discussions. There are both formal and informal spaces for learners to discuss their evolving WBL program plans. UTS advisors, the organization-based WBL coordinators, and the WBL team at UTS take turns to field questions and promote discussion. Given the limited face-to-face support, online learning is a valuable community-building mechanism and can assist participants to engage in peer learning.

The support strategies discussed above are designed to help participants meet a number of challenges and make a number of shifts in their understanding of learning. The first of these challenges is to help learners understand how experience relates to learning. Many WBL learners do not have a clear understanding of what learning is when they begin their WBL program. They tend to understand learning as what one does in classrooms, and they explain their life and work experiences in terms of undertaking tasks rather than the learning those tasks represent. Support strategies for the workshops have therefore been designed to help learners to build the necessary theoretical understanding of learning and to encourage them to reframe their understanding of their life and work experiences as learning rather than as the achievement of tasks.

The second challenge is to help learners gain a holistic understanding of their WBL degree. We have found that if learners invest a great deal of time creating a proposal or portfolio prior to gaining that holistic understanding, it can be especially difficult to shift their mindset and encourage them to write further drafts of work. This can result in a poorly conceptualized WBL program plan. Further, learners need to understand that the WBL degree represents both *what they already know* and *what they need to know*, represented respectively by the portfolio and the Future Learning component of the WBL program plan. In each case, learners also need to identify appropriate titles for each of the areas of learning that will make up their degree.

---

[2]Initially, time frames for the completion of writing tasks were more flexible to accommodate the contingencies of the individual learner's work; however, we found that flexibility in fact impeded their progression through the WBL program. We have since established set time lines and milestones to help them to bring their WBL program plan to completion within the twenty-eight-week period.

Finally, the third challenge is to help learners understand the purpose of the portfolio and implications for the presentation of their case for an RCC claim. In the workshops and in the workbook, learners are provided with an electronic template for the portfolio component as well as an accompanying text to assist them to understand how to structure their WBL portfolio.

The Four Program Planning Workshops

Workshop One: Develop a Conceptual Understanding of Your WBL Degree

The key focus of Workshop One is to help learners begin to grapple conceptually with the idea of learning in general and the WBL degree in particular. Workshop One therefore focuses on an understanding of the difference between experience and learning.

We usually begin by having a short discussion about what reflection means and the relationship between learning and experience. This is useful, as it provides the facilitators with a clear idea about the conceptions the group has. At this stage, the main outcome is to encourage learners to share their thoughts and engage with the topic. We may record the group's ideas on a mind map to help learners to see similarities and differences between various responses.

Many learners find reflection to be a somewhat dubious idea that does not relate to them. To challenge this view, we show learners comments from prior students. For example:

> It is worth noting, perhaps even confessing, that I was not initially sold on the idea of reflection as a legitimate learning process. To my ignorant ears it sounded like a cheap academic trick to fool us experienced, work-hardened professionals, and a complete waste of "real learning." I am glad to say that I had the sense to persevere because I soon came to realize that it was not just an essential part of the program but is now a valuable weapon in my armory which will prepare me better for future learning. (WBL learner, reflective essay, 2000)

Reflection on learning gained from experience is very personal and can be a confrontative process. To gain trust from the learners and also to scaffold the next learning experience, we usually share a story about something we have learnt from our own work of developing and implementing WBL programs at UTS. We then give learners about twenty minutes to write a short reflection of what they have learnt from an experience at work. To help guide their writing, we give them the following questions:

What did the experience involve?

What do you think you learnt?

What did it feel like?

How has it changed the way you think about and do your work?

Is there further related learning that you still need to do?

Learners then share these ideas in small groups. After approximately twenty minutes, we ask learners to refer to their workbook, which gives some advice about reflective writing. Based on the work of Hatton and Smith (1995), it provides one useful way of recognizing different types of writing—descriptive writing, descriptive reflection, and critical reflection.

Descriptive writing is not reflective. It simply describes events and does not attempt to provide reasons for these events or thoughts about their implications. Descriptive writing is useful for recalling what happened, and we'd expect that learners' reflections would include it, but we stress that description alone is not adequate for the critical reflection we expect WBL learners to engage in throughout the WBL program.

> I'm now up to my tenth meeting with the client about the contract. My last meeting was terrible. After the meeting, I talked about it with a colleague who has had a lot more experience in negotiating contracts. She has given me some advice—build on the relationship with the client.

Descriptive reflection includes both a description of events and some reasons for why they occurred. At a more sophisticated level, it might involve using perspectives from external sources to provide these reasons. Again, it is not yet adequate for the critical reflection we expect, but it's closer:

> I'm now up to my tenth meeting with the client about the contract. There is now building animosity between us. This is terrible. I couldn't see my way out of the meeting. We seem to just get bogged down with nitpicking about the wording and passing it from our legal to their legal and back again. It's costing a packet, it's all too time consuming, and plus I can't see where it will all end—probably in losing the contract! I finally decided to talk to a colleague of mine and she was really helpful. She said, "Contracts are so often thought of as a written document but they are really about building and maintaining relationships." She also invited me to sit in on an initial meeting she had with a client to negotiate a contract.

Critical reflection (as in conducting a dialogue with yourself) involves a greater stepping back from events and exploring alternative explanations and courses of action in context. The writing might make more connections with a range of perspectives from the literature and other sources, might begin to reflect back on earlier reflections and challenge earlier assumptions. This is characteristic of the **critical reflection** that we hope your reflections will include.

> After talking to a colleague and watching her set up a contract with a new client, I developed a different perspective on negotiating contracts. I had assumed that somehow I always got landed with the difficult clients that seemed so nitpicky about the wording. I can see a pattern now in the contracts that I have negotiated—I develop a draft contract stipulating our terms of the agreement prior to the initial meeting with the client. I always thought this would seem professional and speed up the process. I realise that another way of thinking about this is that this way of establishing the process doesn't really allow the client to feel ownership for the document. We also usually meet in my office. I've come to realise that space is a really important consideration in negotiating contracts—perhaps we should meet on neutral grounds—possibly even in a more informal setting so that we can feel more relaxed and really work on understanding each other. I always have legal there from the outset too. I thought this was a good idea because it ensured that we were covered right from the start. My colleague by contrast didn't have a document prepared for the initial meeting but rather spent the entire time in the first meeting really clarifying what the client wanted and what we wanted out of the partnership. She also established what both parties will bring to the table. This was all minuted and agreed to before legal was brought into the picture. Negotiating contracts, in this sense, is about building trust relationships.

In the next stage of the small-group activity, participants discuss their own writing in the light of three types of writing outlined above and are encouraged to understand the relationship between each type of writing and its context, purpose, and audience. Workshop One typically includes a group discussion focusing on how and why we should aim to develop a more critical approach to writing about our learning experiences. From this point, we progress to a discussion of different theorists and their conceptions of reflection. The range of readings in the workbook includes selections from Anderson, Boud, Cohen, and Sampson, "Students' Guide to Learning Partnerships" (1998); Binney and Williams, *Learning into the Future: Changing the Way People Change Organizations* (1997) ; Boud, Keogh, and Walker, *Reflection: Turning Experience into Learning* (1985); and Senge, *The Fifth Discipline: Practice of the Learning Organization* (1990).

Many WBL learners have not read scholarly journal articles and other academic texts for some time, if at all. Hence, they may feel quite daunted by reading and understanding these more theoretical materials. A useful scaffolding activity is to do a jigsaw reading task as a workshop activity. This involves learners reading different sections of chapters in a text and explaining ideas discussed in small groups. Learners are encouraged to discuss the extent to which they disagree or agree with the ideas presented by the authors. After the workshop, learners undertake a number of writing tasks. The first writing task requires learners to reflect on the learning they can expect to gain from undertaking a WBL award with reference to their understanding of the readings and the workshop discussion. This involves identifying the shifts in thinking that underpin the Work-Based learning program. Other writing tasks include identifying supportive and potentially disruptive influences impacting the successful completion of their program, beginning their learning journal, and starting to work on identifying the learning focus for their degree. This involves locating relevant sources of information that will help them to identify the learning priorities of each of the three stakeholders in the WBL program. This may include documents or relevant people, that is, business plans, performance agreements, and CVs. Between Workshops One and Two, responses to writing tasks are discussed and refined with advisors, and in online discussion groups.

Workshop Two: Plan Your WBL Degree

In Workshop Two, we help learners to consolidate their understanding of the link between learning and experience by asking them to construct a time line of their learning from prior work experiences. We provide learners with an extract from a learner's time line detailing a number of educational, work-based, and other relevant experiences (Exhibit C10.2). First we talk about the current roles and recent courses attended by the participant and then unpack the key themes of learning that each of these experiences entails. This encourages people to think of how they have gained knowledge from a range of experiences and the connection between disparate experiences.

Learners then work in pairs and help each other to gain a feel for what they have learnt from specific work, education, and other relevant experiences. For this task to work well, it is useful to inform learners prior to the workshop to bring a copy of their Curriculum Vitae (CV) and other relevant resources. Referring to the resources, they ask each other questions such as:

What is your current work position?

What are some of the major roles and responsibilities in your job?

What are the broad themes of learning in these roles/responsibilities?

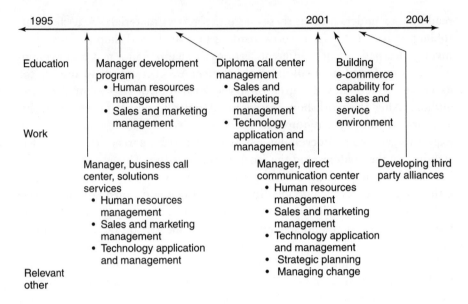

Exhibit C10.2

Can you see similar themes of learning in previous work positions?

How has your learning in your current job built on your learning in previous positions?

What educational experiences have you undertaken that relate to your work?

Have these experiences built on the learning themes that you identified in your current and/or previous jobs? How?

In constructing their time lines, students also focus on their "future learning." They add this dimension to their time line by analyzing their business plans, other strategic documents, and a personal list of learning and career goals that they have identified in one of the writing tasks in between Workshops One and Two. Learners find this to be a very rich learning experience. They have not generally reflected on their skills, knowledge, and understandings so deeply and linked them explicitly either to what they already know or to what they need to learn to improve their work practices and facilitate their career development. After they have completed their time lines, we conduct a whole-group activity in which learners discuss the types of questions that helped them to reflect critically on their experience, explore their findings, and develop the specific components of their WBL program plan.

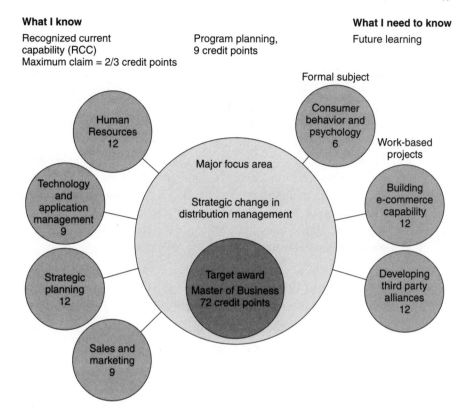

What I know

Recognized current
capability (RCC)
Maximum claim = 2/3 credit points

Program planning,
9 credit points

What I need to know

Future learning

Formal subject

Human Resources
12

Consumer behavior and psychology
6

Work-based projects

Major focus area

Technology and application management
9

Strategic change in distribution management

Building e-commerce capability
12

Strategic planning
12

Target award
Master of Business
72 credit points

Developing third party alliances
12

Sales and marketing
9

Exhibit C10.3

To continue to develop a holistic understanding of their degree, learners undertake an activity in Workshop Two in which they are asked to develop a concept map for their degree. As a scaffolding activity, learners analyze a sample concept map and discuss it in groups. As guides to this exercise, they use two taxonomies provided by the university, one that describes various levels of learning and another that indicates the required distribution of credit points. A sample concept map is included in Exhibit C10.3.

Naming the major focus area and RCC as well as future areas of learning in the degree is a vital part of the program-planning process and one that learners generally confront with both excitement and angst. These feelings are explicitly acknowledged and reflected on in the workshop discussions. Key points raised are that the "naming" of subjects in conventional university degrees is generally beyond a student's control. It is done for them by the lecturer. By "naming" the titles of the areas of learning in their degree, they are taking control of its shape and thus the construction of past and future perspectives of their learning. It is emphasized that this is a very valuable learning experience in itself, and one that has allowed many WBL learners to develop capabilities that equip them to be both more autonomous learners within UTS and "knowledge workers" at the workplace.

Following the development of their own concept map, learners work in pairs to focus on the areas of learning that they identified as forming part of their claim for RCC. Again by asking questions, they help each other tease out the justification for including these areas of prior learning in their program plan. This work is preliminary: The development of the RCC portfolio is the subject of Workshop Three, and at this point in the process the answers are not as important as the questions, which are recorded and shared in a group discussion. Questions usually include the following:

> What do you mean by the title of this area of learning?
>
> What learning does this area of learning represent?
>
> How have you demonstrated this learning?
>
> What evidence do you have for this area of learning?
>
> How do you intend to gain this "future learning"?

The questions that the group has identified are noted by learners and are used as a guide to refine their concept map in subsequent independent writing tasks. Participants also work in groups to analyze samples of participants' proposals, using the criteria outlined in the workbook to discuss the strengths and areas of improvement. One particular challenge is to help participants to write learning outcomes for each of their areas of learning. To help them with this process, we have developed a formula that is as follows:

Learning verb + content + context + purpose

We also provide participants with samples of learning outcomes from participants' work and a series of "learning verbs" with which they may choose to commence their learning outcomes as follows:

Knowledge

"I am able to *state/outline/recall/identify/list/enumerate* . . . (for example) the key principles of . . ."

Understanding

"I can *describe/discuss/explain/clarify/identify . . .*"

Application

"I can *illustrate/demonstrate/apply/relate/adapt . . .*"

Analysis

"I know how to *distinguish/contrast/compare/calculate/analyze . . .*"

Synthesis

"I am able to *organize/synthesize . . .*"

Evaluation

"I know how to *evaluate/appraise/assess/review . . .*"

Abstraction

"I know how to *generalize/hypothesize/theorize/transfer/reflect . . .*"

Workshop Three: Provide Evidence of Prior Learning

In Workshop Three, an additional group activity again focuses learners on the link between learning and experience. Each group is given a statement that relates to learning and experience, for example:

Learning can be gained from positive and negative experiences.

Learning is dependent on the diversity of your experiences not necessarily on the time spent on gaining the experience.

Learning that results from an experience may be unintentional.

Learning needs to align with the level of your target degree.

Reflection on learning can be used to integrate quite disparate experiences.

Learners are asked to discuss the meaning of each statement with other members of their group. They are also asked to refer to their CV and to relate examples from their own experience. Explanations of these statements and a related writing task are provided in the workbook to help learners consolidate the learning that they gained from the workshop activity.

It is in Workshop Three that we most centrally address the task of compiling a portfolio. Although a portfolio can be presented in a variety of ways, we have found that it is very important to provide learners with clear guidelines as to how to structure their portfolio. In Workshop Three, therefore, learners critically review a sample of a learner's portfolio. They focus on its strengths and on the ways in which it could be improved. Analysis of a

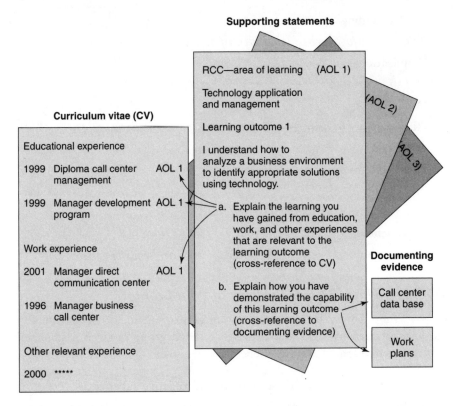

Supporting statements

RCC—area of learning   (AOL 1)

Technology application
and management   (AOL 2)

(AOL 3)

Learning outcome 1

I understand how to
analyze a business environment
to identify appropriate solutions
using technology.

a. Explain the learning you
   have gained from education,
   work, and other experiences
   that are relevant to the
   learning outcome
   (cross-reference to CV)

b. Explain how you have
   demonstrated the capability
   of this learning outcome
   (cross-reference to
   documenting evidence)

Curriculum vitae (CV)

Educational experience

1999   Diploma call center   AOL 1
       management

1999   Manager development   AOL 1
       program

Work experience

2001   Manager direct   AOL 1
       communication center

1996   Manager business
       call center

Other relevant experience

2000   *****

Documenting evidence

Call center
data base

Work
plans

Exhibit C10.4

sample portfolio is a useful strategy to help learners to think about ways of constructing their own portfolio.

Exhibit C10.4 illustrates the structure of the portfolio and the relationship between the three parts it comprises. The three parts of the portfolio are discussed next.

The Curriculum Vitae

The CV provides the assessor with a broad, chronological overview of the participant's whole career, including brief descriptions of education, work, and other relevant experience (i.e., when, where, and how the learning was acquired). Where relevant, participants cross-reference the areas of learning in their RCC claim.

Supporting Statements for Each Area of Learning Included in the RCC Claim

The supporting statements are the most important part of the portfolio. They provide the assessor with a strong case demonstrating the participant's achievement of the learning outcomes for each of the areas of learning (AOLs) in his or her claim for RCC. They also link each of the three parts of the portfolio together. They elaborate on key learning experiences outlined in the CV and explain the documenting evidence.

Reshaping the CV generally poses few problems for the participants. Most participants have a fairly recent CV that they have developed for work purposes; we use this as a base in the workshop to discuss ways in which it needs to be reshaped in order to meet the purposes of the WBL program. This involves restructuring the CV in terms of educational, work, and other relevant experiences and briefly outlining the key learning experiences that will be further elaborated on in the supporting statements.

A Comprehensive Record of Documenting Evidence for Each Area of Learning Included in the RCC Claim

Participants need to provide the assessor with tangible evidence of the learning they have gained for each AOL in their claim for RCC. In selecting documenting evidence that will support their RCC claim, learners first have to understand what documenting evidence they can draw on. Such evidence can be direct or indirect. Some examples taken from work include financial forecasts, work plans, and training materials. Indirect documenting evidence refers to documents that conventionally signify the value of learning. This includes certificates, awards, references, and evaluations.

One particularly useful activity to help learners to clarify the documenting evidence to be included in their portfolio is to develop a matrix for each area of learning and its four to five learning outcomes. The box, "Area of Learning 1 in Claim for RCC," is provided in the workbook as a guide.

The workshops stress that it is not enough for participants to simply include unsupported documenting evidence in their portfolio. It is important to explain why they chose this evidence, how it is relevant to their portfolio, and in what ways it demonstrates their capability in the specified area of learning. The site for this explanation is in their supporting statements. It is often quite difficult to help participants to see that the evidence does not "speak for itself." To help participants come to this realization, we ask them each to bring a piece of evidence that they plan to use in their portfolio claim. In groups, they focus on one person's evidence. In the first part of the

Area of Learning 1 in Claim for RCC

Electronic Information Systems Design

	Education		Work		Other relevant experience	
	Direct documenting evidence	Indirect documenting evidence	Direct documenting evidence	Indirect documenting evidence	Direct documenting evidence	Indirect documenting evidence
Learning outcome 1 Understand how to analyze a business environment to identify appropriate technology-based solutions and the like.	Screen dumps of interface of a call-center database	Diploma: call-center management	Work plans: outlining detailed needs analysis.	Gold Champions award certificate from CEO	Reflection on a range of relevant readings	—
Learning outcome 2, 3, and so on						

activity, all group members (including the person whose evidence it is) write down what they think can be assumed about the learning achieved from the evidence as it stands. In the second part of the activity, group members are encouraged to ask the person whose evidence it is to provide the group with information about the learning that the evidence demonstrates. One person in the group acts as the scribe writing the questions that the group asked. Following this activity, we discuss the questions and also the discrepancy between the assumptions made by the group leader and other members. We then consider that the assessor would be in a very similar position to other members of the group who in many cases could ascertain very little about the learning that the evidence showed without the further explanation gained by the group on asking key questions. This leads into the discussion on the role of the supporting statements in the portfolio.

Learners are required to develop a supporting statement for each of the areas of learning in their claim for RCC. Learners generally find the writing of supporting statements to be the most difficult part of the portfolio. The supporting statements form the site for the argument they present to convince the assessor that they have an understanding of each of the learning outcomes for the areas of learning in their RCC claim. To explain the purpose of the supporting statements, learners are provided with the analogy of a lawyer presenting a case. This analogy is useful because it helps participants to understand that evidence can not stand alone. The strength of the case is built around how convincingly the lawyer can explain the relevance of the evidence in demonstrating his or her argument. WBL learners write drafts of supporting statements as a workshop activity and peer review each other's work. Where possible, we make explicit links with previous activities they have done that can help them to write the supporting statements, that is, the critical reflective writing task in Workshop One and the construction of the timeline in Workshop Two.

Workshop Four: Consolidate the Components of Your WBL Degree

This final workshop focuses on the peer assessment of the work participants have undertaken thus far and also on gaining an overview of what to write in their reflective essay. In workshop groups, we discuss the challenges that the WBL program has involved and what participants learnt from these challenges.

Conclusion

Portfolios have become one of the key pedagogical devices that are both cause and effect of the increasing legitimization of the relationship between work experiences and learning. Indeed Work-Based Learning at UTS is motivated around this relationship, and the development of individual portfolios is an integral component of these degrees. As described in this chapter, portfolio development in WBL degrees is a process through which individual learners make credit claims for the recognition of their current capabilities (prior learning). But, importantly, it is also a process that facilitates the learner's understanding of the relationship between his or her work and learning.

While the relationship between an individual's work and his or her learning has become almost common sense, however, its realization is a complex one. The boundaries between being an employer and being a student, between educational institutions and organizations, have become more permeable, but the emerging overlaps are complex. The language for thinking about and describing one's work at the workplace is not necessarily the same language that is used in universities for thinking about and describing learning. Moreover, once learning is articulated and once it becomes managed and institutionalized, any notion of an unproblematic view of the relationship between being a worker and a learner needs to be challenged.

As we have attempted to demonstrate in this chapter, at UTS we are confronting the challenges. We do so by developing teaching and learning strategies that focus on learning a new language for describing oneself—a language that has currency in both organizations and universities. These strategies are not only relevant to learners. They are also part of a process that is contributing to the development of new professional identities as academics also struggle with many challenges when working in these new programs. At the same time, the design and delivery of WBL programs invariably create epistemological and political tensions. The emergence of these tensions is not surprising given the layers of relationships that are intrinsic to this program and the very different histories and understandings of each of the partners.

For many years, universities have had "business" relationships with organizations, and indeed for many years work practices have been incorporated into students' learning. Yet in this kind of collaborative program, the knowledge discourses and structures taken for granted in more conventional academic programs are in a process of change. The new knowledges and the shifting power relations, while inevitable, disturb not just the nature of the learning but also the systems and policies of universities and the way academics understand themselves and their work.

At the beginning of the chapter, we drew attention to the seductive nature of WBL programs. We described the appeal for each of the partners—the university, the students, and their workplaces. Perhaps the phrase "openness of disciplinary boundaries" best captures the feature that makes it so attractive. Yet it is the very openness of the boundaries that is the cause and effect of many of the complexities and contradictions of work-based learning programs.

Even within a university that foregrounds professional practice, many academics view WBL as problematic. While they may have worked with organizations and employees previously, most often their relationship with the "real" world has been more or less on their own terms. They articulate their concerns in several ways. They describe WBL as an unwelcome symptom of the corporatization of the university and the accompanying loss of the university's status as a primary knowledge producer in contemporary society. They describe their resentment of the increased scrutiny by the university of their everyday work and fear an additional layer of surveillance by the partnership organization. It is not surprising, then, that some academics respond to these new innovations by resisting participation.

However, some academics do take up the opportunity to participate, but in doing so many also struggle with their new roles in WBL programs. Many are confronted by the inadequacy or irrelevance of their disciplinary knowledge and express regret at the loss of their existing expertise and of their previous certainties of their roles and responsibilities. These concerns call for a number of additional strategies. At UTS such strategies involve the design of professional development programs for academics. These programs not only focus on the new ways of teaching and learning in these programs but they also provide a site of debate about the place of disciplinary knowledge in the programs and the accompanying power and control issues.

As described early, many students are drawn to the program by the apparent freedom to develop individual programs that are based on their existing knowledge and experience as well as their current work projects. However, giving students this degree of responsibility often presents a number of challenges. As the majority of students do not have the course design experience of educators, the size and complexity of designing one's own program can be daunting. In addition, unlike in conventional programs, there is little institutional separation between work and university learning in work-based learning programs and thus between the roles of employee and learner. This is manifested in students' relationship with their work supervisor and academic advisor, at times complicated by different expectations. Students and their supervisors need adequate preparation and support in order to work with these complexities. Initial preparation includes participating in information sessions that realistically present the nature of their responsibility.

While partnerships are described as flexible and negotiable, there are limitations to the degree of flexibility. It is essential that the roles and responsibilities of all the partners are negotiated and articulated before the program begins. At UTS we have found that management's desire to be involved in the delivery reduces as the program becomes part of their overall human resource development program. However, if workplace supervisors and management withdraw altogether, care needs to be taken so that academics resist the desire to retreat into conventional subjects and ways of being.

References

Anderson, G., Boud, D., Cohen, R., and Sampson, J. (1998). "Students' Guide to Learning Partnerships." In *Peer Learning: A Guide for Staff and Students.* Sydney: University of Technology Sydney.

Binney, G., and Williams, C. (1997). *Learning into the Future: Changing the Way People Change Organizations.* London: Nicholas Brealey Publishing.

Blake, T. (2000). "Planning and Review Unit." UTS public documents. Sydney: University of Technology, Sydney.

Boud, D., Keogh R., and Walker, D. (1985). *Reflection: Turning Experience into Learning.* London: Kogan Page.

Boud, D., and Solomon, N., eds. (2001). *Work-Based Learning: A New Higher Education?* Milton Keynes, UK: Open University Press.

Gee, J., Hull, G., and Lankshear, C. (1996). *New Work Order: Behind the Language of the New Capitalism.* Crows Nest, NSW, Australia: Allen & Unwin.

Hatton, N., and Smith, D. (1995). "Reflection in Teacher Education: Towards Definition and Implementation." *Teaching and Teacher Education* 11(1), 33–49.

Reich, R. (1991). *The Work of Nation: Preparing Ourselves for 21st Century Capitalism.* New York: Knopf.

Senge, P. M. (1990). *The Fifth Discipline: Practice of the Learning Organization.* New York: Doubleday.

Senge, P. M., et al. (1994). *The Fifth Discipline Fieldbook: Strategies and Tools for Building a Learning Organization.* London: Nicholas Brealey Publishing.

Symes, C., and McIntyre, J., eds. (2000). *Working Knowledge: New Vocationalism in Higher Education.* Milton Keynes, UK: Open University Press.

AFTER APARTHEID

THE RECOGNITION OF PRIOR LEARNING AT THE COLLEGE OF EDUCATION, UNIVERSITY OF THE WITWATERSRAND

Ruksana Osman

The assessment of workers' experiential learning was placed on the national agenda soon after the election of Nelson Mandela and South Africa's transition to democracy. Its stated goals were to help redress the education and wage gap between white and Black South Africans that was one of the major legacies of apartheid. Because of this, the slow implementation of the "recognition of prior learning" has both institutional and social dimensions and is a contested and deeply political terrain.

The Johannesburg College of Education, now part of the University of the Witwatersrand, is typical of the changes to apartheid-era institutions under the new dispensation, including the merger of student bodies across historical racial lines, the imperative to upgrade the skills of those historically denied access to quality education, and the centrality of the relationship between adult learning and social change. As Ruksana Osman says of the early government policy documents, "Through the White Paper, the government indicated that RPL was not just another innovation in education. It was one of the key mechanisms that would bring about educational and vocational redress and contribute to social justice." The South African experience is thus an important case in point of themes that vitalize the assessment of prior learning in all parts of the world.

Acknowledgment: I would like to thank Dr. Jane Castle for comments on an earlier draft of this essay.

Origins of RPL: The South African Education Policy Agenda

In South Africa, the recognition of prior learning (RPL) has emerged in the context of wider societal change. In particular, RPL appeared on the African National Congress (ANC) policy agenda in response to proposals from the Congress of South African Trade Unions (COSATU). COSATU, which has been at the forefront of workers' struggles in South Africa and has championed the rights of workers for education and training, believed that workers could improve their wages and achieve better job grading through RPL.

To this end, COSATU influenced the proposals made in the White Paper on Education and Training released by the postapartheid government in 1995. In particular, the union called for the restructuring and transformation of the education and training system that, under the apartheid government, served to systematically entrench racial inequalities in terms of access to both education and better paying jobs. The trade unions proposed RPL as an intervention through which a large number of experienced workers could be granted a formal qualification based on their experiential learning in order to obtain better wages and access new educational opportunities. In effect, RPL was seen as a tool to narrow the wage and education gap left by the educational system of apartheid (Cooper, 1998).

As is well known, under apartheid, systematic policies of injustice and unequal distribution permeated every aspect of life from employment, to education, to where one could live. To illustrate, the Bantu Urban Areas Act of 1945 was introduced to prevent Blacks[1] from moving into the cities to seek work. The Group Areas Act ensured that Black people could only reside in designated areas, usually far from cities and places of work. The Registration for Employment Act of 1945, and later the In-Service Training Act of 1979, effectively excluded Blacks from opportunities for advancement in the jobs which they occupied.

The Nationalist Party government of the apartheid era (1948–1992) created a system of schooling that produced unskilled and semiskilled workers to serve the labor requirements of an unjust society based on differences of race and class (Christie & Collins, 1984). Education under apartheid was characterized by a racially fragmented framework consisting of separate education departments within the school system for each "race." The education system was used as a tool to maintain and justify oppressive practices. By

---

[1]The term "Black" is used in the context of apartheid and it refers to Indians, Coloureds, and Africans (people that were classified as nonwhite under apartheid).

underfunding education for Blacks and by making education compulsory for white and not for Black children, the apartheid government in effect barred the majority of South Africans from substantive formal education. In cases in Which Black South Africans did manage to complete primary and secondary education, the Extension of the University Education Act of 1959 ensured that students could only attend universities designated for a particular racial group. The passing of this act meant that a Black student could not register at a white university without ministerial consent.

While 1994 brought the first democratic election in our country and a president revered by the world, for the majority of South Africans the economic and the psychological damage caused by apartheid education still lingers (Seepe, 2000, p. 53). Seepe cites Steve Biko[2] on the damage of apartheid education: "In order to destroy completely the structures that were built in the African society and to impose their imperialism with unnerving totality the colonialists were not satisfied merely with holding a people in their grip and emptying the Native's brain of all form and content, they turned to the past of the oppressed people and distorted, disfigured and destroyed it" (2000, pp. 53–54).

This systematic policy of inequality in education, coupled with a policy of undermining the very fabric of African society, has resulted in a situation in which the majority of South Africans have had an incomplete primary and high school education and poor chances of competing in the job market. Discriminatory practices in education were mirrored in the workplace where a policy of so-called job reservation ensured that only whites could occupy particular jobs. This policy also prevented Black workers from obtaining any on-the-job training and restricted the mobility of Black workers in favor of white workers. Presently, South Africa faces an ever-growing unemployment rate. It is the semi- and unskilled workers who bear the brunt of job losses in an economy that favors skilled labor. The legacy of such policies can still be felt today as our young democracy tries to meet competing imperatives of global competition and social justice.

---

[2]Steve Biko, a medical student, was the charismatic leader of the Black Consciousness Movement in South Africa. He was outspoken about the brutality of apartheid and the need for Black people to free themselves economically, psychologically, and socially from the shackles of apartheid and colonial domination. So compelling and unifying was Biko as a leader and Black Consciousness as an ideology that the apartheid police detained him. He died in detention as a direct result of police brutality in September 1980.

Thus, COSATU's proposal for RPL must be seen as a strategy for narrowing this economic gap and for enabling workers to regain their dignity through the recognition of knowledge and skills acquired in the workplace and elsewhere. It was part of a vision that saw education and training as an integrated system that allows mobility from workplace into the university and back into the workplace with improved wages and job prospects. The recognition of knowledge and skills acquired by the workers in contexts other than formal education was central to this model. It sought to validate worker's knowledge as worthwhile knowledge that was worth accrediting in formal contexts such as higher education. As the White Paper on Education and Training (Department of Education, 1995) described it, RPL could "open doors of opportunity for people whose academic or career paths were needlessly blocked because their prior knowledge has not been assessed or certified" (p. 15).

Through the White Paper, the government indicated that RPL was not just another innovation in education. It was one of the key mechanisms that would bring about educational and vocational redress and contribute to social justice. Because of these bold claims, many in South Africa question the capacity of RPL to deliver. Such questioning is especially poignant in an environment like higher education in South Africa, which has a discourse that is distinct from that of the world of work, only has experience with a conventionally aged student body, and generally uses traditional pedagogies implemented by some academics who have limited experience with the academic, personal, and professional needs of adult learners. Clearly, there are many issues that need to be addressed.

Changes in Higher Education in South Africa

Higher education in South Africa, as elsewhere in the world, is under pressure to reinvent and transform itself. Traditionally, it has enjoyed financial support from the government and an autonomous existence. However, recent postapartheid policy changes have required that universities respond to a National Plan (Ministry of Education, 2001) generated by the Ministry of Education that commits them to become cost-effective, streamlined institutions that compete for a dwindling pool of school leavers who qualify for university study.[3] Universities are required to generate strategies that broaden

---

[3]Admission to a university in South Africa is determined by a twelve-year school-based qualification. In the twelfth year of study, matriculation, a candidate is required to pass six subjects on the higher grade to obtain a matriculation exemption.

access routes for disadvantaged groups and at the same time consider curriculum strategies that ensure success to such groups after access. In addition to these daunting challenges, the higher education sector has experienced a decrease in government funding at a time at which national policy is calling for institutions that are responsive to the academic and the vocational needs of the economy and society. Moreover, these institutions are now in direct competition with overseas universities that have established themselves in South Africa. In response to these contextual circumstances and in sharp contrast to the more traditional model of university education in this country, universities across South Africa are having to consider the introduction of vocational qualifications to complement traditional discipline-based academic qualifications. However implicitly, the introduction of such vocational qualifications has required us to engage with the idea of "other knowledges" (such as the practical and the experiential) entering into the university—and with the acceptance of "other" students, too.

It is clear that, given such a context, RPL is gaining a more important profile in at least some institutions in higher education. Coupled with the recognition of such an achievement, however, is the concern that some institutions may use RPL as a competitive, market-driven tool while systematically overlooking the redress and social justice agenda that RPL promises (Buchler, 1999). Others have continued to caution that "the wedding of RPL to a progressive social vision is not automatic" (Michelson, 1999, p. 100).

RPL as a Contested and Controversial Practice

Given the contextual features of the terrain of higher education in South Africa, it is no surprise that RPL is emerging as a contested and controversial practice (Osman & Castle, 2001). First, there is the basic epistemological challenge inherent in the recognition of prior experiential learning. There are those who are critical of RPL and challenge the "site" of knowledge production (everyday life and the workplace), the nature and quality of the knowledge produced there, and its currency in higher education (Breier, 1996; Shalem, 2001). These writers assert that even if such knowledge were allowed into the academy, it would be impossible to agree upon how it could be placed within pre-established academic curricula that are themselves based on strongly held disciplinary assumptions.

A second related issue emerging in this debate on the nature of "real" knowledge relates to the social relations inherent in the assessment process itself. Critics of RPL have suggested that the recognition of prior learning requires an assessor to find broad equivalencies between academic knowledge and practical knowledge. Furthermore, throughout the entire RPL process, a third person, the mentor, is called upon to provide assistance to the student in the articulation of that knowledge. It is the mentor who enables the student to present her practical knowledge by giving it a conceptual frame. The critics have thus asked: "Whose knowledge is it if it was re-framed and re-presented through mentoring? Is it the RPL candidate's or the RPL mentor's?" (Shalem, 2001).

Thus in both the epistemological and the social relational domains, RPL practices and the philosophical ideals that propel them have raised significant questions in South African higher education about what knowledge is, where it comes from, and who names it. Problems and serious controversies in the assessment of RPL especially arise when students have sought to bring into the RPL process insights and experiences that lie outside existing disciplinary knowledge and even outside the experience of assessors. In this way, RPL has forced a discussion about the very issue of "who controls the knowledge" and thus of authority in the university. Indeed, how we deal with learning that is work based and experiential, and with students who may become our teachers for a day or two, lies at the heart of this still controversial practice that is developing unevenly in South Africa.

The College of Education at Wits: A Foray into RPL[4]

The University of the Witwatersrand (Wits) is an Anglophone university situated in Southern Africa's economic heart, Johannesburg. It provides internationally recognized qualifications and graduates who are readily absorbed into foreign economies. Wits attracts not only local school-leavers[5] but also a variety of students from developing countries. While Wits offers a vast range of academic qualifications, the majority of them are offered as full-time programs, most suitable for younger students. However, part-time initiatives are growing at Wits. "Wits Plus" is one such part-time initiative. Established in 1999, its main aim is to attract working adults into higher education and thereby act on Wits' commitment to broadening access to disadvantaged students. In its response to the National Plan, Wits commits itself to "broadening access for students from disadvantaged communities who have the potential to

---

[4]The RPL initiative at the College of Education was a collective effort. I would like to acknowledge my colleagues Marian Baker, Viv Linington, Francis Faller and Dirk Postma for their energy to push the boundaries.

[5]"School-leavers" is the term for secondary-school graduates.

succeed academically" and to playing a "leading role in addressing historically disadvantaged communities in the education of the majority of the population of South Africa" (University of Witwatersrand, 2001, p. 1).

Like other institutions of higher education in South Africa, Wits is undergoing restructuring and rationalization. These changes resulted in its incorporation of the former Johannesburg College of Education (JCE) in 2001. Given this preoccupation with the restructuring process and the incorporation of JCE, which has absorbed vast resources, RPL has not been on the priority list of the institution. However, a RPL pilot project was initiated within the Education Department in the College of Education because of the interest in RPL by some academics within that department who were conscious of and attracted to its "redress" agenda. After a seminar facilitated by the Joint Education Trust (JET), the Education Department chose to participate in a national research and development project funded and facilitated by JET on RPL.

As a result, the Education Department decided to pilot a developmental model of RPL, which contrasted with our existing instrumentalist practice of giving credit for prior formal courses done at other universities. The curriculum for Educational Studies within the Higher Diploma in Education (HDE) consisted of six topics to be covered in two years of study. As part of our pilot, we constructed a six-week module as a portfolio of work to replace one of the six prescribed topics. The module enabled students to compile a portfolio that recorded their prior experiences and also served as an application for advanced standing or exemption from subsequent modules in Educational Studies. The initial cohort of students consisted of seventeen learners, of whom fifteen were women and two were men. All of them wanted to upgrade their initial teaching qualification, and all had extensive teaching experience, ranging from ten to twenty years. English was the first language of only two students. The majority of the students (fifteen of the seventeen) were Black.

The portfolio of work experience was constructed through a series of activities that required students to articulate, analyze, and reflect on their work experience. To enable students to do this, we met once a week for three hours as a group; in addition to this, we also consulted with students individually if they so desired. During the first week of the course, we introduced students to the proposal that we had submitted to JET and informed students of the research agenda and what this meant for them in terms of their coursework. In effect, we explained to them that they would be constructing a portfolio of experience in place of the regular course scheduled for that term. We also introduced students to the notion of RPL as a new policy imperative emerging on the educational scene in South Africa.

This introduction was important because both we and the students were on new territory. This was our first venture into RPL, and it was radically different from the highly structured approaches to education with which students were familiar. Some students felt they would be better off doing the regular course scheduled for the block, because both RPL and the portfolio course sounded very tentative. Students were also concerned about the nature of assessment in the portfolio, which sounded very different from the more known and traditional strategies such as essay writing and examinations. Others felt that the portfolio course could not be equal to or as rigorous as a traditional course if it did not have examinations. Still others felt excited at the prospect of learning about themselves.

In many ways, the fears of students were also fears for the faculty because it was the first time that we as members of an academic department steeped in theories of more conventional education were attempting to work with the kind of learning that went outside our experience. We were anxious about not being able to recognize it and therefore being unable to work with it or through it. Interestingly, when reflecting on our own fears and anxieties, it struck me that the academics in our department always went in groups of two or three to the portfolio course. We never went alone! We drew strength from going as a group. It was in this uncertain climate that we began our journey in RPL.

In our second session, we invited students, in pairs or individually, to "map" their previous learning from formal, informal, and nonformal contexts. I subjected myself to the same exercise in order to gain a sense of the demands that such an activity imposed on individuals in terms of time, emotions, and modality of expression. Some students took well to the mind-mapping of previous learning, but others preferred to give a descriptive account of their experiences, and still others preferred to talk about it. This alerted us to the importance of exploring differences in learning styles among adult learners, an issue that had not been an explicit component of our portfolio-development course, and including a range of assessment methodologies in portfolio courses. We learned, perhaps at the expense of the students, that not all students are able to mind-map their previous learning. At this point in our process, we noted that reviewing Kolb's experiential learning cycle (1984) might have served both us and the students well.

In the third session, students identified and expanded on the learning associated with each item on the map or with each bold heading in the narrative, depending on the mode the student had selected. The students who chose to talk through their experiences were encouraged to make notes under relevant sections that would be more telling than the headings they had identified.

Throughout these sessions, we worked with students as a group, and students were always encouraged to consult staff for private tutorials. In the initial consultations, we found that students' queries were related to "how to" questions. That is, students were trying to find out what we wanted, or what was the "right answer." From their point of view, to succeed in institutions is to know "how to . . ." As the students' and our confidence grew, however, consultations related more to "What do you think of this?" Still, my own sense was that students always felt that there was a right answer and that they had to find it. They continued to feel less free to express themselves in ways that could truly express who they are and what they are made of.

In the fourth and fifth sessions, students were asked to pair off with a classmate. The two men in the group chose to work with each other, and three women chose to work on their own. In pairs or individually, they were encouraged to share their maps or narratives with each other. One person in each pair then reported to the larger group on the work experiences of his or her partner. Those who worked on their own reported on themselves. This emphasis on autobiography helped students to reflect on the significance of their past experiences in the construction of their present professional identity. It also affirmed their competencies in teaching and learning, especially in the classroom. Whether they chose narrative or visual methods, all students carried out the mapping of personal histories with relative ease and confidence because of the supportive group context. Our experience of the value of group process for RPL is corroborated by Fraser who asserts that "learning operates at the interface between the individual and the social . . . and it is a group process [which enables us] to unravel the 'cliches' upon which our sense of our experience is based" (1995, p. 144).

For us as academics, the maps representing students' experiences showed a richness and a diversity that could not be matched by the experiences of the students we were accustomed to teaching in our traditional programs. The maps showed that the RPL students collectively had experience in monitoring peace initiatives in their schools and communities as well as facilitating conflict resolution workshops in strife-torn schools. Their maps also revealed experience in a variety of service learning projects, ranging from establishing vegetable gardens in poor schools to presenting literacy classes for parents whose children were in primary school. More importantly, the maps of experience revealed to us the gaps in our curriculum. It showed clearly what the experienced teachers brought with them, a richness of learning from experience, that had to be discarded and left outside once they chose to enter the academy. And yet, in spite of this richness, there were students who continued to ask about "standards." They worried that all they had done sounded far too personal and with very little academic and expert input. How striking that these students were echoing the same concerns of the faculty who argued against RPL for exactly these reasons!

In the sixth session, students were asked to relate their experiential learning to theory, especially theories related to Studies in Education. We attempted to enable students to critically reflect on their learning from experience and to do so in the context of the kind of theories that would be taught in a formal curriculum. This was very difficult because the discourse of learning from experience did not resemble theories of education either in terms of language or coherence. Learning from experience was not a tight theoretical account that had a beginning, a middle, and an end. This led to one important insight into the contradictions and tensions within RPL, the fact that the students had been right all along. There *was* a right answer! The answer was that their experience had to be re-presented in the context of disciplinary theory if we were going to be able to recognize and accredit it! Given the challenges encountered with this activity—and our commitment to valuing knowledge outside of formal academic theoretical norms—we thought of another way in which we could get students to relate learning from experience to theories of education that grew out of their own professional practices.

In the seventh session, therefore, we asked students to analyze critical incidents drawn from their classroom experiences, an approach well documented in Mezirow (1991) and Boud, Keogh, and Walker (1985). Students were asked to select an issue that emerged in their daily teaching practice. The unanimous choice of an issue was "discipline." Corporal punishment had just been outlawed in South Africa at the time, and most teachers felt that the discipline problems they experienced were directly attributable to its banning, which disempowered them as teachers.

Students identified a critical incident in which they exercised discipline in their classrooms. This time students worked individually on their critical incidents. Each student described a critical incident and then subjected it to "why" questions in order to analyze aspects of the incident. Students were then given readings on three approaches to teaching and learning. These readings represented a behaviorist, a humanist, and a constructivist approach, and students were asked to locate themselves within these perspectives depending on the kind of discipline upon which they relied. The conversations again showed the capacity of some of the students to be able to interrogate their practices. The conversations also reflected their thoughtfulness about teaching and learning.

Next, they were asked to consider the role of discipline in facilitating or inhibiting learning. Students' accounts were both idiosyncratic and universal, particularistic and yet familiar. Their stories reflected the messy and unexpected qualities of teaching and learning, but they also provoked thought and discussion about good teaching. These reflective activities also encouraged these teachers to generate their own views on what it means to teach well. Their reflective accounts were assessed by us for evidence of academic writing and for their clarity in describing what they had done and why.

This approach to RPL was "developmental" (Butterworth and McKelvey, 1997), meaning that there was a strong commitment to in-depth reflection on past experiences and support for such reflection, including the integration of this reflection with the discourse of the disciplines in Educational Studies. The aim was to record learning experiences in order to reflect on and integrate these experiences with other ideas about teaching and learning, encouraging personal growth, and nurturing professional consciousness. Grummet (1987) suggests critical consideration of such material from the perspectives of educational psychology, sociology, history, and philosophy of education. She sees this as linking the realm of private thought with public knowledge. In this way personal thought is validated and becomes part of professional education and practice. The developmental approach embodied in this portfolio course provided an opportunity and a means for students to express themselves in a creative, narrative mode, which was different from conventional modes of assessment such as examinations.

Tensions and Contradictions with Reflection in the RPL Process

The portfolio activity based on critical incidents in students' prior work experience required an articulation of embedded theory and a reflection on teaching and learning practices. Many students found this difficult to do. Indeed, sometimes a process that was designed to affirm and empower candidates had the opposite effect. One student said angrily, "I know what I know!" She found it difficult to engage with the idea that her own learning could be considered a social and communicative act. The reflective activities in the portfolio course were a dramatic change for most of the students, themselves products of the apartheid education system in which being passive, compliant recipients of taken-for-granted knowledge was the norm. In contrast, these students were being asked to be active creators and participants in the construction of knowledge and of their professional identity.

These were also difficulties for us as teachers because what was being generated by the students was in a format that was different from what we were accustomed to from young students with no professional experience and limited life experience. Furthermore, while the critical incidents contained an invitation for self-exploration and reflection on embedded theories, there was always a requirement to do this in the context of other relevant and established theories, and in the discourse of the disciplines in education. This seemed to students to confirm their suspicion that there must be a "right" answer, so they tended to respond according to their perceptions of what the academic wanted. In this sense, and for the most part in an unintended way, we were actually re-inscribing academic ways of knowing and were asserting our power by defining what counts as academic learning. We were asking the students to "talk the talk," even though they were "walking the walk" in their daily lives as experienced practitioners.

Conclusions

Our brief foray into RPL at the College of Education at Wits has shown us that RPL resonates with the many challenges faced by higher education in South Africa. In terms of new policy imperatives, higher education is challenged to become more responsive to disadvantaged students by broadening access and facilitating curriculum change in order for this population of students to enjoy success at universities. If higher education is to respond to these imperatives in a sustained way, the challenges around different knowledge discourses, flexible curricula, and intensive student support will need immediate attention. These issues happen to be the same ones that have to be engaged for the implementation of RPL. The future of RPL in higher education in South Africa depends heavily on how we approach and work with the question of academic and experiential knowledge. This question forces a confrontation between two worlds that hold different perspectives on the question of experience and on the basic question of how to define knowledge.

Second, our brief experience tells us that RPL and its implementation should not just be about responding to policy imperatives and widening access. It is also about facilitating success after access and thus remaining true to the equity and redress agenda that RPL brings with it. That is, merely creating places in the university for RPL students will not change the nature of their participation in the academy. The academy needs to recognize and respond to the need for significant changes to teaching and learning framed in the discourse of adult learning and development.

Third, our experience has shown that RPL requires student support services in the form of advice, guidance, and counseling, and, in some instances, academic support for writing. This process can be time-consuming for the assessor and the student alike. Our experience points us to the realization that RPL requires a flexible institutional structure that provides a range of entry and exit routes and pathways through academic programs. It demands a range of curricular offerings from which students may make selections—itself a still-radical notion in South African higher education—and this flexibility requires student counseling so that students can make informed choices. It requires trained assessors whose work is factored into workload models, and that work in RPL is recognized for appraisal. All of this in turn requires an institutional culture that values learning derived from experience. Presently, however, the organizational structure of higher education restricts political will and adventurousness in terms of recognizing learning from nonformal and informal contexts. Wits now has a draft RPL policy but does not implement RPL widely across the institution. Within the College of Education, RPL is implemented on a case-by-case basis, and implementation is generally heavily dependent on the will and capacity of individual departments.

In terms of the portfolio of work experience, our experience tells us that we relied heavily on reflective processes, a process fraught with ambiguities. While a portfolio of experience can be an enabling process, valuing a range of individual and social learning experiences and helping learners find creative outlets for their expression, it can also be a process that is coercive and confrontational. It can be a technical device, seeking commonalties between two situations for the sole purpose of claiming credit or exemption for prior learning. Given the diversity of students' educational backgrounds and life experiences, an important question that arises is "What are the most appropriate processes to assist both students and assessors to identify the learning from experience, and especially the knowledge component thereof?" Various forms of self-representation, including oral and visual modes, could enhance and enrich reflective activities used in portfolio applications. However, using a variety of methods places additional demands on mentors and assessors, who are often unaccustomed to working experientially with students. We thus regularly asked ourselves whether a reflective portfolio is always an appropriate indicator of competency. Would observations of actual performance in classroom contexts not supply better evidence of the teacher's professional repertoire, and could they be more revealing of their attitudes to teaching and learning (Osman & Castle, 2001)? A reflective portfolio provides useful information about students' academic literacy and their capacity for formal reflection, but may not provide the best evidence of their capacity to act as a participant in a community of practice (Luckett, 1999). All our students were full participants as experienced and practicing teachers, albeit undercredentialed ones.

The experience of the Educational Studies Department indicates that no single RPL process will be suitable for all individuals, departments, or subject areas within the College of Education. For this reason, RPL needs to be an evolving activity in which individual departments retain a sense of control over assessment procedures and the proportion of students who are admitted. This can lead to a range of approaches to RPL, influenced by issues such as the nature of the subject, the traditions and leadership style of the department, its recruitment needs, and the degree to which departments are responsive to adult students' needs and aspirations.

It is clear that a considerable investment in research, policy development, and advocacy is needed to establish RPL in teacher education in South Africa because it seeks to reshape fundamental values, beliefs, and paradigms for change in higher education. RPL forces the negotiation of two worlds—the world of experience and the world of academia. People who span boundaries, who understand the culture of both worlds, are vital in linking formal and informal sites of learning in viable collaboration.

References

Boud, D., Keogh, R., and Walker, D. (1985). *Reflection: Turning Experience into Learning.* London: Kogan Page.

Breier, M. (1996, October). *Whose Learning? Whose Knowledge? Recognition of Prior Learning and the National Qualifications Framework (NQF).* Paper presented at the Kenton Conference, South Africa.

Buchler, M. (1999, November 11–13). *Pushing the Boundaries: Prior Learning and Educational Transformation in South Africa.* Paper presented at the Building the Future through Learning conference, Council for Adult and Experiential Learning, Seattle.

Butterworth, C., and McKelvey, C. (1997). "A Study of APEL at Four Universities." *Journal of Access Studies* 12, 153–175.

Christie, P., and Collins, C. (1984). " 'Bantu Education': Apartheid Ideology and Labour Reproduction." In *Apartheid and Education* edited by P. Kallaway, 160–183. Johannesburg: Ravan Press.

Cooper, L. (1998). "From 'Rolling Mass Action' to 'RPL': The Changing Discourse of Experience and Learning in the South African Labour Movement." *Studies in Continuing Education* 20 (2), 143–157.

Department of Education. (1995). *White Paper on Education and Training.* Department of Education, Government Gazette, Vol. 357, No. 16312, Cape Town.

Fraser, W. (1995). "Making Experience Count . . . Towards What?" In *Adult Learning, Critical Intelligence and Social Change* edited by M. Mayo and J. Thompson, 137–146. Leicester, UK: National Institute of Adult Continuing Education.

Grummet, M. (1987). "The Politics of Personal Knowledge." *Curriculum Inquiry* 7 (13), 319–335.

Kolb, D. A. (1984). *Experiential Learning: Experience as the Source of Learning and Development.* Englewood Cliffs, NJ: Prentice Hall.

Luckett, K. (1999). "Ways of Recognizing the Prior Learning of Rural Development Workers." *South African Journal of Higher Education* 13 (2), 68–79.

Mezirow, J. (1991). *Transformative Dimensions of Adult Learning.* San Francisco: Jossey-Bass.

Michelson, E. (1999). "Social Transformation and the Recognition of Prior Learning: Lessons for and from South Africa." *South African Journal of Higher Education* 13 (2), 99–102.

Ministry of Education. (2001). *The National Plan for Higher Education.* Pretoria: Government Printer.

Osman, R., and Castle, J. (2001). "The Recognition of Prior Learning: Early Lessons, Challenges and Promise." *South African Journal of Higher Education* 15 (1), 54–60.

Seepe, S. (2000). "Higher Education and Africanisation." *Perspectives in Education* 8 (3), 52–71.

Shalem, Y. (2001). "The Recognition of Prior Learning in and through the Field of Academic Practice." *Perspectives in Education* 19 (1), 53–72.

University of the Witwatersrand. (2001). *Strategic Plan.* Johannesburg: Author.

THE COMPONENTS OF LEARNING

STATEWIDE ASSESSMENT OF PRIOR LEARNING AT THE VERMONT STATE COLLEGES

Judy Fitch

The Assessment of Prior Learning (APL) program of the Vermont State Colleges is an example of a single assessment program serving a variety of regional institutions. Managed by the Office of External Programs (OEP), the APL course is offered at almost twenty locations across the state, and each institution who participates is able to award the recommended credit according to its own policies. This credit, which is considered transfer credit by the various institutions, is not articulated on a course-match basis. Rather, students' experiential learning is organized according to broad academic criteria. Judy Fitch explains: "Our assessment policies are broad enough to encourage students to request credit for college-level learning that is nontraditional in scope. . . . Students are directed to present their learning in its own authentic terms rather than try to wedge it into the prescribed mold of a potentially constricting course title, yet their requests for credit must remain within the standards for college-level learning." She adds, "This is often a challenging balance to achieve."

This model of a regional assessment center is particularly important at a time of shrinking academic budgets. The portfolio-mediated assessment of prior learning can be an expensive item. Establishing a single quality program across institutions is an alternative to narrowing the range of student options and compromising the quality of student support.

In the last three decades, the Vermont State Colleges' Assessment of Prior Learning Program has become one of the largest and most successful assessment programs in the country. In a small rural state with a population of only a half million people, over 6,000 students have enrolled in the Assessment of

Prior Learning (APL) course and have had experiential learning assessed for college credit. The APL program is a part of the state culture, with thousands of APL alumni who continue to live and work in the state, hundreds of people serving as learning documentors, and another hundred faculty and practitioners annually serving on Advanced Standing Committees that evaluate portfolios. While there is still resistance to credentialing experiential learning in some of the more traditional pockets of higher education in Vermont, by and large there is a favorable climate for and acceptance of the philosophy and practice of awarding college credit to adults with verified experiential learning.

The Vermont State Colleges system is composed of five colleges. Four are traditional "campus colleges": Castleton State College, Johnson State College, Lyndon State College, and Vermont Technical College. The fifth college, Community College of Vermont (CCV), serves primarily part-time adult learners with twelve learning locations around the state in key geographical areas. The APL program is managed by the Office of External Programs (OEP), which operates under the administrative auspices of CCV and serves the whole Vermont State Colleges system. The three-credit, fifteen-week APL course is offered at fifteen state college locations—three campus colleges and twelve CCV locations—with additional offerings at the private Burlington College and the State of Vermont's training center, as well as in-house offerings for businesses and state agencies. In 1998, an online APL course was piloted, which will be discussed later in this model.

In part because OEP serves a range of institutions, credit is not awarded on a "course-match" basis. Students receive credit for all verified college-level learning, not just courses that correspond to a particular college's catalog. Students' experiential learning requests are generally broken down into three-credit "areas of study," with titles that fit within academic disciplines. College-level learning is clearly defined for APL students and for the committees who evaluate the students' credit requests. OEP's assessment policies are broad enough to encourage students to request credit for college-level learning that is nontraditional in scope, such as Practicum in Market Research, Community Volunteer Service, or Diversified Agriculture. Students are directed to present their learning in its own authentic terms rather than try to wedge it into the prescribed mold of a potentially constricting course title, yet their requests for credit must remain within the standards for college-level learning. This is often a challenging balance to achieve. The end result is a transcript with an interesting and often varied list of areas of study for which each student has received credit.

Again, because OEP serves multiple institutions, the credit awarded through portfolio assessment is not institutionally based and is considered *transfer* credit. The receiving institution determines whether or not to accept the credit students earn through APL. Transferability of assessed credit is always a concern for students, for the advisors who help them navigate the world of higher education, and for OEP. APL students are advised to research the college they plan to attend to ensure that participating in the APL program will be worthwhile and will help them move toward their academic goals. Depending on the institution, APL credit often can meet elective requirements or fulfill requirements for a particular major. The three-credit APL course itself serves as an elective at some colleges (for example, CCV's communication degree requirement) but at a few colleges is not accepted because these institutions offer no equivalent course. APL students are encouraged to keep a copy of their portfolio. The complete document, impressive as it often can be, is often helpful in negotiating acceptance of credit with department chairs and registrars at students' future institutions.

Pre-Enrollment Advising: A Key to Student Success

One key to students' success in the APL program is sound advising before enrolling in the course. Students are encouraged to attend an interactive television presentation presented by OEP each semester. They are required to meet with an advisor familiar with the program at the college that is sponsoring the APL course or to speak with an OEP coordinator to ensure that the APL course and program will help them meet their goals.

Four key questions must be answered when advising the potential APL student. First, does the student have significant experiential learning that could potentially "overlap" with college-level learning? This is easier to determine in some cases than in others. For example, a student in her thirties who has successfully managed a business or office for years, who is a volunteer public speaker for an organization, and who has significant training in computers yet has little or no previously earned college credit is an ideal APL candidate. A younger student with two years of college who has no long-term work experience or significant avocations and who is perhaps only looking for a way to "speed up" the degree is a questionable candidate.

Second, does the student have existing college credit in the same academic area as the experiential learning that may complicate the assessment process? If a student has already earned a significant number of credits in business and wants to assess learning obtained while managing a retail store, the Advanced Standing Committee may have difficulty determining the source of the learning. Was the knowledge acquired in the college course or gained in the role of manager at the store? The committee must never award credit that overlaps or duplicates previously earned college credit. Yet, the student may have significant learning above and beyond what was gained in the college business courses. In this situation, it takes skilled advising, based on an interview with a student, to ferret out potentially legitimate credit requests.

Third, does the student have the necessary writing skills? Students should be able to write at the college level. This is determined by a formal writing assessment through a college advisor or by successful completion of college writing courses. Many students are advised to complete English Composition before enrolling in the APL course. The portfolio is a demanding writing project, and students do not want to be struggling with basic writing skills while articulating experiential learning. It is because of this strong emphasis on writing in the APL course that CCV allows the course to fulfill a communication degree requirement.

Finally, does the student have a sufficiently high level of commitment and the focused time needed for the course? Students who are going through major life transitions such as geographical moves, family crises, or illness are discouraged from taking the course. They are told to expect to spend 12–15 hours per week on the course during the first five weeks, which for many working parents and busy adults is a heavy sacrifice and daunting prospect.

Assessment of Prior Learning: The Course

The students who ultimately enroll in the APL course have a varied profile, but the typical APL student is in his or her thirties, has significant career and life learning, may have already earned credit for some college courses, has adequate writing skills, and is ready for a change. There are more women than men (72 percent women/28 percent men), and a significant number of students have business backgrounds. The APL student typically wants to move forward in his or her education and career and wants to make sense of jobs, training, military service, hobbies, workshops, independent study, and volunteer activities—to see how and if all of this might be pulled together in a format that will help make a leap forward toward a degree. It is through the creation of a portfolio in the APL course that the student weaves the strands of his or her background into a cohesive whole.

Students often enroll in the APL course with a clearly defined goal: to earn college credit quickly in order to save time and money in the quest for a degree. While this is a worthy, pragmatic goal, the APL course is purposefully designed to address broader learning objectives. Once enrolled in the APL course, students are often surprised to learn that they will be required to reflect more deeply on their lives and learning, to trace turning points and significant setbacks, and to identify personal, educational, and career goals that are aligned with their values and interests. Students are expected to identify past experiences; reflect on, write about, and discuss these experiences; and then extract and articulate the learning.

As a course, APL is described as "front loaded": The first five weeks require total dedication and concentration, with a little more flexibility built in as the semester continues. Students receive a packet of materials that includes a letter of welcome from OEP staff; the OEP-published textbook, *Earning College Credit for Prior Experiential Learning* (Office of External Programs, 1990a); information about the program and transfer policies; forms to be filled out; templates for parts of the portfolio; samples of letters of documentation; and other pertinent handouts.

The first in-class assignment, after ice breaking and "getting-to-know you" exercises, asks students to "free write" a page without concern for grammar and punctuation, perhaps describing their reason for taking the course. This begins the writing process in a nonthreatening manner and gets students in the habit of putting the pen to the page. The writing assignments increase in complexity as the weeks progress. The first take-home assignment requires students to list every job, hobby, volunteer stint, area of interest developed, significant travel activity, and major family change since high school. This "experience list," from which learning is later "extracted," is the foundational source from which the portfolio is built. Each student is also assigned to write a one-page goal statement that addresses personal, educational, and career aspirations.

One successful first-class activity is to have the group break into pairs or threesomes and write the definitions of "experience" and "learning" on sheets of newsprint. When students reconvene to compare notes, the class discussion that grows out of the exercise is very fruitful. Often students discover (and draw!) a circle that represents how experience leads to learning, which in turn leads to a new experience on a deeper or higher level, which leads to richer learning—a spiral of experience and learning, continually increasing in scope. This exercise accomplishes several things: Students get to talk in a smaller group and begin to feel more comfortable; they are encouraged to think critically and come up with their own definitions; they debate definitions of experience and learning, which leads to clearer thinking; and, importantly, they begin to understand that there is a difference between experience and learning. It is understanding this difference that raises the students' experiences from a laundry list of activities to a document that describes what they have *learned* over the years. While writing and discussing definitions of "learning" and "experience" begin to help students clarify differences at an intellectual level, students find it is more challenging later in the course to analyze their personal experiences and distinguish experience from the learning derived from that experience. This is often the most labor-intensive and frustrating task in developing the portfolio.

In the second and third weeks of the course, when the experience lists are complete, it is time to turn to the task of prioritizing significant experiences and "extracting" the learning from them. This is accomplished through group discussions and exercises, assignments from the textbook, and handouts provided in the instructors' manual. This is a methodical process, taking each experience listed, analyzing it, and asking questions that determine what exactly was *learned*. Questions that help students with this analysis process include "What did I learn that I didn't know before? What can I do now that I could not do before? Do I have different beliefs or feelings than I had before this experience? If I had to train someone in this area, what skills, knowledge, attitudes, or qualities would they need to develop? How does this learning apply to my personal, educational, or career goals? Did I attend training sessions? Did I read books related to this area? Could I teach others about this area? Did I have to make decisions? Did I have to solve difficult problems?"

To illustrate this process, let us imagine a student who selects the significant learning experience of having "worked as an office manager at IBM." The learning extracted from this experience might be described as knowledge and skills in the areas of "organization; computer skills such as word processing, spreadsheets, and database management; communication with colleagues and the public; planning and leading meetings; negotiating personnel issues; public speaking and training; and leadership skills." This extracted learning can be further analyzed and described in writing until a range of areas of study and learning components emerges.

At this initial stage, students often feel as if they are groping through pages and pages of words. Nothing is quite making sense; the learning is not congealing into tidy blocks. The process seems overwhelming, and experiences and learning are difficult to break down. It is not unusual for class discussions to include venting frustrations and students wondering aloud if all this work and apparent confusion will really be worth it in the end. The instructor starts repeating the message, "Trust the process."

One productive class activity at this point is to have the group brainstorm questions for a student about a particular experience. Choosing one nonthreatening significant experience and allowing the class to analyze it as a group helps to demonstrate analytical thinking, decreases the sense of isolation for students reflecting on their own experiences, and serves as a model as students move forward and analyze other significant experiences on their lists. For example, a student may have "worked as a teacher's aide for students with learning disabilities," and the APL students may brainstorm questions such as: "What types of disabilities did the students have? What types of tasks did they work on in class? Did you create and use individualized educational plans for the children? Did you see progress in the children? What techniques did you use to maintain students' interest?"

"Clustering" is another group exercise that helps students begin to organize and categorize experience and learning into manageable areas of study with learning components. The instructor selects from the group a sample of a significant experience from the group, such as "Ran my own business." She then creates a spiderweb cluster drawing, beginning by writing "ran my own business" in the center of the blackboard inside a circle. Then, branching off in lines to new bubbles, the group brainstorms possible learning from this experience, such as *accounting, supervision, marketing,* and *finance.* Then, from these subcategories, new lines can be drawn to the next layer of circles. For example, "supervision" might lead to new subcategories of *defining jobs, interviewing, hiring, training, maintaining personnel records,* and so on. Students are able to see clearly from the map on the board that "ran my own business" was the significant experience, "supervision" is a potential area of study, and the sublayer of *interviewing, hiring,* and so on can be turned into supporting learning components.

At this point in the course, helping students grasp the definition of college-level learning is most important. OEP has published two handbooks, one for students and one for portfolio evaluators. According to the APL textbook, *Earning College Credit for Prior Experiential Learning* (Office of External Programs, 1990a), and the handbook for evaluators, *Guidelines to Be Used in Assessing Portfolios and in Awarding College Credit for Prior-Experiential Learning* (Office of External Programs, 1990b), college-level learning can be defined by six descriptors. College-level learning is (a) describable, (b) applicable outside the context in which it was learned, (c) within the realm of recognizable academic disciplines, (d) inclusive of both theoretical and practical understandings of a subject area, (e) more than common knowledge, and (f) verifiable.

A thorough discussion of the definition helps students discern if the learning they are describing truly meets the definition provided in the textbook. As students delve deeper into the process of analyzing their life learning, there is excitement as they realize how much they really *do* know that they have undervalued. But there is also the recognition that some experiences will not translate into college credit, and this can be disappointing, Years of entry-level manual labor may suddenly appear "wasted" because it is not deemed creditable in the academic realm. Students often feel that their personal experiences, such as giving birth and raising children, are not adequately respected by the APL program. Instructors try to be sensitive as they explain that, unless a parent can prove he or she has studied parenting and child development with some formality and academic rigor, with theoretical knowledge and a healthy reading list of experts in the field, the experience of family life will not be credited through the portfolio. This is often difficult for students to understand and accept, especially if years have been spent focused solely on childrearing. Similarly, lifelong hobbies such as crafts and woodworking may not be creditable, depending on the level of expertise and knowledge.

As part of this discussion, the terms "college-level" and "college-type" are distinguished in hopes of removing a sense of hierarchy. The instructor encourages students to value and honor *all* their learning, whether or not it fits within the parameters of the academic world. In the end, students usually surmise that it is often the most valuable learning garnered through parenting, religious experiences, and deep personal exploration that cannot be translated into college credit. Thus, while OEP materials refer to college-*level* learning, instructors try to help students in the APL course think in terms of college-*type* learning, a term that does not judge the worth or value of their learning.

At approximately the third week of the semester, students begin to use a summary of Bloom's *Taxonomy of Educational Objectives* (1956–1964), as provided in *Earning College Credit for Prior Experiential Learning* (Office of External Programs, 1990a). Bloom's taxonomy helps students write the learning components that describe experiential learning. "Experience and Learning," the third chapter in *Earning College Credit for Prior Experiential Learning,* explains that Bloom's taxonomy categorizes verbs describing intellectual operations according to level of learning. Verbs are listed reflecting sequentially more complex levels of knowledge, demonstrated through (a) memorization and naming, (b) comprehension, (c) application, (d) analysis, (e) synthesis, and (f) evaluation, which involves judging, appraising, assessing, and comparing.

Thus, APL instructors try to help students see that the development of learning components is more than a rhetorical exercise. Students must be able to articulate their learning in order to prove they have learning at the college level. The ability to construct meaningful, coherent learning components is a critical aspect of the students' naming and claiming their knowledge. Well-written and thoughtful learning components, coupled with strong documentation, convince the evaluation committee that the students have the learning they claim and thus deserve college credit.

Students are taught that effectively articulated learning components are made up of three parts: a verb, a description of learning, and the conditions of learning. For example, in the learning component "Interpret data on financial statements to determine accuracy of budget," "interpret" is the learning verb, "data on financial statements" is the content of the learning being described, and "to determine accuracy of budget" is the *how* or *why*—the condition of the learning. This learning component might appear under the area of study of "financial management" or "accounting."

This complex concept of using verbs describing intellectual operations in order to write learning components is simplified through another assignment. Students are asked to make a list of steps describing a relatively simple task, such as changing a tire or cooking a pizza. They must then add the verbs offered by Bloom to the steps: for example, "Recognize the tire is flat; identify tools in trunk; calculate amount of strength necessary to remove rusty bolts." While at first this appears to be a silly exercise, it demystifies the verb selection process by using learning content that is not intimidating. Students are then able to move on to more challenging areas of learning.

When students have developed lists of learning components, they begin to group them into areas of study and assign credit request amounts for each area of study. Areas of study are typically clustered in three-credit requests that replicate actual college course titles, such as Microcomputer Applications or Child Development. Six to twelve credits can be requested for areas of study that describe and document learning that is the equivalent of an internship or practicum. Typically, a total credit request per portfolio is between fifteen and forty-five credits.

Some areas of study will resemble course equivalents: Office Management, Introduction to Photography, Supervision. Many areas of study, however, do not fall into easily recognizable course look-alikes and may have titles such as Practicum in Alternative Secondary Education or Foodborne Pathogenic Bacteriology with Lab. After the first few weeks of the course, students are encouraged to research college catalogs to find programs and courses that will help them organize their learning into academic disciplines. APL instructors discourage them from doing this early in the course, however, to give them time to identify and reflect on their own learning instead of trying to "copy" from catalogs or artificially fit their learning into the predesigned structure of college courses.

Another method for developing areas of study for assessment is for students to write down the title of a course and brainstorm learning components that might fall under that title. Still, students are encouraged to review their own learning first and see where it overlaps with college-level learning, rather than try to "invent" learning that happens to match a course they may need for their degree requirements.

An OEP representative visits each APL class in the fifth week, a point at which frustrations are often running high. The OEP visitor reassures the students, encourages them to stay with the process, and discusses the documentation process in detail. The visitor explains that each area of study in the students' portfolios must be supported by a letter from an expert, verifying that the student has the learning described. In many cases, the OEP representative takes the heat from the students that would otherwise be directed at the instructor. The visitor underscores much of what the instructor has been teaching throughout the first five weeks, and students often gain a deeper understanding simply from hearing the same words repeated by a newcomer or by hearing suggestions phrased in a different way.

Midway through the course, while students are analyzing their learning and identifying people to write letters of documentation, another dynamic is simultaneously occurring in the class. The students are beginning to act as a support to each other. Students with similar backgrounds do homework together during the week between classes. Stories of students' pasts have inevitably been shared—of disappointments in high school or frustrations of being passed over for promotions, of the sacrifices being made to take the APL class, of the childcare needed or the missed family dinners or children's baseball games. All this tends to build a sense of kinship that for some groups has continued on in class reunions and lifetime friendships.

The group format also appears to be key in building skills for future academic success. Through discussion and writing, students are able to put their pasts into perspective and clarify future academic and professional goals. They practice critical thinking, intellectual inquiry, interpersonal communication, analytical writing and discourse, and academic self-discipline. These skills are best developed within a supportive group, and it is clear that these skills help students succeed in subsequent college courses and make earning a degree an attainable goal.

In the fifth through tenth weeks of the course, students focus on requesting and collecting letters of documentation, writing a resume, and completing the autobiographical essay. The essay provides a context for the learning that is described in the portfolio. It is an opportunity for each student to infuse the portfolio with his or her own voice, to tell the story of his or her life and learning, and to demonstrate writing skills. As part of the portfolio, students submit the 7–12 pages that describe where they have been since high school, where they are now, and where they are headed in terms of personal, academic, and career goals.

In the tenth week of class, students participate in the "mock Advanced Standing Committee." Students read a sample portfolio provided by OEP and then act as evaluation committee members, defending their reasons for either awarding or not awarding credit to the sample student. This provides students with an opportunity to gain some distance from their own portfolio and to get a better understanding of the role of the Advanced Standing Committee.

In the last month of the course, students pull all the parts of the portfolio together into one complete document: the table of contents, the summary transcript that includes areas of study with the specific amounts of credit requested, the essay, the resume, primary letters of documentation, secondary documentation, and the bibliography. Students review letters of documentation to determine if the letters are strong enough to stand alone or need supplementation. Students finalize the collection of secondary documentation such as workshop certificates, lists of trainings, and letters of reference. If they choose, students create bibliographies of relevant academic reading. Students also discuss future goals in more depth. Representatives from various colleges are invited to the class to describe programs and offerings. APL students are often surprised to find their role has reversed since the time when they first enrolled in the course just three months earlier. Rather that viewing themselves as outsiders trying to enter the lofty ivory tower, they now realize they are savvy consumers, students coveted by competing colleges.

The Advanced Standing Committees: Portfolio Evaluation

Once the portfolios are completed at the end of the semester, they are delivered to OEP and then organized by academic discipline. Advanced Standing Committees are convened each semester to evaluate the portfolios produced by the previous semester's APL students. Approximately thirty Advanced Standing Committees meet each year. The committees typically consist of an OEP facilitator, two faculty or staff from the state college system, a faculty member from a private college, and a practitioner with expertise in the field related to the group of portfolios being evaluated. Each committee reads seven to ten portfolios, which have been grouped by similarity of content such as health sciences, business, or the arts. Committee members receive a modest stipend and a meal for what is typically a half-day meeting. There is never more than one inexperienced evaluator on the committee. Each member receives the *Guidelines to Be Used in Assessing Portfolios and in Awarding College Credit for Prior-Experiential Learning* (Office of External Programs, 1990b), which details the program, the definition of college-level learning, and the procedures for decision making in regard to awarding credit. The OEP facilitator acts as a neutral guide to the process and is not involved in decisions about awarding or denying credit. Consensus must be reached for every requested area of study.

The committee structure brings faculty and practitioners together in a unique format that produces collegial camaraderie and cross-fertilization of ideas about curriculum. This is another significant outcome of our APL program. Discussions are often lively as the committee analyzes the areas of study and scrutinizes letters of documentation. More often than not, the committee members reach decisions quickly and have similar responses to requests even though they may represent different colleges and departments, varied disciplines, and contrasting teaching styles. If students' requests in the portfolios do not meet a standard that convinces the committee that the learning is college-level learning, credit is not awarded. The committee denies requests that are not well articulated, that have weak or no documentation, or that don't fit into an academic discipline. The student must demonstrate through the portfolio that the learning is at the equivalent of a "C minus" or better, the passing grade for typical college courses.

Students receive results of the evaluation of their portfolios the semester following their enrollment. Students rarely receive all the credit they request, and usually the committee has altered area of study titles and credit amounts to more accurately reflect the learning the student has described. On average, students receive 67 percent of the credits requested. The results arrive in the mail: a letter from OEP and a transcript of the awarded credit. Students are encouraged to call OEP staff within thirty days to discuss results. There is an appeals process for students who believe they were unfairly evaluated, though not more than one or two students per year usually appeal.

Students' Next Steps

Once students have successfully completed the APL program and have chosen a college where they want to earn a degree, most students bring the OEP transcript to an academic advisor at the college to have the credits integrated into an official degree plan. More often than not, this is an advisor at CCV who is very familiar with the APL program and can work with the students to maximize use of the assessed credit toward an associate degree. Many students go on to the Johnson State College External Degree Program, which is designed for adult students and has flexible degree plans that easily incorporate assessed credit.

Former OEP Director Brent Sargent conducted research examining APL students' subsequent degree participation, persistence, and attainment. He targeted students who had successfully completed APL and who had requested an OEP transcript. Sargent found that 80 percent of research respondents indicated that the APL program was "much" or "very much" a factor in their decision to pursue a degree. Of the 253 APL student respondents, 88.9 percent had participated in a degree program. Two hundred and seventeen students had attained a college degree: Eighty-two earned the associate degree, 104 the baccalaureate degree, and thirty-one the master's degree. Four students were involved in doctoral programs (Sargent, 1998). This research supports the theory that enrollment in the APL program is critical to a student's future academic success.

Looking toward the Future

The Vermont State College APL process was designed almost thirty years ago with these assumptions and values: (a) Adults should not be marginalized at the edges of academia, but welcomed into higher education through programs that build on adult learners' strengths and help them meet learning challenges; (b) the experiential learning of adults must be valued and, with appropriate procedures, accredited; and (c) the APL program must provide students an opportunity to build academic skills, gain an overview of higher education, create a portfolio that articulates and documents their college-type learning, and receive support from staff and fellow students as they enter academia. These values and assumptions were challenged when OEP experimented with a new model for delivering the APL course.

In 1998, OEP piloted an online APL course. Time and effort were taken to try to replicate the classroom structure on the Web. Text was written for the online version of the course and loaded into the online system so that students could access instructional notes and handouts at the classroom Internet site. The technology allowed students and instructors to engage in ongoing discussions through messages posted sequentially, with no specific class time. Students enrolled from around the state. For some students, the online format was convenient, assignments were completed in a timely fashion, and excellent portfolios were produced. For others, the online format was a technological challenge; they avoided engaging in their online "class" each week, fell behind, and either completed with a struggle or dropped the course.

Based on initial experiences with this latter group, the online format was modified as a "hybrid" course that offered both classroom time and online communication. The extensive online text was significantly reduced, and students relied more on the published textbook and online discussion. A first class in-person meeting was introduced to develop more group rapport, and individual midsemester meetings with the instructor were added to encourage appropriate progress. The learning technology improved as well, and became more fluid and user-friendly.

The online pilot raised questions that have made OEP staff review the underlying values and assumptions of the entire APL program. For example, the online format tended to "streamline" the APL experience, cutting it down to the bare essentials. In the piloted APL courses, the learning became more mechanical, less dialectical or dialogic experience. For some students, this posed no problem for successful completion of the course and producing quality portfolios. For others, it appeared that the face-to-face support group atmosphere, with the camaraderie of a first-year cohort, was a key ingredient to success, and without it they could not succeed. It was clear that some aspects of the course did not translate well from the classroom to the online format. For example, the OEP representative visit becomes students reading a page of text rather than a dynamic two-hour classroom discussion. Visits from college admissions representatives were cumbersome online and do not give students the face-to-face contact that often makes them feel welcome to a new institution. In-class discussions in which students process their past experiences and future goals in a personal way rarely occurred online in the piloted APL courses. Perhaps with more experimentation in online delivery techniques and more sophisticated technology, these obstacles could be overcome.

Overall, the APL online course, after the first few weeks of the course, seemed to become a group independent study, with students having difficulty engaging with one another in the same way they do in the APL classroom. John Christensen, coordinator of online learning at CCV, says, "Online education is viable, practical and pedagogically sound only if certain conditions are understood and met by both faculty and administrators. Online educators must strive to compensate for the lack of the human element in online teaching. The communication and sense of community in traditional education are important elements of the college experience that are difficult to replicate online" (2000).

Also, another challenge for OEP staff is the routine scrutinizing of the expense of the program, which is viewed as a "loss leader." The program is costly to the organization in the short term, but as students complete the program and enroll in degree programs (degree programs in which they would not have enrolled without APL), the APL program becomes financially viable in the long term.

The tensions and debates playing out in relation to the APL program mirror those of higher education in general. How do colleges implement learning technologies in ways that enhance learning? How do educators measure and determine what may be lost and gained when learning technologies are implemented? How does higher education continue to welcome and serve marginalized learners whose backgrounds and needs are increasingly diverse and complex? How do colleges provide high-quality education at the most economical cost?

As the OEP staff grapple with the questions, they keep in mind the foundational values held at the program's inception: that the program must welcome and serve adult learners, honor their learning, and help them reach their educational goals.

References

Bloom, B. S., Committee of College and University Examiner, et al., ed. (1956–1964). *Taxonomy of Educational Objectives: The Classification of Educational Goals.* New York: D. McKay.

Christensen, J. (2000). Personal communication with the author.

Office of External Programs. (1990a). *Earning College Credit for Prior Experiential Learning.* Montpelier, VT: Author.

Office of External Programs. (1990b). *Guidelines to Be Used in Assessing Portfolios and in Awarding College Credit for Prior-Experiential Learning.* Montpelier, VT: Author.

Sargent, B. (1998). *An Examination of the Relationship between Completion of a Prior Learning Assessment Program and Subsequent Degree Program Participation, Persistence, and Attainment.* Sarasota, FL: University of Sarasota Press.

CONTRIBUTORS

ELANA MICHELSON is a mentor and professor of cultural studies at Empire State College and the chair of the Master of Arts in Liberal Studies program. She has consulted extensively in the field of adult and experiential learning, most recently in opening opportunities for adult learners in postapartheid South Africa. She is the author of numerous articles and book chapters on issues of multiculturalism, feminism, epistemology, and adult learning.

ALAN MANDELL is a mentor and professor in the social sciences and director of the Mentoring Institute of Empire State College, where he has worked for almost thirty years. He has regularly written about and guided workshops on adult and experiential learning. With his colleague Lee Herman, he is the author of *From Teaching to Mentoring: Principle and Practice, Dialogue and Life in Adult Education* (Routledge, 2004).

MARIXSA ALICEA, an associate professor at the School for New Learning, DePaul University, earned her Ph.D. in sociology from Northwestern University. She teaches Foundations and Research Seminar courses as well as courses related to U.S. Latina women's lives and immigration issues. Marixsa is an active member of the DePaul University's Center for Latino Research and serves as an associate editor of *Dialogo*—a periodical published by the Center. She is coauthor of *Surviving Heroin: Interviews with Women in Methadone Clinics* and has published articles concerning the Puerto Rican transnational migration experience, adult education, and women's drug use. She is currently coediting a volume on international immigration issues.

KATE CROWE coordinated the prior learning program at the Evergreen State College for more than ten years. She serves as an adjunct faculty member who teaches poetry, short story writing, novel writing, autobiographical writing, and courses related to prior learning.

BERNARDIN DEUTSCH is professor of psychology at Alverno College. She has worked with the transfer of learning curriculum for returning adult and transfer students since the early 1980s. She holds a Ph.D. from The Catholic University of America in Washington, D.C.

JUDY FITCH is the director of public relations and development at the Community College of Vermont. She served as coordinator of assessment services at the Office of External Programs for the Vermont State Colleges and taught the VSC's Assessment of Prior Learning course.

SUZANN GARDNER is associate professor of education at Alverno College. She collaboratively developed the transfer of learning curriculum and has been instrumental in assisting students to adapt their prior experience to Alverno's ability-based focus. She holds a master's degree in curriculum and instruction from the University of Wisconsin–Milwaukee, where she is currently completing her Ph.D.

JULIE GUSTAVS is learning development manager of Work-Based Learning programs, Faculty of Business, University of Technology, Sydney. She is responsible for developing and implementing learning support strategies for the Work-Based Learning programs in the Faculty of Business and Faculty of Information Technology (IT). Her research interests focus on exploring critical perspectives to learning partnerships in higher education and industry.

Since 1979, **LEE HERMAN** has been an Empire State College mentor and the coordinator of one of its small-town sites, Auburn, in New York State. He has done educational planning and other forms of mentoring with students concentrating in every area of study for which Empire State awards degrees. A cofounder of the ESC Mentoring Institute, he frequently writes about mentoring, often with his longtime friend and colleague, Alan Mandell. They have recently published *From Teaching to Mentoring: Principle and Practice, Dialogue and Life in Adult Education* (Routledge, 2004).

DIANE HILL is a Mohawk from the Grand River Territory of the Six Nations Iroquois people situated in Ontario, Canada. She has worked for the past seventeen years as an adult educator, independent consultant, writer, and Native traditional healer. Currently, Diane works on contract with the First Nations Technical Institute as a consultant in Aboriginal education and the use of PLAR within a holistic model of learning and teaching. Her work focuses on the design, development, and delivery of community-based educational training programs for First Nations people in Canada.

THERESA (TERRY) HOFFMANN, assistant professor and licensed certified professional counselor (LCPC), has worked with adult students at University of Maryland University College (UMUC) for almost twenty years.

Her university roles included teaching the portfolio-development course (EXCEL) and courses in behavioral sciences, faculty development, and career counseling, and serving as director of academic support and director of prior learning for twelve years. PLA presentations include CAEL, CAPLA, and PLAR Centre international conferences. She also served as president of the Experiential Learning Assessment Network (ELAN), which was established in 1987 and consists of educators from four- and two-year institutions.

Theresa Hoffmann's publications include her written constructions to the prior learning Web Course, the EXCEL Video, "Puzzling through Prior Learning Assessment: The Faculty Evaluator's Manual," and "Extracting Knowledge from Experience: The Prior Learning Challenge." Her degrees include ones in the areas of biological sciences and community counseling. She is a therapist in a private counseling practice.

DEBORAH W. HOLTON, an associate professor at the School for New Learning, DePaul University, is also a member of the SNL Center for Distance Education faculty. In both programs she teaches Foundations courses. She also teaches courses in American literature and drama, culture, and creativity. She holds a B.F.A. degree with honors in theatre from Howard University, an M.A. in English from Atlanta (Atlanta-Clark) University, and a Ph.D. in American theatre studies from University of Wisconsin–Madison. Dr. Holton has served as writer-in-residence for the District of Columbia, and as dramaturge for such distinguished companies as the Great Lakes Shakespeare Festival and Pegasus Players. Her publications include essays regarding dramatic literature and adult learning, as well as poetry and fiction.

LINDA JOHNSON is academic leader, subject field director–business law at London Metropolitan University and is also program leader for B.A. Business Studies and M.A. European and International Business Law. She has considerable experience in admissions and access developments and in teaching business law, business skills, and student skills at foundation and undergraduate level. Recently she developed an interest in APEL and has contributed to a couple of conference papers and the development of a university-wide taught module in this area. Her degrees include the L.L.B., L.L.M., M.Phil., and Certificate of Education Diploma Access Studies in Higher Education.

GEORGINE LOACKER, who directed the Council for Student Assessment at Alverno College from 1973 to 2003, is professor of English. Her research and publications are on the process of assessing individual students, a topic on which she has given presentations and workshops nationally and internationally—most recently in Hong Kong and South Africa. Her doctorate in English is from the University of Chicago.

CAROLYN MANN, professor of experience based education at Sinclair Community College, Dayton, Ohio, has been involved with prior learning assessment for more than twenty years. She began her career as an instructor assisting adults with the identification, articulation, and documentation of college-level learning in a portfolio format. In 1983, she developed the Academic Credit Assessment Information Center, which expanded Sinclair's assessment of prior learning to a comprehensive program providing students with a complete range of assessment options. In 1986, she became responsible for the administration and marketing of Sinclair's prior learning assessment program. In 1994, she was asked to direct the Ohio office for the American Council on Education's (ACE) College Credit Recommendation Services program. She is responsible for marketing and coordinating the review of corporate training programs for college credit. Carolyn has been an active member of the college-wide assessment committee since 1994. She has worked with numerous colleges and universities to develop prior learning assessment programs in the United States and Canada. Carolyn is currently chair of the Experience Based Education Department, which provides learning and assessment options geared to adult learners.

BARBARA NEVERS is assistant professor of liberal studies at Alverno College. She collaboratively developed and piloted the transfer of learning curriculum for Alverno's weekend college students. She has been instrumental in developing strategies for prior learning assessment. She holds a master's degree in communication from Marquette University.

RUKSANA OSMAN is an associate professor at the University of the Witwatersrand, Johannesburg, South Africa. Her teaching and research interests are varied and include adult learning, recognition of prior learning, and service learning in higher education.

HELEN PETERS is a senior lecturer at London Metropolitan University, UK, involved in accreditation of prior experiential learning (APEL), learning and language development, and international programs. She spent a semester researching the potential for Recognition of Prior Learning (RPL) at University of Cape Town, South Africa, and has published papers on APEL, on women learning at university, and on student writing. She is currently researching in the field of language and APEL for a doctorate in education (Ed.D.) with the Open University, UK.

HELEN POKORNY is a learning and teaching coordinator at London Metropolitan University, UK. She has worked within the field of APEL for many years, contributing to the development and delivery of APEL guidance for students across the university. She also works with colleagues to promote the development of institutional APEL policy and practice. Her research interests are in the field of APEL.

JAMES ROTH is professor of history at Alverno College, where he has taught since 1976 and formerly served as head of the division of arts and humanities. He has contributed to several texts on teaching, learning, and assessment in higher education, including the *Handbook of the Undergraduate Curriculum* and *Learning that Lasts*. He holds a Ph.D. in history from the University of California, Berkeley.

SUSAN RYDELL is a charter faculty member of Metropolitan State University where she has held a number of faculty and administrative positions. She was on the team that developed the university's prior learning assessment program and the original Individualized Educational Planning course, the precursor to Perspectives. From 1999 to 2002, she served as interim dean of the First College, which houses the individualized baccalaureate degree, coordinates the university's alternative learning and assessment strategies, and coordinates university-wide faculty development programs through the Center for Teaching and Learning.

NICKY SOLOMON is associate professor and senior research fellow in the Faculty of Education, University of Technology, Sydney. She is also coordinator for the Work-Based Learning programs within the faculty. Her current research interests focus on new understandings of knowledge and learning, particularly those that support the emerging knowledge economy. She is currently attempting to theorize these new understandings by drawing on the concept of "working knowledge" in order to explore the new research and teaching relations between universities and workplaces.

DERISE E. TOLLIVER is an associate professor at the School for New Learning, DePaul University. She is a clinical psychologist by training. Her professional and research pursuits fall within the broad category of growth, healing, and transformation in the context of culture and spirituality. She is particularly interested in African-centered psychology and the role of culture and spirituality in effective teaching and learning. She has given numerous presentations and has published on HIV/AIDS in the African American community; learning about race and racism through study abroad in Africa; and culture, spirituality, and teaching for transformation in adult education.

INDEX